Colección Támesis

SERIE A: MONOGRAFÍAS, 237

CONTEMPORARY SPANISH AMERICAN NOVELS BY WOMEN

MAPPING THE NARRATIVE

Space is critical to imaginative writing. As English novelist Elizabeth Bowen has observed: 'nothing can happen nowhere'. This book offers an interdisciplinary framework for reading novels, and in particular women's fiction in Spanish America, with a focus on geoplot, on space rather than time as the narrative engine. Following the work of Lefebvre and Friedman, the author examines recent works by Spanish America's most visible women novelists – Angeles Mastretta (Mexico), Isabel Allende (Chile), Rosario Ferré (Puerto Rico), Sara Sefchovich (Mexico) and Laura Restrepo (Colombia) – and the ways in which their female protagonists challenge the spatial barriers erected by capitalist hegemony. Margins, borders, liminal spaces, the chora-space, and the body are emphasized as potential sites of transgression. The analysis identifies spatial negotiation as a mechanism both for cementing and for undermining authority, thus exposing the strategies through which literature constructs and represents power.

SUSAN CARVALHO is Associate Professor of Hispanic Studies at the University of Kentucky, and Director of the Middlebury College Spanish School.

SUSAN E. CARVALHO

CONTEMPORARY SPANISH AMERICAN NOVELS BY WOMEN

MAPPING THE NARRATIVE

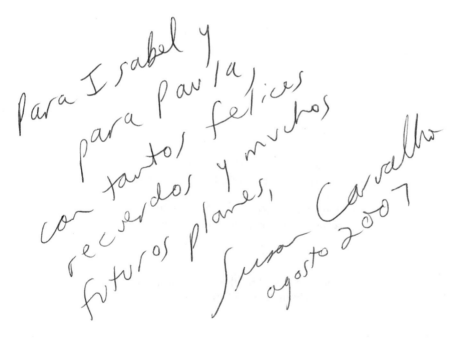

Para Isabel y
para Paula)
con tantos felices
recuerdos y muchos
futuros planes,
Susan Carvalho
agosto 2007

TAMESIS

First published 2007 by Tamesis, Woodbridge

ISBN 978–1–85566–142–4

Tamesis is an imprint of Boydell & Brewer Ltd
PO Box 9, Woodbridge, Suffolk IP12 3DF, UK
and of Boydell & Brewer Inc.
668 Mt Hope Avenue, Rochester, NY 14620, USA
website: www.boydellandbrewer.com

A CIP catalogue record for this book is available
from the British Library

This publication is printed on acid-free paper

Printed in Great Britain by
Antony Rowe Ltd, Chippenham, Wiltshire

CONTENTS

ACKNOWLEDGMENTS

This project is truly the product of a community, and my brief words here cannot convey the depth of my gratitude to all of those who supported this endeavor and its author through its years of conceptualization. For their very tangible support of this project I am grateful to the College of Arts and Sciences at the University of Kentucky; my thanks to Steve Hoch and Mike Nietzel for their guidance throughout my career. I thank all those who thought I could and all those who hoped I would – my parents, Arnaldo and Grace Carvalho; my other set of parents, George and Annabelle Chumney; my godparents, Jim and Jean Smith; and my extended family in Illinois, Maine and Ohio. With best wishes for his own projects, I also thank my brother, Arnie Carvalho, for his patient and constructive advice. I would not have completed this project without the support of my coaches, cheerleaders and dear friends – Carla van Hoose, Melinda Hanley, Gina Kirwan, and Rusty Kreider, along with my graduate school colleagues whose belief in me still serves as a source of nourishment. For the gift of their time and their acute critical eye, I express my heartfelt thanks to Enrico M. Santí, Margaret E. W. Jones, and Donald L. Shaw. Above all I am grateful to my husband David, whose faith never ends. And finally, I wish this book to commemorate three strong women who taught me to take my place: my grandmother Doris H. Storey, my mentor Mary Jo Gies, and my friend Paula Frías.

For David, גהג
the architect of my dreams

… how can we reveal our place, first as it is bequeathed to us by tradition, and then as we want to transform it?

Julia Kristeva, 'Women's Time', p. 24

INTRODUCTION: TAKING HER PLACE

Space has always played an important role in imaginative writing. As English novelist Elizabeth Bowen observed in 1973, 'nothing can happen nowhere.'[1] Yet studies of the novel have traditionally foregrounded time over space, discussing plot as a sequence of actions. This book intends to offer a different framework for reading novels, and in particular women's popular fiction in Spanish America, with a focus on space rather than time as the narrative engine. We will examine five novels in which the female protagonists stake out a place for themselves within societies that are intentionally structured to work against this occupation of place. The analysis which follows will offer a way of reading that emphasizes spatial negotiation as a mechanism both of cementing and of undermining authority, thus exposing the strategies through which literature constructs and re-presents power.

Fundamental to this way of reading are the ideas of recent geographers and humanists who explore the negotiation and contestation of assigned social space. Questioning, subversion, and transgression constantly threaten the territorial boundaries erected for purposes of hegemonic stability. Geographic reality is converted into lived experience, through what geographers Michael Keith and Steve Pile term 'the spatialized politics of identity': 'the rhetoric of origins, of exclusion, of boundary-marking, of invasion and succession, of purity and contamination' (p. 20), and ultimately of the possibilities for individual or collective autonomy. Most contemporary cultural geographers, and the humanists who have benefited from and expanded upon their work, now recognize that the identity of the individual and the texture of her landscape are inseparable and reciprocally influential. In the words of feminist geographer Liz Bondi, 'the question "Who am I?" ... becomes "Where am I?"' (p. 98). The writers included in our study ask not only where she is but who put her there, with what authority and methodology, whether that placement is tolerable, and whether it is alterable. They articulate these questions through the creation of a three-dimensional imagined geography, the verbal construction of spaces which both reflect and exercise power.

The geographic theories to be utilized in the current study build on the groundbreaking study of Henri Lefebvre, *The Production of Space*,[2] and later explora-

---

[1] Elizabeth Bowen, *Pictures and Conversations* (1973), quoted in Tindall, p. 2.

[2] *The Production of Space*, published in French in 1974, was not translated into English until 1991; its reappearance at that time is both testament and impetus to the re-thinking of

tions of these concepts by theorists such as Edward Soja and Susan S. Friedman. Central to all of these studies is the concept of dynamic flows of power and their constitutive role in the establishment of places. Space is both a tool of power and the canvas of power; it is 'at once a precondition and a result of social super-structures' (Lefebvre, p. 85). Identity as well should be understood in terms of movement: in the words of Smith and Katz, 'the flow of travel not the putative fixity of space donates identity' (p. 78). In other words, location must be viewed as dynamic rather than static, and correspondingly, identity should also be seen as dynamic.

A compelling image for conceiving space in this way is offered by Lefebvre's image of a house's place-ness. A house may be viewed as stationary and solid: it has walls, concrete and glass, it seems 'the epitome of immovability,' as mapped by the architect in a blueprint. Yet, as Lefebvre points out, an electrician or a plumber would map the house very differently, 'as permeated from every direction by streams of energy which run in and out of it by every imaginable route: water, gas, electricity, telephone lines, radio and television signals, and so on. Its image of immobility would then be replaced by an image of a complex of mobilities, a nexus of in and out conduits' (pp. 92–3). This is the type of map that should guide us through the spaces we live and read – resulting in an alternative vision of physical space which does not deny materiality, but rather sees that materiality as a site of convergence for the various forces which contend for power.

Lefebvre attempts to resist past binarisms by setting up what he calls a *conceptual triad* (p. 33), what W. J. T. Mitchell terms a *dialectical triad* (p. x), and what Soja's enlightened re-reading of Lefebvre defines as a *trialectics* of space: they propose to understand further the traditional categories of 'perceived space' and 'conceived space' by viewing them through the lens of 'lived space' (Soja, *Thirdspace*, p. 11). This theoretical triangulation, or 'thirding' (to use Soja's term),[3] not only better enables the mental configuration of flows and relations, but also satisfyingly restores the third dimension to the discussion of space.[4]

As Soja observes, 'trialectical thinking is difficult, for it challenges all conventional modes of thought and taken-for-granted epistemologies. It is disorderly, unruly, constantly evolving, unfixed, never presentable in permanent constructions' (*Thirdspace*, p. 70). Patricia Yaeger, in *The Geography of Identity*, applies a similar idea to traditional ways of thinking about narrative, whether fictional, geographic, or historical. She notes that while linear thinking and the process of

---

space in more political terms during the past fifteen years. In Soja's view, upon its original publication Lefebvre's paradigm-shattering study 'was obliviously sucked back into unchanged disciplinary cocoons' and its implications were 'almost entirely missed by nearly all' (*Thirdspace*, p. 11). Soja's 1996 study *Thirdspace*, as well as other contemporary geographic discussions of power, have explored the far-reaching implications of Lefebvre's observations.

3   *Thirdspace*, p. 11.

4   Mathematically, a space of one dimension 'has length but no breadth or thickness,' a space of two dimensions 'has length and breadth, but no thickness,' and a space of three dimensions 'has length, breadth, and thickness' ('Dimension,' *Webster's 1913 Dictionary*).

writing have a natural affinity, as both are sequential, space 'resists traditional patterns of narrative. Space is a fragmentary field of action, a jurisdiction scattered and deranged, which appears to be negotiable or continuous but is actually peppered with chasms of economic and cultural disjunctions ... [S]pace moves out in all directions at once, and it is difficult to imagine a narrative structure capable of capturing this multiplicity' (p. 4).[5] We are accustomed to reading in two dimensions. The text is also composed in two dimensions; however, it is meant to reflect and to evoke a reality in three dimensions. Analyses such as the present one attempt to foreground the study of space in order to restore this three-dimensionality to our reading process, to conceive of events that happen through space as well as through time and that are shaped by space as well as by action.

We might therefore postulate a set of *trialectics* for the reading of space in literature. In analyses where plot, the 'sequence of events,' takes the fore-ground, setting has served primarily as backdrop.[6] The current study, along with other contemporary applications of spatial theory to literary texts, proposes to view the built environment, the body, the natural environment, and movements through space as both agent and consequence of the novel's depicted actions. It also proposes to examine the role of space within the textual practice of the novel. 'Popular fiction' of the type here studied tends to be viewed as more trans-parent than the intellectualized texts of the postmodern era. However, narrated space, like lived space, is not at all transparent. Its aesthetic construction involves and reflects an attention to context, a dialectic between protagonist and society, and a reflection of the flows of power within the narrated society.

Foucault proposed, in opposition to traditional linear history, a new disci-pline which Soja termed *geohistory*,[7] one which includes synchronic as well as diachronic visions, considering space in relation to time and event. This trian-gulation restores the unruly third dimension to our methods of analysis. Here I propose that we study the novel as *geoplot*. Plot is linear, but plot through space becomes three-dimensional, disrupted but also more vivid. Instead of concep-tualizing two-dimensional linear or even triangulated models, we borrow from Foucault the image of the 'polyhedron of intelligibility,' a structure which empha-sizes 'facets and intersections' rather than causal continuums.[8] We shall view the plots of these novels as narrative arrangements of tours rather than maps,[9] of

5   Yaeger does acknowledge the work of scholars such as Hayden White who demonstrate that time is in fact also not as linear and sequential as we have assumed (p. 4).

6   Lefebvre calls this 'the illusion of transparency,' the idea that space serves primarily as a backdrop and gives action 'free rein' (p. 27).

7   Summarized by Soja as 'an inseparable combination of heterotopologies and hetero-chronies that explicitly focused on the spatio-temporal interpretation of the power–knowledge relation' (*Thirdspace*, p. 170).

8   Foucault, 'Questions of Method,' p. 77. Referenced in Bordo, p. 32.

9   See Michel de Certeau, who defines a *map* as description, but a *tour* as experienced space. A map involves seeing, but a tour involves acting (p. 119).

actions through space, and of space as a sign of the power struggle between hegemonic forces and the individual or local expression of autonomy.

Soja concludes *Thirdspace* with a prose-poem, a portion of which we borrow
to summarize the geographic focus of our study of textually constructed spaces:

> a politics in which arguments over   SPACE   its enclosures
>   exclusions   internments
> become subjects for debate and discussion,
> and more important, for
>   resistance
>   and
>   transgression ...   (p. 320)

Of course, all stories happen *somewhere*; with varying degrees of verisimili-
tude, all stories confect some kind of place in which the action occurs. Both
spatial and literary theorists have noted the necessary connection between place
and plot. Tzvetan Todorov, in 'The Journey and its Narratives,' points out that
the journey – spiritual, material, and (usually) both – is a constitutive ingredient
of stories, for 'movement in space is the first sign, the easiest sign, of change;
in this sense journey and narrative imply one another' (p. 287). Spatial theorist
Michel de Certeau concurs, writing that 'every story is a travel story – a spatial
practice' (p. 115).[10] He further points to the dialectical nature of the relationship
between action and setting, noting that stories are marked out 'by the "citation"
of the places that result from them or authorize them' (p. 120). Such conceptualizations lead us towards consideration of the geoplot, which will seek to decipher
the ideological via the optical (Fitter, p. 22) and to link the question 'Who am I?'
with the question 'Where am I?' (Bondi, p. 98, cited above).

An illuminating articulation of the nexus between geography and literature
is found in Susan Stanford Friedman's 1998 study *Mappings: Feminism and the
Cultural Geographies of Encounter*. A scholar of English as well as Women's
Studies, Friedman proposes that all texts – literary or not – function on the basis
of identity juxtaposition and, correlatively, spatial juxtaposition. She identifies
shifting contact zones as the narrative engine which actively advances the events
of the plot (p. 144), and she thus postulates identity as geopolitical: 'Identity often
requires some form of displacement – literal or figurative – to come to consciousness' (p. 151). Thus, arguing against traditional notions of time as movement and

---

[10] De Certeau calls all stories 'spatial trajectories': 'stories [...] traverse and organize
places; they select and link them together; they make sentences and itineraries out of them'
(p. 115). Cultural geographers Daniels and Rycroft also note that the novel has always been
inherently geographical:

> The world of the novel is made up of locations and settings, arenas and boundaries,
> perspectives and horizons. Various places and spaces are occupied by the novel's char-
> acters, by the narrator and by audiences as they read. Any one novel may present a field
> of different, sometimes competing, forms of geographical knowledge, from a sensuous
> awareness of place to an educated idea of region and nation.   (p. 460)

space as stasis, she posits space as a series of encounters, as the basis for an alternative exploration of 'narrative kinesis': 'How does the narrative get from one cultural location to another? What propels its motion, its travel? ... How does each space reflect the cultural production of spatialized meaning? Or, determine the nature of or changes in character? Or, provide the conditions within which the agency of the characters must maneuver?' (p. 139).[11] Friedman postulates a *topochrone* in response to Bakhtin's *chronotope* (p. 137),[12] because the spatial emphasis allows for a closer examination of juxtaposed cultural difference, of cultural location as represented by material location. This allows for a revolutionary way of reading, one which will 'break open and expose ... the difference *difference* – specifically geopolitical and cultural difference – can make in our theorizations of narrative' and of identity (p. 133).

This approach substitutes anthropology for psychoanalysis in the study of desire. Rather than conceiving desire as represented in family and relationship, Friedman postulates this concept in terms of 'desire for the other, the different, the alien; desire to connect across or bridge difference; desire for difference as a mark of one's own lack or projection onto others of what is repressed in the self; desire propelled by curiosity, desire to fabulate, fantasize, dream, or create' (p. 134). In this sense, space represents the ultimate field of transgression. Space both separates and connects people. For those who are comfortable with their assigned social place, space – for example, traditional conceptualizations of home and homeland – provides reassuring boundaries which protect as well as proclaim. But for those who desire something else, something individually generated and therefore socially destabilizing, traditional spatial structures become constricting, and new places must be articulated. Space must be traversed, even transgressed, and places must be appropriated – either wrested in some sense from their prior possessors, or else reinvented.

The term 'identity' is also analyzed by Friedman, since its etymology implies both 'the same as' and 'relationally different from' (p. 143). The process of identity negotiation involves establishing both similarities and differences, and this 'oscillation between sameness and difference' is, for Friedman, the essence of ethnographic encounter. Thus, 'travel – a form of movement through space –

11 Friedman acknowledges that time must still be considered alongside space as a narrative engine; but she opts to emphasize the spatial dimension because it has so long been ignored, and thus has much to reveal (p. 138).

12 Michail Bakhtin's 1975 essay *The Dialogic Imagination* identifies the 'chronotope' (time-space) as an important element of narrative construction. Bakhtin postulates that different literary genres employ different categories of chronotopes, and he identifies as specific to the novel such time-spaces as crossroads, railway stations, thresholds, and marketplaces. The chronotopes unify literary genres across times, and serve as vehicles for 'cultural memory,' according to Katharina Hansen-Löve (p. 31). Hansen-Löve notes that Bakhtin conceived the idea of the chronotope during the 1930s but did not publish his analysis of the concept (in Russian) until 1975 (p. 30). According to Friedman, traditional literary scholarship has 'privilege[d] the temporal over the spatial axis, subtly turning Bakhtin's chronotope into chrono*type*' (p. 137).

brings about an engagement with the other or others in a liminal space materially, psychologically, or culturally in between' (p. 143). Since travel is the underlying structure of most, if not all, stories, then stories may be seen primarily as the exploration of ethnographic encounter, of 'intercultural blending and clashing' (p. 136). Friedman wonders at the fact that literary criticism has delayed so long in recognizing the centrality of such spatial readings; she cites Sabina Sawhney, who writes: 'crossracial/ethnic encounter itself seems so knotty, so tangled with conflicting concerns and desire, that it seems to demand a narrative unraveling, a fiction of explanation' (Friedman, p. 60). The present study will view five current novels as such fictions of explanation, utilizing the examination of spatial constructs within the novel as a basis for deciphering the work's judgment on the place of women in Spanish America, at the turn of the millennium.

For all of this approach's reliance on recent cultural geography as well as spatial theory, it does not propose the erasure of disciplinary distinctions. Instead, observations such as these allow for the examination of fictional narratives as purposeful aesthetic constructs, not obscured but rather illuminated by the obser-vational and interpretative practices of cultural geography, gender studies, and ethnography. Friedman's chapter title 'Telling Contacts' (p. 132), with its double entendre, summarizes an entirely new way of breaking open the literary text.

Feminist geographer Doreen Massey states that her concern 'is not with the geography of women but with the construction of gender and gender relations' (*Space, Place, and Gender*, p. 12). Similarly, this study will focus on the narrative configuration of geography as it pertains to structures of power and, in particular, how those structures operate on and through the female protagonist. We shall examine representations of displacement, and the ways in which this displace-ment can lead to the creation of new, more fluid spaces in which identity can potentially be self-articulated. Most of the women represented in these novels do travel, whether within a town, between towns, or between countries; but the focus of our study will be on the navigational strategies involved in this spatial movement, the relation between autonomy and spatial norms or restrictions, and considerations of embodiment as a point of contact between identity and place. Again we turn to Massey for an articulation of gendered geographical study as a way of building on Lefebvrean concepts, but with a consciousness of power exercised through race and gender as well as class, thus further illuminating the polyhedron of intelligibility involved in social construction:

> what gives a place its specificity is not some long internalized history but the fact that it is constructed out of a particular constellation of social relations, meeting and weaving together at a particular locus. ... It is, indeed, a meeting place. Instead, then, of thinking of places as areas with boundaries around, they can be imagined as articulated moments in networks of social relations and understandings ... constructed on a far larger scale than what we happen to define for that moment as the place itself. ...
>
> (*Space, Place, and Gender*, p. 154)

Since literary constructions of space are at once mimetic and symbolic, we shall examine margins, borders, the liminal space, and the imaginary realm of the *chora*, as well as the self-articulated body, as chosen sites of resistance, as what bell hooks calls 'locations of radical openness and possibility' (*Yearning*, p. 153). We will read through descriptions of ordinary existence for the construction of surveillance and control that produced space makes manifest, as well as for the strategies of resistance that also take place, for as Gillian Rose notes, 'the everyday is the arena through which patriarchy is (re)-created – and contested' (p. 17). The female protagonist in the Spanish American novel will thus be studied as both object and subject of spatial control; and paramount to our analysis will be the discursive strategies of this verbal chorography. While Susan Griffin's 1978 essay *Woman and Nature: The Roaring Inside Her* has been – correctly – criticized by contemporary feminists for its essentializing equation of women with nature, we nonetheless borrow from her here to summarize our novelists' constructions of the ways in which women take place:

> We are no longer pleading for the right to speak: we have spoken; space has changed; we are living in a matrix of our own sounds; our words resonate, by our echoes we chart a new geography; we recognize this new landscape as our birthplace, where we invented names for ourselves; here language does not contradict what we know; by what we hear, we are moved again and again to speak.   (Griffin, p. 195; quoted in Rose, p. 80)

The idea of studying women rather than Woman is central to the examination of feminism within the novels to be considered here. Because we will discuss novels from different countries, by writers from distinct social, cultural, and class situations, we shall attempt to draw conclusions not about the geographical situation or mobility of 'the Latin American woman,' but rather the situations of certain fictional women within hypothetical communities; their situations serve as examples of ways in which subjectivity can be negotiated in the face of opposing forces of power. The protagonists all strive to construct a place for themselves, but each invents her own strategies for doing so. Additionally, the novelists represent in an intentional way the oppositional forces which attempt to enforce conformity and homogeneity, often through the control of physical space, but differently for each author. Thus, the observations of contemporary feminist theorists in general, and feminist geographers in particular, can serve as a useful guide for avoiding generalizations that erase situated ways of knowing and responding to the world. Adrienne Rich's conceptualization of women's geographic, and thus social, specificity is again useful: 'Tribal loyalties aside, and even if nation-states are now just pretexts used by multinational conglomerates to serve their interests, I need to understand how a place on the map is also a place in history within which as a woman, a Jew, a lesbian, a feminist I am created and trying to create' (p. 212).

One stereotype that is undermined in all of the novels we shall examine is the idea of a 'women's space.' While past feminist theory has celebrated the strategic importance of alliances among women, some of which manifest themselves in spatial groupings, we shall see in all of these novels a disintegration of that concept. While women certainly associate with each other, their alliances are shifting and provisional, as ultimately they must negotiate their own individual space. Such plotting is consistent with contemporary locational feminism, which emphasizes 'the multiplicity of ways of being a woman, of "doing gender"' (McDowell and Sharp, *Space, Gender, Knowledge*, p. 3).

Indeed, warning against constructions of universalization, Donna Haraway in 'Situated Knowledges' equates unlocatable knowledge claims with irresponsibility, defining irresponsible as 'unable to be called into account' (p. 583); thus unlocated figurations, those which appear placeless and bodyless, often tell us nothing about the real world in which we live. We must instead ask not only what happens, but where it happens, under what circumstances, and to which specific person(s). Friedman most clearly articulates the inescapable connection between geographical and socio-cultural positioning:

> A locational approach to feminism incorporates diverse formations because its positional analysis requires a kind of geopolitical literacy built out of a recognition of how different times and places produce different and changing gender systems as these intersect with other different and changing societal stratifications and movements for social justice. Locational feminism thus encourages the study of difference in all its manifestations without being limited to it, without establishing impermeable borders that inhibit the production and visibility of ongoing exchange and hybridity. (p. 5)

While our female protagonists may be considered as representative of a particular gendered or cultural situation, they should be seen as case studies rather than universal models, as women grounded in bodily and geographic specificity rather than as archetypes of a postulated, universalized feminist agenda.

Towards this end, our authors portray secondary female characters and posit their differences from the woman protagonist as well as their similarities to her. Female 'communities' are represented, but as heterogeneous rather than unified. Judith Butler posits, in *Gender Trouble: Feminism and the Subversion of Identity* that gender coherence is a regulatory fiction, that the construction of Woman is a consequence of invented norms intended further to direct the paths and choices of women within patriarchy (pp. 32–3). As we shall see, the female protagonist in these novels does not feel 'at home' among other women, but continues restless and roaming, as she seeks to make a place not for her gender but for herself.

Another simultaneous development in both feminist theory and recent literature by Spanish American women is a geographic de-centering, consonant with the emphasis on locational politics, which focuses on conceptualizations such as diaspora and borderlands. These imagined geographies offer the space for an examination of marginalized populations, of those who have either been expelled from the center (geographic and/or metaphorical) or are unable to reach it, and whose positions of resistance or difference are thus more definitive. Such populations offer fertile ground for explorations of counter-hegemony and self-articulation, often combine racial with gender and class conflicts, and represent the strategic role of the margin in subverting the control of the center.[13] Homi Bhabha's study of postcolonial identity, *The Location of Culture*, explores similar ideas from a cultural rather than a gendered perspective; he postulates a 'third space' of localized hybrid identity 'where the negotiation of incommensurable differences creates a tension peculiar to borderline existences' (p. 218). The intersection of postcolonial with feminist theory, and of both with the production of recent novels by Spanish American women, further illuminates the complex web of power flows that operate through and upon space.[14]

Consonant with the above-described 'boom' in spatial theory as well as the newly mined affinities between geography and literature, studies of the configuration of narrative space in Spanish American fiction have begun to appear. The literary production of Spanish America lends itself in a very particular way to analysis from the geographic perspective, because it has for centuries functioned as a contact zone in terms of race, class, and economic interests. In the novels to be examined here, the issue of contact between the Spanish American countries and the United States plays a fundamental role. Class and gender lines have also been more strongly delineated in Spanish America than in, for example, the North American culture. However, all cultures are of course inherently heterogeneous. Thus, while the contact zone between the United States and Spanish America, in terms of politics, economics, and culture, is often evident in Spanish American fiction, this is not the only intercultural difference to be marked by spatial discursive strategies. Instead, each individual is depicted in 'contact' with her surroundings – with those postulated as her social equals, with those who promote and who impede her movement, with both 'home' and the territory that lies beyond. The concepts of borderlands and boundaries, then, can be expanded to include all space which lies between an individual and her surroundings. All of those spaces, including even the surface of her body, form a contact zone to be mapped and negotiated.

Many recent applications of spatial studies to Spanish American literature continue earlier lines of investigation, further developing the kind of geographical determinism, or equations of natural environment with national character, so prevalent in nineteenth-century fiction (particularly of the Southern Cone).[15]

---

13 bell hooks' essay 'Choosing the Margin' in *Feminist Theory: From Margin to Center* (1984) is particularly helpful here.

14 See Linda McDowell, 'Spatializing Feminism: Geographic Perspectives' (1996), for a discussion of convergences between contemporary feminism and postcolonial theory.

15 For example, Javier de Navascués edited in 2002 a collection of essays entitled *De Arcadia a Babel: naturaleza y ciudad en la literatura hispanoamericana*. While the studies contained in this collection do make astute observations regarding particular spatial constructions in Spanish American literature, they continue to see space in terms of the grand binary

However, other critical explorations begin to examine the more dialectical stances outlined in this Introduction. Some of the most fruitful studies of space are grounded in contemporary postcolonial thought. These studies focus on questions of national identity, in particular in the face of European cultural presences which continue to overshadow and direct continental self-perceptions of collective identity.[16]

A study more closely aligned with our own perspectives of situated and localized knowledge and place is Claire Lindsay's *Locating Latin American Women Writers: Cristina Peri Rossi, Rosario Ferré, Albalucía Angel, and Isabel Allende* (2003). Grounding her study in Adrienne Rich's insights on positionality as well as Jean Franco's study of the simultaneous political and literary emergence of Latin American women,[17] Lindsay discusses the intersections of gender, ethnicity, sexuality, and other sociocultural factors in establishing the identity and perspectives of the writers themselves. She works to situate the authors and their geographical locations with questions of textual production, including the literary marketplace; the central focus of her analysis is the question of *from where* the texts are produced, where the writer herself stands as she generates her text. This study marks an important advance in Spanish American spatial studies, as it foregrounds the formative role of cultural and national positioning in the production of literature by women. The literary texts themselves are not analyzed in terms of their articulation of material places. Nonetheless, Lindsay's work demonstrates that this theoretical stance can be useful for various potential interrogations of Latin American women's literary production.

Various article-length studies also mark the growing awareness of spatialized studies in their potential for examining Spanish American literature in general.[18]

---

opposition of natural against built environment, as descended from colonial and nineteenth-century traditions. Questions of space as a construct and an engine of power negotiation are not considered, nor is the question of individual positioning within a particular spatial context.

[16] Marcy Schwartz produces a fascinating study of various representations of Paris by Spanish American writers, in her book *Writing Paris: Urban Topographies of Desire in Contemporary Latin American Fiction* (1999). This work examines the discursive strategies through which Paris is narrated as a social image, to be navigated by American characters who have often sought to define themselves in terms of, or in opposition to, Europe. Schwartz's postcolonial approach focuses on 'Latin America's geohistorical relationships through their continuing cross-Atlantic intersections' (p. 4). In an equally illuminating postcolonial study which incorporates a gendered perspective, Ileana Rodríguez explores the connections between land, gender, and nationhood in *House/Garden/Nation: Space, Gender, and Ethnicity in Post-colonial Latin American Literatures by Women* (1994). Her vision of a 'continental narratology' (p. 4) corresponds with the focus of Schwartz, in the analysis of Spanish American literary and cultural declarations of independence through verbal constructions of particular symbolic places.

[17] Jean Franco, 'Going Public: Reinhabiting the Private' (first published 1992).

[18] Within the above-mentioned 1987 collection *Geography and Literature: A Meeting of the Disciplines*, César Caviedes publishes a study of José María Arguedas's novel *El zorro de arriba y el zorro de abajo*. And Luz Aurora Pimentel's essay 'The Ideological Value of Description in Latin American Narrative' (1995) explores the ideological significance of

Again, however, these discussions do not closely examine the aesthetic structuring of space; and while they may incorporate issues of class distinctions, they do not view space as gendered as well as class-constituted. Nonetheless, studies such as the ones mentioned here demonstrate the increasing awareness of the relevance of spatial theory to Spanish American literary study. Because questions of borderlands and boundaries have been of particular relevance in that region, because the shadow of the United States' economic, political, and cultural expansion makes postcolonial theories of juxtaposition and hegemony particularly illuminating, and because of an increased awareness of racial and gendered positional stances as well as a corresponding surge in literary exploration of such themes, there is certainly a place for geographic study in the analysis of Spanish American narrative. The present study is intended to serve as a model for future explorations of feminist geography and contemporary Spanish American prose, as we explore texts by five of the most widely read women novelists at the turn of the twenty-first century, from four distinct regions of Spanish America: Laura Restrepo (Colombia), Isabel Allende (Chile), Angeles Mastretta (Mexico), Sara Sefchovich (Mexico), and Rosario Ferré (Puerto Rico).

Women's writing in Spanish America remains a relatively recent phenomenon, with novels by Spanish American women appearing on international bestseller lists only since the 1980s. Texts since that time may be grouped into two broad categories: avant-garde works which create radically amimetic spaces to articulate postmodern theories of nation and identity;[19] and more popular novels which appear to follow a relatively 'traditional' novelistic structure and narrative perspective. These latter works, consonant with the so-called 'post-boom' movement (in contrast to the contemporary postmodern vein of novels), reject the inaccessibility of the previous generation's novels, and instead avail themselves of quotidian imagery and a level of discourse intended to attract a broad readership base. In spite of their greater accessibility, however, this latter group should not be considered inferior in terms of technical and thematic innovation, since subversions of traditional discursive strategies and perspectives continue to undergird both types of narrative. This study will focus on examples of the 'popular novel,' both because of its more referential articulation of geographic

diegetic space as the articulation of a political stance, emphasizing that the narrative representation of space transcends the functions of ornamentation or backdrop (p. 60). While her study includes application only to one work – José Donoso's *Casa de campo* – her observations are nonetheless valid for many other literary works of Latin America.

[19] Examples include the novels of Chilean writer Diamela Eltit, Mexican novelist Carmen Boullosa, or Uruguayan novelist Cristina Peri Rossi. For a full discussion of the post-boom and postmodernity in Spanish American fiction, see Donald L. Shaw, *The Post-Boom in Spanish American Fiction* (1998), chapters 2 and 8. He notes, in summary: 'Postmodernism's delegitimation of ideology, in other words, threatens the social agenda of some Post-Boom writers and would in fact tend to promote the idea of complete heterogeneity in the literary arena, with no dominant tendencies. By contrast, use of the term *Post-Boom* implies emphasis on the importance of a separate group of writers, identifiable by reference to a set of (loose) criteria' (p. 178).

(regional) spaces, and because its broader readership arguably gives it a greater role in shaping as well as reflecting views of space and place in the Latin American cultural, political, and economic context.

The writers to be studied in this work share particular characteristics in both their approaches to reality and their aesthetics. They do not question the nature of reality, nor do they believe it to be unintelligible. Rather, their work carries a committed social agenda, intent upon examining the sources of contemporary national problems and, implicitly or explicitly, postulating conceivable solutions to those problems. Consonant with this intent, their aesthetics aim for originality and (modest) narrative experimentation, but maintain a constant goal of accessibility. They all tell a good story. In conscious reaction to the perceived elitism of the Boom period of Spanish American fiction, they hope through their novels both to portray and to attract a broad readership base, and thus to effect real social and political shifts in the consumers' view of their own world. The five writers studied here are, in market terms, the most successful Spanish American women writers of their generation. All have won major literary awards, have been (or are being) widely translated, and have had their work issued in numerous editions. All have transcended the often constraining bounds of their own national publishing houses, and are widely read throughout Latin America and abroad. In sum, they are either the agents or the products of a major marketing trend in Spanish American fiction. Significantly for the purposes of this study, their work embodies an attempt to change the way their (female) readers see, and by extension appropriate, their own places within their nations and societies.

Our first discussion, in Chapter 2, will deal with the Colombian novelist Laura Restrepo, whose openly political fiction appropriates techniques of female popular fiction to interrogate paralegal power structures and confront the military as well as the economic violence of contemporary Colombia. The following chapter will focus on the most successful writer of popular fiction in Spanish America, Chilean novelist Isabel Allende, whose female protagonists utilize various strategies for entering forbidden territory – cross-dressing, the disguise of the camera, business negotiations behind 'front-men,' and the act of writing – as they demand their place within a male-dominated economic, political, social and romantic arena. The subsequent chapter will treat the fiction of the most popular Caribbean woman writer, Rosario Ferré, whose most recent novels, published first in English and then in Spanish, trace familial dynasties and changing gender dynamics alongside Puerto Rico's political and social evolution since 1898. Our discussion of Mexican writer Sara Sefchovich, in Chapter 5, will revisit the discussion of sexual transgression, posing the final question of whether the voluntary cessation of movement should be interpreted as resistance or surrender. And the final chapter will deal with Mexican writer Angeles Mastretta, whose adoption of the genres of melodrama appears to offer more traditional portraits of Hispanic femininity, and whose novels offer intriguing rewritings of public versus private space.

Isabel Allende (b. 1942) put Spanish American women's fiction 'on the map,' with the publication of the blockbuster *La casa de los espíritus* in 1982. Building on the legacy of magical realism popularized by Gabriel García Márquez, Allende added a strong dose of melodrama along with the context of Salvador Allende's rise and fall, in order to trace the history of four generations of upper-class Chilean women. This novel, as well as some of the works which followed (*De amor y de sombra*, *Eva Luna*), was criticized by feminist critics because of its traditional portrayals of gender roles and the optimism that some readers found ingenuous. However, Allende has survived these critiques and continued as a major figure in Spanish American letters, having published to date twelve full-length fictional works,[20] a collection of short stories, and her autobiography, *Mi país inventado* (2003). Two of her recent novels are designed as prequels to *La casa de los espíritus*, and at the same time explore the nineteenth-century ties between Chile (Allende's homeland) and California (her current home). *Hija de la fortuna* (1999) follows the protagonist Eliza Sommers from Valparaíso to California during the Gold Rush of 1849; *Retrato en sepia* (2000) tells the story of her granddaughter Aurora as she returns to Chile and maps her own trajectory. Our discussion will focus on this latter novel, and the central figure of the photographer-protagonist who develops her unique way of seeing bodies and places, and then 'captures' them in her portraits. Additionally, Aurora uncovers her own roots by examining postcards and old photos, thus constructing a territory of memory that parallels her explorations of her own identity. Taking possession of space through travel and through the photographic eye, Aurora moves from the margin to the center and, by the novel's end, feels empowered to wander where she will, independent of the traditional male escort figure.

Like Allende, Laura Restrepo (b. 1950) began her writing career as a journalist, gaining significant visibility through her investigative reporting on paramilitary forces and drug cartels in Colombia. In addition to four nonfiction collections, to date she has published six novels, the most recent of which (*Delirio*, 2003) received the prestigious Premio Alfaguara; earlier works were recognized by Mexico's Premio Sor Juana Inés de la Cruz and the French prize awarded to the best foreign novel, the Prix France Culture. *La novia oscura* (1999) tells the story of a prostitute of unknown origins, Sayonara, who becomes the fantasy object of desire for hundreds of petroleum workers in the region of Colombia's interior controlled by Standard Oil Company. Eventually the *barrio* of the prostitutes is dismantled by the oil company, and replaced by US-style suburbs, in an attempt to quiet a restless worker population. The portrayal of these societies erected and dismantled according to the interests of the international conglomerate reflects a geography of power within which individuals struggle to maintain some degree of autonomy. The fragmented nature of the story's telling reflects

---

[20] In addition to the primary novels, these works include three children's novels, the chronicle of her daughter's illness and death (*Paula*, 1995), and the comic mixture of autobiography, recipes, and fiction in *Afrodita* (1997).

the various perspectives from which the men and women attempt to make sense of the systems that direct their lifecourses.

The most recent works of Rosario Ferré (b. 1938) are unique within the canon of Spanish American fiction, in that she writes and publishes first in English and then translates her work into Spanish. This cultural positioning as well as a stance widely perceived as pro-US have made her the target of much criticism from the Spanish American academy. While Ferré first appeared on the literary scene in the 1970s with the publication of popular short stories (eventually published as *Papeles de Pandora* 1976), she has continued to develop as an essayist, poet, and novelist. Her recent novel, *The House on the Lagoon* (1995) won her a nomination for the National Book Award, received the Critic's Choice Award and was selected for the Book of the Month Club. That work explores the complex cultural relationships between the US and Puerto Rico, through several generations of women. Her most recent novel, *Flight of the Swan* (2001), explores the trajectory of a Russian ballet dancer who leaves behind the tumult of her own homeland in 1917, only to face a different kind of upheaval on an unnamed Caribbean island.

Sara Sefchovich (b. 1949) established her reputation as a scholar and essayist before publishing her first novel, *Demasiado amor*, in 1989. Throughout her career, her nonfiction writings have focused on the interconnected questions of national literature and the role of women. Indeed, the role that reading and literature play in the formation of a woman's sense of agency figures as a prominent theme in all three of her novels. *Demasiado amor* met with resounding popular success as well as literary acclaim; it was awarded the Premio AgustínYáñez and has been reissued in several editions, and was recently adapted into a major motion picture (dir. Ernesto Rimoch, 2002). The novel intertwines two written texts – the protagonist's letters to her sister in Italy, and the same woman's personal memoir of her weekends touring the country with her lover. The inviting but intricate narrative style lays before the reader two competing spatial trajectories, as the epistolary narrator explores the sex industry at the same time as the traveling narrator tires of the peripatetic life and struggles to come to terms with a future on her own terms.

Finally, Angeles Mastretta (b. 1949) rivals Laura Esquivel as Mexico's most visible contemporary woman writer. The author of four collections of short stories and three best-selling novels, she has also won several international literary awards. Her most recent novel, *Mal de amores* (1996), received the prestigious Premio Rómulo Gallegos, the first time that it was ever awarded to a woman writer. Her novels combine historical realism with melodrama as they explore the links between power and love. *Mal de amores*, set during the Mexican Revolution, explores the open possibilities for women's activity as the *porfiriato* – the rule of Porfirio Díaz – disintegrated and the post-Revolution environment lent itself to gynocentric restructuring.

All of these writers explore female protagonists who stake a claim for autonomy within geographic territories that are contested on the basis of race, class, gender or ethnicity. While the rhetorical strategies differ, the focus consistently returns to questions which can be illuminated through the framework of cultural geography: Where are these women, how did they get there, and where can they go from there? Our analysis will focus not only on the thematic treatment of these issues but on the structural and aesthetic techniques which turn their trajectories into stories, thereby (re)writing cultural and territorial maps within the mind of the reader.

1

Textual Situations:
At the Crossroads of Literature and Geography

Geographical foundations

Discussions of locatedness often begin by establishing useful definitions and distinctions between the concepts of 'space' and 'place.' There being so much groundwork on the topic, we shall not attempt here to revise the terms, but merely to establish our use of them for the current study. The terms are difficult to define except in relation to each other. Gaston Bachelard claimed correctly that 'Inhabited space transcends geometrical space' (p. 47). This inhabited or lived-in space embodies that concept now denoted by the word 'place.' Or, as W. J. T. Mitchell notes, 'space has connotations of abstraction and geometry, while place resonates with particularity and qualitative density' (p. ix).[1]

For our purposes, a more useful distinction between the terms is established by David Harvey, who begins from the premise that 'change is a characteristic of all systems,' of place no less than of space, and that the task of the scholar is to explore this *appearance* of stability (*Justice*, p. 54).[2] His conceptualization is the one upon which the present study will rely: that our challenge is 'to understand places as internally heterogeneous, dialectical and dynamic configurations of *relative* "permanence" within the overall spatio-temporal dynamics of socio-ecological processes' (p. 244, emphasis mine).[3] This concept of place as a site of interaction and negotiation rather than as a monument functions to explain many of our metaphors of positionality and identity, as well as the forces of change that constantly recontour our physical environment. Spatial metaphors of hierarchy generally use the word *place* rather than *space*: we know (or are reminded of) our

---

[1] See also Harvey's citation of theologian Walter Brueggemann (*The Land: Place as Gift, Promise, and Challenge in Biblical Faith* [1977], p. 4): 'Place is space that has historical meanings, where some things have happened that are now remembered and that provide continuity and identity across generations. Place is space in which important words have been spoken that have established identity, defined vocation, and envisioned destiny. Place is space in which vows have been exchanged, promises have been made, and demands have been issued' (Harvey, *Justice*, p. 304).

[2] Here Harvey references Richard Levins and Richard Lewontin, *The Dialectical Biologist* (1985), p. 275.

[3] However, Harvey's use of the word 'permanence' is problematic, as our study will focus on the constant pressure on space to adapt, or be adapted, to the intentions – the social and personal agendas – of its owners or its inhabitants.

place, we refer to 'a woman's place,' events take place (implying the flow of time momentarily trapped by the fixity of material space). Successful plans 'fall into place,' upstarts 'usurp place' and subsequently must be 'put in their place,' the powerless are 'going no place,' the disoriented 'lose their place,' the discomfited are feeling 'out of place,' the homeless are 'displaced,' and dispensable people are 'replaced.' We thus, philosophically and linguistically, equate place with the assignment of power. In some ways one controls one's place, but in other ways one is subject to the rules and confines of that place. Either one carves out one's place or one knows one's assigned place. Thus place is that space which has become tied to issues of social, cultural, and personal identity.[4]

In order to clarify the framework of our analysis, we begin by offering a brief overview of the tendencies in Marxist and feminist geography that have opened doors to this kind of cross-disciplinary study. The concept of place as a site of intersection and interaction is central to our consideration of its literary construction. It is essential to view places as processes of ongoing negotiation, as continuous advances and retreats in the establishment of individual or collective autonomy. As Robert David Sack notes in *Homo Geographicus*, 'place and self help construct and activate each other' (p. 132). Edward Soja has best captured the far-reaching implications of the dynamics at work in the space/place nexus. He writes:

> As we approach the fin de siècle, there is a growing awareness of the simulta-neity and interwoven complexity of the social, the historical, and the spatial, their inseparability and interdependence. And this three-sided sensibility of spatiality–historicality–sociality is not only bringing about a profound change in the ways we think about space, it is also beginning to lead to major revisions in how we study history and society. (*Thirdspace*, p. 3)

This observation applies not only to how we study history and society, but also to aesthetics, and indeed an entire range of individual responses to the exercising of cultural authority.

Geography – and in particular contemporary cultural geography – must be recognized not in such generic terms as the writing or the study of space, but as a broad-based study of how space is lived in, how cultures construct them-selves within space and how those spaces in turn influence the development and control of those cultures. Edward Said, in his 2002 essay 'Invention, Memory, and Place,' defines geography as 'a socially constructed and maintained sense of place' (pp. 245–6), as a recognition and an exploration of 'the extraordinary constitutive role of space in human affairs' (p. 246).[5] Not only the built environ-

---

[4] Tuan endorses this concept, speaking of space as scientific and measurable, but place as 'full of human interpretation and significance' (*Space*, p. 54), a 'concretion of value' (*Space*, p. 12) incarnating 'the experiences and aspirations of a people' ('Space and Place,' p. 213).

[5] Common to the vast majority of spatial theorizations since 1970, including Said's, is the view of spaces not as a neutral force of nature or 'empty mediums or containers distinct from

ment but also the natural landscape is useful as a commodity, as a possession that connotes and lends power,[6] as the site of natural resources, and as an expanse to be used. Kenneth Olwig defines landscape as 'the expression of the practices of habitation through which the habitus of place is generated and laid down as custom and law upon the physical fabric of the land' (p. 226). In other words, landscape involves the integration of human existence into the natural environ- ment, and when we contemplate a real or a textualized landscape we view not topography but 'a historical document containing evidence of a long process of interaction between society and its material environs' (Olwig, p. 226). Dolores Hayden concurs, when she refers to a 'cultural landscape' as both cultural docu- ment and physical landscape: 'human patterns impressed upon the contours of the natural environment. It is the story of how places are planned, designed, built, inhabited, appropriated, celebrated, despoiled, and discarded' (p. 15). From this basis, Hayden speaks of 'reading' landscapes, cityscapes, and even bodyscapes as embedded and embodied 'narratives of cultural identity' (p. 13).

Space as template, as an engraving through which the hand of the engravers can be revisualized, represents one important component of contemporary cultural geography.[7] However, theorists such as Foucault, Lefebvre and Soja go further, in postulating that space is more than the canvas on which humanity writes its story; it functions also as an agent of identity formation.[8] Its role in shaping rather than just containing human activity is articulated in *The Dictionary of Human Geography*'s definition of 'spatial structure,' which emphasizes the multidimen- sionality of the space/society question: 'spatial structure [is] seen not merely as an arena *in which* social life unfolds but as a medium *through which* social life is produced and reproduced.'[9] As such a medium, space serves as a site of juncture of political, economic, and social forces, creating what Soja, following Lefe- bvre, calls 'the socio-spatial dialectic' of interdependence between social life and territory (p. 207). Into this dynamic must be incorporated the effects of time, of a series of events that superimpose one another on a single territory, creating a three-dimensional 'geographical puzzle' which geographers Wolch and Dear characterize as follows:

> Any locale is ... at once a complex synthesis of objects, patterns, and proc- esses derived from the simultaneous interaction of *different levels of social*

their contents' (Lefebvre, p. 87) but as a process of interaction between the individual and the surrounding hegemonic forces which propose and impose identities.

6   This power is both economic and political, both individual and collective.

7   'an already produced space can be decoded, can be *read*. Such a space implies a process of signification' (Lefebvre, p. 17).

8   In Lefebvre's words, 'social space can in no way be compared to a blank page upon which a specific message has been inscribed' (p. 87); it is not 'innocent and decipherable' (p. 28) but rather offers an illusion of transparency.

9   D. Gregory, 'Spatial structure,' in *The Dictionary of Human Geography*, ed. R. J. John- ston et al., p. 451; cited in Gillian Rose, *Feminism and Geography*, p. 19.

process, operating at *varying geographical scales and chronological stages*.
It is as though a multi-tiered sequence of events had been telescoped into a
single dimension; many levels and scales of process are simply collapsed on to
a single territory.   (p. 7)

A key element of this analysis involves the reciprocal relationship between individuals and social forces, a process which is complex and multi-directional. In
other words, while we shall argue that large-scale economic and political forces
influence the inhabitants of any geographical region – on both the public and
the private levels – at the same time individual persons or groups can transgress
the territorial boundaries which these institutions attempt to impose; they can
establish ad hoc or formal sites of resistance; they can exercise a certain degree
of autonomy in the face of opposite pressures. Yet in most cases, and in particular
in the works that our discussion will address, it is difficult to declare victory for
either side of this struggle. As W. T. J. Mitchell has succinctly summarized the
central question, 'Do we make places, or do they make us?' (p. xii).[10]

The answer, of course, is both. The central mechanism which operates the
dialectic between individual identity and social forces is the exercise of power
– hegemonic vs. autonomic – whenever the sometimes dissonant voices of individual behaviors and attitudes come up against the homogenizing forces of social
control. While Lefebvre and other Marxist geographers configure these hegemonic forces always as capitalist,[11] feminist theorists in particular identify other

---

[10] Mitchell points out that this question is based in Heideggerean questions of place 'as
simultaneously determined by and determining our "being in the world," Dasein' (p. xii).

[11] Marxist social scientists, grounding their work in Lefebvre's presentation of spatial
dialectics, view the organization of space as the province of capitalist hegemonic forces.
Lefebvre defines his thesis as follows: 'I shall show how space serves, and how hegemony
makes use of it, in the establishment, on the basis of an underlying logic and with the help of
knowledge and technical expertise, of a "system"' (p. 11). He does acknowledge the existence
and subversive effect of spaces of rebellion and resistance (p. 26), of what he calls 'counter-
spaces' (p. 349) and Foucault terms 'counter-sites' ('Of Other Spaces,' p. 24). See also Doreen
Massey, who writes that 'spatial form can alter the future course of the very histories which
have produced it' ('Politics and Space/Time,' p. 155). In contrast to Soja and other theorists
who focus more on the negotiated nature of social space, David Harvey postulates that the
capitalist forces of globalization are in the end irresistible, that the leveling effect of world-
wide capitalism moves us increasingly towards an erasure of the local and the personal and
towards a culture of reproduceable, efficient mediocrity (*The Condition of Postmodernity*, pp.
346–9). This results in the erosion of specificity and a push towards faceless homogeneity.
   However, the writers to be examined in our study do not conform to this image of the inexorable fashioning of identity from above, or to Harvey's view of the unproductive results of
what he calls 'identity politics.' Rather, for the present analysis we can find more useful models
of the space–identity dialectic in those cultural studies focused on feminist and marginalized
cultures, such as Dolores Hayden's analysis of Los Angeles (*The Power of Place*) and Raúl
Homero Villa's *Barrio-Logos: Space and Place in Urban Chicano Literature and Culture*,
which address more directly those ways in which individual persons or groups successfully
maintain their own threateningly different identities, in opposition to the social codes that
hegemony's spaces attempt to impose.

entities which seek the rule of order and the silencing of dissenters: patriarchal tradition, social convention, political affiliation, religious oppression, racial conflict, etc.[12] For the hegemons and the dissenters, 'taking place' serves as a statement of presence and of power.[13]

Keith and Pile's discussion of the politics of identity effectively confronts the multi-directional flow of spatial construction and reconstruction, as a site of negotiated identities. They define spatiality as 'the name for the surfaces of articulation between regimes of power,' including the displaced or oppressed collectivities as one of those regimes of power (p. 224), and they point out that spatiality is constructed out of those very 'asymmetrical relations of power' (p. 38). In their emphasis on the bidirectionality of spatial construction, they demand that we challenge the 'hegemonic constructions of place, of politics and of identity' that occur at times in theoretical conceptualizations as well as in practice (p. 38).

Literary texts can enter into the sphere of cultural reproduction, as sites of resistance, counter-spaces, ways of both exposing the agents that control space (from behind the scene, so to speak) and positing a change in the ways that space can be appropriated individually and collectively.[14] In imagery evocative of Foucault's studies on surveillance and control, Lefebvre writes: 'a counter-space can insert itself into spatial reality: against the Eye and the Gaze, against quantity and homogeneity, against power and the arrogance of power, against the endless expansion of the "private" and of industrial profitability; and against specialized spaces and a narrow localization of function' (p. 382). However, his conceptualization of the potential of individual or local demands for change, for the opportunity to assign or to take over place, leads to a rather bleak conclusion:

12 It should be noted that Lefebvre et al. would subsume all of these homogenizing forces of social control under the heading of capitalism, with its economic energies of production and the social energies of reproduction which enable and protect it. Because of the varying political and cultural situations of the authors here to be studied, I will attempt to limit the attribution of capitalist control per se only to those situations where it is explicit or most evident – for example, in the globalization issues confronted in Laura Restrepo's work.

13 Edward Said, in an essay on the Palestine/Israel conflict, speaks of world history, and in particular colonialism, as a continual series of *displacements* – 'the replacement of one geographical sovereignty ... by another' (p. 247). Within this conceptualization, time overlies space in a sequence of struggles for control over a single territory. Geography is inseparable from conquest. Said links both concepts to memory, and thence to 'culture,' in the configuration of history, of national allegiances and collective identities. He finds memory embodied in the built environment as well as in narratives and other texts which present acceptable versions of the territorial transaction.

14 Lefebvre, pondering the revolutionary visual images of Picasso and other contemporary artists, recognizes their potentially subversive role in the fabric of reproduction, when he says that social space 'contains potentialities – of works and of reappropriation – existing to begin with in the artistic sphere but responding above all to the demands of a body ... which by putting up resistance inaugurates the project of a different space (either the space of a counter-culture, or a counter-space in the sense of an initially utopian alternative to actually existing "real" space)' (p. 349).

'Inevitably such resistance or counter-action will tend to strengthen or create independent territorial entities capable to some degree of self-management. Just as inevitably, the central state will muster its own forces in order to reduce any such local autonomy by exploiting isolation and weakness' (p. 382). Nonetheless, Lefebvre sees the continuation of this local resistance as the only possible path before the inexorability of capitalist expansion, and he thus urges 'counter-plans and counter-projects designed to thwart strategies, plans and programmes imposed from above' (p. 383). Soja revisits the issue in a more energetic tone, suggesting that the counter-spaces' very positioning as subordinate – the stigma of difference and Otherness that was imposed and then sustained by the global forces that propose to benefit from that difference – can enable the marginalized to penetrate the interstices of power and disrupt it effectively from beneath:

> Those who are territorially subjugated by the workings of hegemonic power have two inherent choices: either accept their imposed differentiation and division, making the best of it; or mobilize to resist, drawing upon their putative positioning, their assigned 'otherness,' to struggle against this power-filled imposition. These choices are inherently spatial responses, individual and collective reactions to the ordered workings of power in perceived, conceived, and lived spaces.   (*Thirdspace*, p. 87)

Cultural geographer John Paul Jones has noted that 'for every segmentation there is always a disobedient flow' (p. 127), and feminist critiques often represent that resistance which continues to question and then to undermine the fictional foundation of homogeneity on which so many power structures rest.

As we have noted, the fundamental conceptualizations of space on which feminist geographers have built are those offered by Marxist spatial theory. As Rose observes in *Feminism and Geography*, 'marxist geography has from its inception focused on the differentiation of spaces; and this is one reason for the feminist turn towards it' (p. 118). She also notes that the unevenness between the empowered and the disempowered, central to feminist theory, is also 'already implicit if under-theorized in marxism' (p. 118). However, the level of abstraction as well as the almost exclusive emphasis on class over race, gender, and other situational factors has resulted in a demand from feminist thinkers to expand the 'polyhedron of intelligibility' to encompass greater diversity, specificity, and materiality.[15]

Two of the feminists most outspoken against the Marxist vision of space are Doreen Massey, as we have seen above, and Linda McDowell. Massey, in *Space, Place, and Gender*, claims that theorists such as Harvey and Soja, while claiming positions of authority and breadth, nonetheless 'ignore what feminists have been arguing now for a considerable number of years' in terms of the significance

---

[15] Note the geographical connotations of the word 'situated.' This idea is explored in an illuminating way in Donna Haraway's essay 'Situated Knowledges: The Science Question in Feminism and the Privilege of Partial Perspective' (1988).

of gender to all aspects of social configuration (p. 213). She demonstrates that women's positioning cannot be explained solely through the mechanisms of capitalist production and reproduction, and points the finger squarely at another source of power unacknowledged by Marxian universalizing theory – masculinity:

> The degree to which we can move between countries, or walk about the streets at night, or venture out of hotels in foreign cities, is not just influenced by 'capital'. Survey after survey has shown how women's mobility, for instance, is restricted – in a thousand different ways, from physical violence to being ogled at or made to feel quite simply 'out of place' – not by 'capital', but by men.   (pp. 147–8)

She also argues that the effects of globalization emphasized by Marxian theorists are valid only for certain segments of the population, for there are many regions of the world that remain untouched by transnational corporations and the proliferation of globalization; yet racial and gender oppression continue in these areas as they do in regions dominated by first-world capitalism (p. 148). The way in which universalist theorists elide those regions is symptomatic of the way in which their abstractions erase the coordinates of specific subject positioning. However, Massey's wholesale condemnation of class-based conceptualizations of inequality dismisses many of the revolutions that these thinkers have contributed to both feminist and geographic theorizations.[16]

Linda McDowell is less condemning in her view of Marxian spatial theory, and rightly acknowledges its foundational contributions to contemporary ways of envisioning space; but she insists that its view of oppression must be expanded, beyond those categories demarcated by capitalist accumulation.[17] She refers to

---

[16] While the work of Edward Soja is sometimes criticized by feminist geographers as one which contributes to this configuration of the 'master subject,' he does nonetheless bring to our attention the contributions of feminist geographers in contemporary revisions not only of geographic theory, but of feminism itself. He points out that while geographers may have learned from feminist theory for decades, it was only recently that the perspective of feminist geographers began to contribute in a significant way to feminist theorizing in general. As he observes, Gillian Rose's landmark *Feminism and Geography*, in its last chapter, references almost no geographers, but rather introduces 'the feminist geographer's own critical geographical imagination' to the work of feminist theorists in general (*Thirdspace*, p. 120). In turn, contemporary feminism now carries with it a set of spatial metaphors, grounded in materiality, which should be attributed directly to the contributions of feminist geography and the spatial imagination in studying the intersections between space, power, gender, and identity. Additionally, not all spatial imaging in contemporary feminism can be traced to geographical theorists. For example, bell hooks's *Feminist Theory: From Margin to Center* (1984) is an often-cited example of material positionality in relation to women's negotiation of identity. And Rose herself relies on feminist Adrienne Rich's conceptualization of the body as a geographic entity (Rich, 'Notes Towards a Politics of Location,' p. 212).

[17] bell hooks offers a concise definition of oppression in *Feminist Theory: From Margin to Center*: 'Being oppressed means the *absence of choices*,' regardless of causal factors (p. 5).

the work of Iris Marion Young, who in *Justice and the Politics of Difference* (1990) 'constructs a multiple definition of injustice or oppression to replace the belief that inequalities in the distribution of material goods and resources are the basis of injustice ... [adding] ideas about social prestige, physical power, and stereotypes about idealized bodies' (McDowell, *Gender, Identity and Place*, p. 178). Young identifies five categories of oppression – exploitation (of workers by capitalism *or* of women by men), marginalization, powerlessness, cultural imperialism (for example, the confinement of 'others' within their bodies), and violence. For Young, these 'five faces of oppression' involve 'social structures and relations beyond distribution' and 'create hierarchical divisions between people by "othering" an inferior group ... by defining it as different from and inferior to the "norm"' (quoted in McDowell, p. 178). McDowell's reelaboration of these categories demonstrates that while the first three may (or may not) be examined in terms of capitalist categories of power, the latter two transcend Marxian explanations of social difference and must be explored in terms of race, gender, and other cultural constructs. McDowell emphasizes what she calls 'the difference perspective,' which focuses on social relations beyond those encapsulated by categories of economic class. [18]

Finally, it is useful to consider Adrienne Rich's observation that feminism itself, as a discipline, has committed some of the same errors that Marxian theorists have fallen into, in their attempts to universalize a category 'Woman' to the exclusion of 'women.' As she writes in her foundational essay on positionality and the difference perspective, 'Notes toward a Politics of Location,' contemporary feminism has had to transcend the same ways of thinking that led to the creation of the master subject: 'The faceless, sexless, raceless proletariat. The faceless, raceless, classless category of "all women." Both creations of white Western self-centeredness' (p. 219). The feminist geographers whose work is most useful to us are those whose visions of space incorporate the contributions of theorists such as Lefebvre and Soja – particularly their visions of space as an arena of flows and dialectics (or trialectics) – while at the same time considering that the situation of any one woman nonetheless is firmly grounded in social and cultural positioning.

The limitations of dualistic thinking explored by Soja in *Thirdspace*[19] have been even more usefully articulated by contemporary feminist theorists, who perceive behind all Western binary constructions the fundamental opposition Male/Female. Within this opposition A/not-A, as Massey argues, 'only one can be defined positively' while the other is necessarily characterized through 'lack,' and such categorizations only serve to perpetuate the power of the already dominant group (*Space, Place, and Gender*, p. 256). Corollaries to the Male/

[18] Indeed, as McDowell points out, these other constructs in many ways affect the economy, as they are affected by it (p. 180).

[19] See in particular pp. 11 and 70, although the argument against binarism is fundamental throughout Soja's study.

Female dichotomy include empowered/disempowered, center/margin, same/ other, mind/body, active/passive, progress/stasis, and time/space.[20] Each of these binary assumptions serves to consolidate the dominant role of hegemony over its subjects, in schemes of class (owner/worker) but also in terms of race (white/other) and, most significantly for us, gender. Two primary dualisms which may be linked directly to geographic theory, and which are interrogated by the contemporary Spanish American women's novel, are the traditional demarcation of public/private as male/female space, and the culture/nature dichotomy also historically aligned with male/female.

Nancy Duncan conceives the public/private dualism as the 'spatial counter-part' of the mind/body dualism (p. 3), for in the modern Western era it is the idea of woman as body that has confined women to the home environment while men 'go to work,' to do things, to make history. Much Marxist economic theory appears to reinforce this dualism in its imaging of social reproduction, which configures the worker as male and the homemaker as the agent of domestic order. The feminism of difference re-examines the delineation between public and private, in observing that the archetype of the domestic housewife was only valid for women of a certain social class and a certain race (Blunt and Rose, p. 3). Locational feminism includes more precise alternatives to this binarism, for example African-American women whose workplace was a white home, or regions of the world where women have long operated as agents in the market-place or the agricultural arena. The public/private dichotomy proves insufficient to describe, or to circumscribe, the female spatial experience. Indeed, the home is seldom seen as a place of refuge or control within texts by women; female characters move with equal difficulty, or with equal ease, in both arenas.

The association of women with the natural environment, a longstanding fixture in Western literature[21] as well as in westernized ways of thinking, has been used to demonstrate the innate superiority of men in their ability to reason and to transcend their corporeal state. Because women are seen as tied to nature's cycles, to the demands of their bodies, their sphere of activity – mental and phys-ical – is restricted.[22] Because of its inherent bias against women, this dualism is also actively deconstructed both in contemporary feminist theory and in recent

---

[20] In this binarism, time (male) is conceived as forward momentum – as the making of history – and space (female) as passive arena.

[21] See, for example, discussion of the 'green world archetype' in Annis Pratt's *Archetypal Patterns in Women's Fiction* (1981).

[22] An example of this prejudicial association is found in Lutwack's 1984 study *The Role of Place in Literature*, where in discussing natural space he reverts to this limiting stereotype of innate biological difference: 'The female body is more commonly associated with earth than the male, probably because woman has functions of reproduction and alimentation similar to earth's and her menstrual cycle corresponds to the movements of ... the moon. Because child-bearing and child-raising require repose rather than motion, woman is more intimately tied to fixed places than men. Agoraphobia has a much higher incidence among women than among men' (p. 82).

novels by Spanish American women.[23] Instead, both nature and identity are seen as social constructions; biology is shown as an invention intended to demonstrate the 'validity' of ideology; and notions of place now can be employed as an 'empowering but fluid, unstable, and provisional means of liberation,' whether 'place' refers to the natural or the built environment (Nash, p. 239).

As mentioned above, it is now commonplace to include considerations of the body as an integral part of conceptualizations not only of identity but also of geography. Yi-fu Tuan and David Harvey present intriguingly contrasting, yet similar visions of the relation between the individual body and the physical world, when Harvey observes that the body 'is only a peculiarly intimate bit of the world' (*Justice, Nature*, p. 248), and Tuan writes that 'The earth is the human body writ large' (*Space and Place*, p. 36).

The body, Adrienne Rich's 'geography closest in' (p. 212), serves as the physical connection between identity and world, the surface on which the culture inscribes itself as well as the entity which reaches out to shape the surrounding world.[24] It is also inscribed by itself, of one's own volition, although this volition is inextricably tied to the values, ideologies, and practices of the surrounding culture. As individuals seek to find their place in the world, they also express self-definition through the form, the dress, and the activities of the body. Here Edward Casey's essay, 'Body, Self, and Landscape,' proves particularly insightful, as he writes that 'what lingers in the body is how it felt to be in a place' (p. 414). As the body responds to place, it also impacts, and sometimes threatens, that larger place. It thus becomes one more space that societal forces must control, segregate, direct, in order to maintain control over the collective population.

At the same time, the body can be more difficult to dominate than is the built environment. It has its own indomitable rhythms. It bears deeply embedded – although not unchangeable – markers of race and gender, which conspire to determine the places to which it has access; and it can be the receptacle for punishment when those boundaries are transgressed. Its behaviors are almost always socially coded, often in conflict with its own – conscious or unconscious – desires and appetites, and the individual's degree of autonomy meshes with the degree of exercised social control in determining to what extent those appetites will be sated. At the same time, the body is one of the fundamental images manipulated by economic forces of production in order to *create* appetites and desires.

In sum, the body, in so many ways uncontrollable, still must be a dominated

[23] The relatively recent trend of ecofeminism, which attempted to capitalize on the binary by maintaining the association but inverting its positive and negative characteristics, privileging the female as an entity with an innate biological connection to nature, is now generally seen as essentializing in the same way that the more negative binary did, and is thus now rejected by most contemporary feminist theorists.

[24] For Lefebvre, space is both perceived and produced by the body: 'it is by means of the body that space is perceived, lived – and produced' (p. 162); it serves 'both as point of departure and as destination' (p. 194).

territory if larger societal forces are to maintain their sway. Soja quotes an unpublished essay by Barbara Hooper in his discussion of this subject, as she studies the movements of the body in support of and against the flows directed by the broader society; she writes that hegemony is obsessed with controlling unruly and dangerous bodies, for example those seen as polluted or contaminated. Following on Foucault's observation that 'in the first instance, discipline proceeds from the distribution of individuals in space,' she observes that 'when borders are crossed, disturbed, contested, and so become a threat to order, hegemonic power acts to reinforce them: the boundaries around territory, nation, ethnicity, race, gender, sex, class, erotic practice, are trotted out and vigorously disciplined' (quoted in *Thirdspace*, pp. 114–15). The body as a contested site is a concept of particular interest for feminist scholars across the disciplines. Feminist geographers in particular examine the body as a physical territory upon which the forces of power collide, and which, while marked by these struggles, at the same time may attempt to exert its own controlling influence, over itself, over surrounding space, and over surrounding bodies. Some of the most interesting contemporary theory focuses on the body as the repository of the spatial dialectic – both shaped by and shaping the society around it and the identity within it.

Foucault's work on domination through spatial control included considerations of the body that continue to undergird corporeal theory. Two of his observations in particular have merited comment from feminist scholarship. One, cited by Susan Bordo in her groundbreaking study of female embodiment, *Unbearable Weight: Feminism, Western Culture, and the Body*, is the idea that external control of bodily formation – and thence identity – is not necessary as the primary means of social control, because the mechanisms of assessment are so deeply internalized that self-surveillance and self-correction, to the point of self-destruction, take over the task of controlling the female body in particular (p. 27).[25] In other words, a subject's actions upon her own body should not be simplified as 'self-motivated' or self-inflicted, because the normative force of societal expectation controls her relationship even to her own bodily geography. The second Foucauldian notion on which feminists have capitalized is that of resistance.[26] Some aspects of the body remain beyond control; it grows, it ages, it ails, it dies, all regardless of the will of any social or political authority, or even necessarily of the self. It desires and demands, in ways that challenge reason's capacity to direct it. Furthermore, it always carries the potential for self-destruction, which is the ultimate form of resistance to the forces of production.

Such observations have particular meaning for feminism, because of the overemphasis on female physicality implicit in the mind/body, culture/nature dual-

[25] Here Bordo references Foucault's 'The Eye of Power,' in *Power/Knowledge* (1980).

[26] Elizabeth Grosz notes that the body continues to represent a threat to hegemony, because 'it exerts a recalcitrance, and always entails the possibility of a counterstrategic reinscription, for it is capable of being self-marked, self-represented in alternative ways' ('Inscriptions,' p. 238).

isms. However, contemporary feminists also note that the universalizing nature of these earlier theorists erased bodily specificity, particularly in terms of race and gender, along the lines we discussed earlier. Grosz encapsulates the error of this type of constructed generalization, when she defines phallocentrism as 'not so much the dominance of the phallus as the pervasive unacknowledged use of the male or masculine to represent the human' ('Bodies–Cities,' p. 247). Ignoring the ways in which the female body in particular is commodified, inscribed, and surveyed undercuts the usefulness of corporeal theory in accurately envisioning the flows and the effects of power upon individual identity.[27]

Again, a particular phase of feminism committed the same error, when theorists such as Simone de Beauvoir suggested that women might aspire to transcend their biological constraints entirely.[28] Instead, the female body must be studied as it is situated, within the polyhedron of social intelligibility, at the intersection between various personal and social agendas, between will and biology, between surveillance and autonomy, between constraint and the daring statement of independence, between hegemonic inscription and defiant self-definition. It must also be examined in the specific context of race, class, and culture as well as gender. Grosz, in *Volatile Bodies: Toward a Corporeal Feminism*, asserts that 'indeed, there is no body as such: there are only *bodies* – male or female, black, brown, white, large or small – and the gradations in between' (p. 19). The study of bodies rather than the body allows for the exploration of identity as individually negotiated in physical terms, rather than as Woman in opposition to Man. Through corporeality, women – in life and in literature – assert their right to exist and to move, sometimes as spectacle and other times in a mode of fictive invisibility,[29] as they attempt to maintain control of their own most personal territory.

Perhaps because the body appears to make some of its own decisions regardless of the will of its indweller or its spectators, efforts to control it, especially for Westerners, inform every aspect of social life. Teather notes that 'the sort of body that we have prescribes the particular map that we use to navigate our life worlds' (p. 12). At the same time, the existence of an imagined 'idealized body' requires the (female) individual's constant comparison of her physicality to that ideal. Bordo and Grosz in particular discuss the lengths to which women go to conform their bodies to others', and their own, notions of perfection. However, these extremes of beauty standards, of 'dieting, working out, picking, pruning,

---

[27] Linda McDowell, in *Gender, Identity and Place* (1999), correctly observes that it is equally important to study the male body in gender-specific ways, since 'both women and men are subject to disciplinary power and regimes of corporeal production, albeit to different degrees and in different ways' (p. 50).

[28] As Gillian Rose summarizes, de Beauvoir and her contemporaries suggested that 'women's emancipation would happen when they escaped the constraints of their bodily immanence: women would be freed by becoming like men.' But, Rose notes, 'This erasure of the body is as insidious as the biologism of radical feminism' (p. 82).

[29] This term, 'fictive invisibility,' is borrowed from Shirley Ardener's 1981 study, *Women and Space: Ground Rules and Social Maps*, p. 21.

squeezing and decorating,'[30] are not a principal factor in the novels to be studied here. Much more central are questions of corporeal mobility (for example, the freedom to travel unaccompanied, to ride horses, or to dance) and of possession – who owns the female body. We see also the purposeful foregrounding of alternative bodies – aging women, those who bear the corporeal scars of lived experience, and transvestite bodies. Finally, we see in several of these novels the prostitute body, with its flagrant transgression of the confining norms of acceptable femininity. In most cases, the prostitute is seen not as a victim of patriarchal commodification, but rather as a sexualized woman who balances her sensitivity to official disapproval with a celebratory and defiant assumption of her own identity and behavior. When these Spanish American novels do portray the female body in front of the mirror, the character's response is not one of critical assessment in relation to a posited ideal, but rather one of self-actualization.[31] Consequently, the female body is seen, in the contemporary Spanish American novel by women, as a physical space where hegemony confronts autonomy, where one force yields before the other, and where the struggle inscribes its own traces.

Liminoids, nomads, *chora*, heterotopia

Four concepts articulated by feminist geographers have particular relevance to Spanish American women's fiction, and will be defined briefly here in order to clarify our discussion. Ideas regarding *liminoids* and *nomads* help to identify the patterns of movement undertaken by female protagonists. The imaginary space of the *chora* is also a recurrent device in narrative configurations of women's geography. And finally, Foucault's concept of *heterotopia* is often illuminating in the texts to be discussed.

Liminoids and rites of passage

'Rites of passage,' a spatial metaphor, refers to those transitional events that mark development or change in the lifecourse. Teather points out that both academic and creative artists have tended to focus on these periods, as we 'find the personal turmoil involved at such turning points to be the driving impetus for creative expression' (p. 1). The spatial configuration often associated with these moments, in works of fiction, is a discursive strategy that serves to correlate exterior with interior change, and to connect the reader to the material nature of the character's development. Thus the association of narrated geography with character development illumines the analysis of personal worlds and the process of their

---

[30] This quotation is from McDowell and Sharp's editorial introduction, within *Space, Gender, Knowledge* (1997), to the section entitled 'Body Maps,' p. 203.

[31] Bordo notes that 'the pleasures of shaping and decorating the body' are often interpreted as internalized patriarchy, but in many cases should be acknowledged as a legitimate statement of identity, of ownership of one's own body (p. 31).

negotiation, within the novel. These periods of crisis have been of interest to both male and female writers, in the characterization of both male and female protagonists; but like representations of the body they take on a particular significance for women writers, who navigate a lifecourse that is often counter-hegemonic, and that attempts to open up choices in the face of social conditions that delimit those options.

Arnold van Gennep's 1908 study *The Rites of Passage* establishes the link between geography – both metaphorical and material – and transitional stages of development, when he notes that rites of passage mark the stages during which 'a person leaves one world behind him and enters a new one' (p. 19). He studies liminal rites, in both figurative and literal terms, identifying rituals associated with doorways and barriers, and observing that 'to cross the threshold is to unite oneself with a new world' (p. 20). Examples of such crossings or spatial separations include traditions surrounding changes of social condition – for example, baptism or dedication, betrothal, pregnancy and birth, purification, and death. Modern moments of transition identified by more recent scholars such as Teather and Ardener include student matriculation, boarding schools, or terms of military service (Teather, p. 1; Ardener, p. 21). Van Gennep also postulates the existence of geographic 'neutral zones' which can prolong the transitional passage: 'Who ever passes from one [territory] to the other finds himself physically and magico-religiously in a special situation for a certain length of time: he wavers between two worlds. It is this situation which I have designated a transition ... a symbolic and spatial area' (p. 18). Pointing to the destabilizing threat of these moments of transition, he claims that socially homogeneous rituals accompanying these crises help to reduce their harmful effects (p. 11). He articulates three types of rites of passage: those of separation (preliminal), the transition rites themselves (liminal), and the rites of incorporation (postliminal). The novels we shall study emphasize preliminal and liminal passages, but seldom present a postliminal incorporation, as will be demonstrated through our analysis. Additionally the rites accompanying these preliminal and liminal moments are not socially established but individually constructed, thus amplifying rather than reducing their potentially destabilizing effects.

Van Gennep, with an ethnocentrism typical of his time, identifies major liminal segregation as a practice of more primitive societies: 'for the semicivilized the passage is actually a territorial passage' (p. 192). However, in literature the territorial passage serves as an effective textual practice for marking significant moments of change. Additionally, for women characters, geographical mobility is itself a statement of defiance or independence, even if that mobility is the desire to flee from the societally approved but personally unacceptable options presented to them. Flight allows the female protagonist to invent new options, in a space at least temporarily removed from the normative gaze and restrictions of autonomy of the society from which she escapes. She might linger in a 'neutral zone,' or find a space where she can reconstruct her identity. These rebirths are generally marked by territorial passage.

Victor Turner (1974) and John W. Schouten (1991) build on van Gennep's study to focus on the liminal phase as 'a period of personal ambiguity, of non-status, and of unanchored identity' (Schouten, p. 49). Both scholars point to the painful nature of such transitions, in particular for the modern individual who is often deprived of the sense of '"communitas" or shared psychological support throughout major status passages' (Schouten, p. 49). Schouten points to the absence of 'communitas' as the reason that individuals construct their own personal rites of passage, as they are 'devoid of ... supportive rites' and 'left to their own devices' (p. 49). And he notes that failure results in an entrapment in the 'liminoid state,' thus impeding 'normal development' (p. 50). However, for women novelists the prolongation of the liminoid state is in fact a useful tool of aesthetic structuring. A refusal to 're-incorporate' into phallocentric norms of embodiment and conduct, constructing instead the option to remain liminoid, constitutes a statement of victory rather than surrender. Several of the protagonists we shall study may be termed liminoids, as they opt to remain in a neutral zone or to prolong the phase of 'identity play' (Schouten, p. 49), experimenting with alternative identities and utilizing their personal navigational skills, opting to remain in the liminal region rather than to settle 'in place.'

Nomads

A construction corollary to the situation of the permanent or indefinite liminoid is that of the nomad. The nomadic figure is one which chooses mobility over stasis, in a geographic sense as well as in the sense of identity or social position. Rosi Braidotti's study *Nomadic Subjects: Embodiment and Sexual Difference in Contemporary Feminist Theory* articulates the nomadic position as one of independence and resistance. While many of her conclusions have to do with metaphorical nomadism, she – like several of the authors we will study – consistently frames her discussion in terms of physical mobility. She conceptualizes nomadism as 'the kind of critical consciousness that resists settling into socially coded modes of thought and behavior' (p. 5). In geographic terms, Braidotti depicts a kind of restless movement not only without destination, but without any vestige of the concept of destination: 'The nomad does not stand for homelessness, or compulsive displacement; it is rather a figuration for the kind of subject who has relinquished all idea, desire, or nostalgia for fixity. This figuration expresses the desire for an identity made of transitions, successive shifts, and coordinated changes, without and against an essential unity' (p. 22).

The female nomad in particular rejects the categories that phallocentrism has carved out for her, opting instead for mobility. Braidotti concedes that the nomadic consciousness does not necessarily require physical mobility: 'Not all nomads are world travelers; some of the greatest trips can take place without physically moving from one's habitat. It is the subversion of set conventions that defines the nomadic state, not the literal act of traveling' (p. 5). However, travel remains a useful discursive device in Spanish American women's novels, in order to denote discomfort with the available identity options, and the destabilizing counter-option of remaining mobile. Female protagonists generally travel alone, without maps or destinations, articulating their identity more through the process of travel than through the goal of the journey. Unlike the migrant and the exile, the nomad does not exhibit nostalgia for the point of origin, or have a fixed image to which it intends to return (p. 22). Instead, 'the nomad's relationship to the earth is one of transitory attachment and cyclical frequentation' (p. 25).

The nomad, like the liminoid, is not necessarily a female figuration; but like the liminoid construct, nomadic subjectivity takes on a distinct connotation for women. As Braidotti observes, the nomad 'has the potential for positive renaming, for opening up new possibilities for life and thought' (p. 8), and for 'resisting assimilation or homologation into dominant ways of representing the self' (p. 25). The geographical trope thus once again serves as an effective narrative strategy for representing self-discovery, experience with the world, and a way of carving out one's own place in the world.

The absence of nostalgia should not be read as an absence of origins, in novels by Spanish American women. On the contrary, we read as very significant the context of birth and childhood, and the experiences which caused an initial forced expulsion into mobility. But once mobile, the female protagonist often finds the condition of nomadism preferable to that of stasis – and a fertile ground for continued identity play. Or, she attempts to settle into various roles that each prove unsatisfactory, and once having explored the nomadic route, she easily returns to it. Braidotti, in the opening passages of her study, quotes Gertrude Stein in a statement which proves relevant to the narrative constructions we will examine: 'It's great to have roots, as long as you can take them with you' (p. 1). While the specific conditions of origin as well as the mechanism of expulsion or flight will be closely examined in our study, the newly constructed options of prolonged liminality or nomadism will be seen as the fundamental lifecourses of the contemporary Spanish American female protagonist.

Chora

The concept of *chora* has undergone considerable development since its initial postulation by Plato. It has carried distinct symbolic meanings for philosophers particularly since its re-exploration by Julia Kristeva and Jacques Derrida, but has also been appropriated by geographers, and in particular some feminist geographers, as a useful way of conceptualizing a particular imagined space that recurs in women's narrative, both oral and written. Because of its recurrence in several of the novels here to be studied, we will provide a brief context for its use.

Plato, in the *Timaeus*, used the masculine word *choros* to refer to land/country, and more particularly to demarcated places (Olwig, p. 34). But he also conceived of an amorphous intermediate space, somewhere between the mythological realm and material reality, a region that Olwig summarizes as a 'primordial, feminine, bodily receptacle' (p. 34); through this imaginary space he supposed the material world to have been generated. He thus implicitly characterized this space as female, *chora*. Elizabeth Grosz, in her article 'Women, *Chora*, Dwelling,' contests the phallocentrism of this spatial theory, noting that the *chora* shares characteristics with the female womb as a 'placeless place, obliterating itself to make others possible and actual' (p. 51), as it brings the masculine world into being without itself being quite real. For Grosz, '*Chora* may well serve as one of the earliest models of this appropriation and disenfranchisement of femininity' (p. 57).[32]

However, Julia Kristeva's essay 'The Semiotic *Chora* Ordering the Drives,' published in 1974, appropriates the term in a different way, one that aligns itself with feminist theory of that era in its assertion of the feminine as an active part of identity creation. Building on semiotic theory, Kristeva's binary construct of human thought labels the preconscious and preverbal stage (that of instinctive drives) as 'semiotic' and the conscious, linguistic stage (dominated by social constructs) as 'symbolic.' The binary structure corresponds roughly to the 'nature/culture' dualism, instinct versus consciousness. Based on this construct, she conceives of *chora* – the prioritization of drives over control – as a geographic metaphor for the semiotic world, one which is 'pregnant with as yet unrealized possibilities' (*Revolution*, p. 4). Kristeva thus privileges the *chora* as a space of potential, which language then struggles to articulate, and one with which the Woman implicitly continues to have greater affinity. For Kristeva the space remains amorphous and conceptual; but she theorizes that poetic language, in particular, attempts to 'lend a topology' to the *chora* (*Revolution*, p. 26).

Elizabeth Teather in *Embodied Geographies* (1999) and John Lechte in '(Not) Belonging in Postmodern Space' (1995) revisit the concept of the *chora* from a stricter spatial perspective, and appropriate the term in a way which will be more directly relevant to our study of the construction of narrated spaces. Both theorists imagine the *chora* as a place of retreat for the conscious mind, which seeks an escape from or transcendence of the restrictive ordering of topological reality. Both Teather and Lechte turn to artistic works in order to explain their configuration of the *chora*. Lechte refers to a painting by Turner, which Michel Serres has linked to the concept of *chora* because of its hazy representational strategies, 'random, unordered distributions' of smoke, steam, flames, and clouds. For Lechte, 'Here, then, would be another exemplification of Kristeva's *chora*, only now, the drive-element of the semiotic gives way to the indeterminacy of topological space' (p. 102); Lechte equates this indeterminacy with conceptualizations of postmodern space. Teather draws a similar analogy, with reference to Emily Brontë's poem 'Caged Bird.' In her brief analysis of this poem, she points to the fantasies of flight and freedom articulated there, and interprets them from the feminist perspective of resistance to phallocentric spatial control; she notes that women are often 'desperate not just for death but for the liberation of the mind and spirit that is also implied in the concept of the *chora*' (p. 5).

---

[32] Jacques Derrida's 1993 exploration of the term closely follows Plato's, and he reiterates the equation of the *chora* space with mother, nurse, and receptacle; he conceives of it as an 'imprint-bearer' but not as a force which itself can imprint (p. 93).

This latter concept is the one which we shall see repeatedly represented in the fiction of contemporary Spanish American writers. Female protagonists, through flights of fantasy, dreams, or delirium, escape to a space that precedes or transcends the order and confinement of topological reality. While one can find similar narrative representations in novels by and about men, the appropriation of this space by women takes on particular significance in that it represents a gyno-centric, individually constructed space, where the woman can give herself free rein. Aesthetic construction of the *chora* is of particular interest to our analysis, for, as the realm that precedes articulation, it is often narrated in a tone distinct from that of the rest of the novel. Representing a different level of awareness or of being, it also carries with it unique discursive strategies. Because our analysis of these novels will never be separate from considerations of their textual practices, the verbal construction of the *chora*, the order of this 'unordered space' (Lechte, p. 100), will be closely examined.

The Counter-force of heterotopology

Foucault, in his landmark study 'Of Other Spaces,' proposes a concept that proves particularly illuminating in our study of Spanish American fiction. In his discussion of potential counter-sites which can serve, as discussed above, as loci of resistance, material places which allow individuals physical protection from the leveling forces of general and daily society, he presents the idea of the *heterotopia*, a site whose subversive nature stems from its radical juxta-positioning of individuals or elements normally segregated and controlled. He mentions two types of heterotopias that function to preserve social stability: the crisis heterotopia (places that exert vigilance over potentially dangerous liminal change – boarding schools, military service, homes for pregnant women) and the heterotopia of deviation (prisons, rest homes, asylums). Both types of location contain individuals of disparate origins, who are thrown together under an institutional structure which allows them to be governed effectively ('Of Other Spaces,' pp. 24–5).

However, other heterotopias occur through juxtapositions that are not socially or institutionally sanctioned. These places can serve as dangerous sites of contact, where local resistance can take root, where comparisons can foment dissatis-faction, where creative energies can build to a threatening level, or where the governing hand of power temporarily cannot find its grip. Foucault's examples of these locales of juxtaposition, fertile ground for transgression, include the theater or the cinema, museums, libraries, fairgrounds, bars, brothels, colonies, and boats (a 'floating piece of space, a place without a place') ('Of Other Spaces,' p. 27). Countless other examples may be cited; Teather mentions carnival (p. 61), and Hayden discusses festivals and parades (p. 38), as counter-sites of dangerous contact which temporarily convert controlled places into volatile and uncontrol-lable space. Foucault points to the heterotopia as a site 'in which the real sites, all the other real sites that can be found within the culture, are simultaneously represented, contested, and inverted' ('Of Other Spaces,' p. 24).

Narrative fiction has always exploited the idea of the heterotopia, without necessarily recognizing it as such. These spaces of encounter, ripe with possibilities for contact and revelation, have long drawn the attention of creative writers. The present study will focus in particular on the presence of heterotopias in terms of their implications for the assignment and subversion of place within social hierarchies. The heterotopias we shall examine are often sites where sexually transgressive behavior is tolerated or even approved. They allow temporary illuminations that later grow into stronger forms of resistance. They make permeable the boundaries of gender, class, and race, and these possibilities, once glimpsed or experienced, often create or feed the desire for a broader restructuring of social space.[33] Finally, by way of conclusion, we shall consider the ways in which it is useful to imagine these texts themselves as verbal heterotopias, a place where identities, spaces, and often times, are juxtaposed and where opportunities for resistance, grounded in the conquest and control of places, can take root and grow.

Literature and geography

Geographical determinism has figured prominently in literary analysis, and perhaps to a greater degree in Spanish American writing than in other traditions. However, this was a unidirectional flow; a national character was determined as a result of the configuration of the nation's physical environment – both its oppositional challenges and its rich resources. D. H. Lawrence echoes this view in a 1923 essay:

> Every continent has its own great spirit of place. Every people is polarized in some particular locality, which is home, the homeland. Different places on the face of the earth have different vital effluence, different vibration, different chemical exhalation, different polarity with different stars: call it what you like. But the spirit of place is a great reality.[34]

Such studies of place involve the influence of the environment on character formation, but seldom reflect the geographical and architectural setting as constructed 'texts,' which are both written and read in culturally and socially specific ways, and which can be resisted by the particular appropriations and movements of its inhabitants.

Even more recent studies such as Gillian Tindall's *Countries of the Mind: The Meaning of Place to Writers* (1991) still view physical setting primarily as a metaphor or emblem for 'ideas that transcend that particular time and place' (p. 10). Such descriptive readings are important in linking a writer's thematic preoccupa-

---

33 Examples include the boat and the photography studio in Allende's work, the brothel and the cemetery in Restrepo's novel, the hospital in Mastretta's novel, the Vips restaurant in Sefchovich's work and the carnival in Ferré's.

34 *Studies in Classic American Literature* (1923), pp. 8–9. Quoted in Lutwack, p. 140.

tions with particular geographic representations, but they do not expose hitherto unseen dimensions of the novel's discursive tactics or see the representation of space as part and parcel of the novel's constructive engine. In fact, the novel's use of space is an element which most firmly links the work to a specific time and place, as it reflects an entire structure of social relations which undergirds plot, characterization, and theme. Lutwack, in gauging the varying importance of space to literary works, postulates as an example that 'Fielding's Tom Jones is not at all influenced in his behavior by the places he happens to be in' (p. 38), but we would argue that a re-reading from the perspective of cultural geography would demonstrate that Fielding's protagonist is indeed deeply influenced by the political and economic climate of his narrated surroundings. We prefer instead the insight of Chris Fitter, in his 1995 study *Poetry, Space, Landscape: Toward a New Theory*: 'I wish to argue that perception of a landscape can never be "disinterested": that it ... has always a structuring, desiring agenda of needs and hopes and warinesses, conscious or otherwise' (p. 11).[35]

Recent studies on the discursive aspect of geographical study have helped to bridge the historical gap between geography and literature. Discourse is defined by geographer J. B. Harley as 'a system which provides a set of rules for the representation of knowledge' (p. 243).[36] In this light, no discourse can consider itself empirical or documentary. Instead, these rules – consciously or not – are constructed to privilege a particular theoretical positioning, to convey an embedded ideology, and to manipulate in some way the reader's vision of the world. Maps, as Harley demonstrates, are an example of a graphic discourse – 'the map is never neutral,' but always reinforces a particular political and ideological structure (p. 247).[37]

Neither literary nor geographic writers are empiricists, but rather both are cultural producers. Their subjective renderings of place not only reflect their own particular positioning, but also influence the way their readers subsequently *see* places.[38] An example of the way in which literary texts can be used, wittingly

---

[35] It should be noted that later in his study, Fitter attempts to identify a particular 'nature-sensibility' for each of various literary periods or movements. Analyses such as the current one will attempt to avoid such tacit assumptions of cultural homogeneity.

[36] See also Hayden White, *Tropics of Discourse* (1978): 'it does not matter whether the world is conceived to be real or only imagined; the manner of making sense of it is the same' (p. 98).

[37] Harley points out the textual features of the map: 'the steps in making a map – selection, omission, simplification, classification, the creation of hierarchies and "symbolization" – are all inherently rhetorical' (p. 243).

[38] Nigel Thrift makes this provocative point in 1983, when he notes in the geographic journal *Antipode* that literature imposes social meanings on a place (p. 15). Using the European Front of World War I as his illustration, he examines how literary representations of that place constructed an image that came to represent reality – the Front 'acquired meaning' and became a paradigm: 'It has become a signification of place, not the remembrance of the experience of place itself. It has become the idea of the Front, not its archaeology' (p. 18). While Thrift acknowledges that geographic writing also plays such a role, he points to literature

or not, to create cultural meaning is found in a journal dedicated to geographic education; Susan R. Brooker-Gross, in a 1991 article entitled 'Teaching about Race, Gender, Class and Geography through Fiction,' observes that the reading of a novel – if considered in its social and political particularities – can 'substitute for field experience': 'The first-person account, even if a fictional voice, may substitute for direct encounters' (p. 36). Beyond the academic setting, we may assume that literature, and in particular popular fiction of the type to be examined in this study, plays a similar role. Literary representations of place construct obvious as well as latent systems of power relations which then can become part and parcel of the reader's subsequent way of seeing places. The dialectic between cultural representation and cultural production is a complex one, but it should be carefully considered when one is tempted to simplify questions of claims to truth, in literature and in the social sciences.

Such emphases on geographical discursive strategies heighten our awareness of the ways in which the observing eye sees, interprets, and reconstructs places. In particular, this focus on geography as ideologically and rhetorically strategized heightens our awareness of all texts as cultural producers as well as documents of a particular culture. Two excellent geographical collections which problematize the question of spatial representation are Barnes and Duncan's *Writing Worlds: Discourse, Text and Metaphor in the Representation of Landscape* (1992) and Patricia Yaeger's *The Geography of Identity* (1996). Both collections demand the invention of a 'poetics of geography: a site for investigating the metaphors and narrative strategies that we use to talk about space' (Yaeger, p. 5). This poetics of geography will also be extremely illuminating for our reading of literary texts, since both geography and literature in the end present imaged and therefore imagined worlds, which will legitimate particular ideologies and elide the representation of those aspects of reality which do not serve those aims.[39]

With this in mind, literary criticism as well as both literature and geography – all equally, as forms of discourse – should avoid 'discursive violence,' which geographers Jones, Nast, and Roberts define as 'scripting groups or persons in

as a particularly effective means of creating a mutual structure of signification between 'the truly social in the individual and the truly individual in the social' (p. 19). He points out the centrality of spatial, material experience in evoking a host of other responses in the readers: 'an appeal to place experience will also simultaneously materialize other social and cultural relations that would otherwise remain outside the linguistic realm' (p. 18), and he emphasizes the literary text's constitutive role in cultural construction: 'the literary meaning of the experience of place and the literary experience of that meaning of place are both part of an active process of cultural creation and destruction. ... They are all moments in a historically cumulative spiral of signification' (p. 12).

[39] See also Said, who comments extensively on the notion of 'imaginative geography' in his cultural analyses of the West's configuration of the Orient: 'invention must occur if there is recollection' ('Invention, Memory, and Place,' p. 248). All writers of places rechart the past, erecting a new space that represents not a place but a *version* of a place, one that carries some kind of social, metaphorical meaning as the represented material space reflects the personal and social dynamics perceived by the writer.

places in ways that counter how they would define themselves – and obscuring the socio-spatial relations through which a group is subordinated,' thus casting them into subaltern positions (pp. 393–4). This warning is based on the recognition that texts not only reflect power structures, but exert power as well. Thus, our study will not attempt to generalize a national (much less a continental) situation or context based on the socio-spatial representation within a particular novel; rather, each novel will be read as the articulation of one position, one self-representation which is itself asserting an ideological stance at the same time that it critiques broader hegemonic forces of marginalization from the situated vantage point of a particular race, class, and/or gender.

Finally, the focus on geography as earth-representing rather than earth-reproducing allows for a narrowing of Mallory and Simpson-Housley's (and others') categorization of literature as imaginative – read imaginary – and geography as empirical. An articulate summary of a new, more nuanced focus is provided by geographers Daniels and Rycroft in their analysis of novels by English writer Alan Sillitoe; they write:

> We consider geography and literature not as the conjunction of two essentially distinct, coherent disciplines, or orders of knowledge – objective and subjective, real and imaginative, and so on – but as a field of textual genres – the novel, the poem, the travel guide, the map, the regional monograph – with complex overlaps and interconnections. We have brought out both the worldliness of literary texts and the imaginativeness of geographical texts. The imaginativeness of texts consists in the images they express and in the way they construct, through modes of writing or composition – however empirically – particular and partial views of the world. The worldliness of texts consists in the various contexts – biographical, economic, institutional, geographical – which are entailed by them and make them intelligible.   (p. 461)

Narrative artists need not be aware of this kind of spatial theorization in order to reflect verbally the dynamic between space/place and identity. Their characters evolve over time – this is part of the very definition of the novel[40] – but those characters also develop across and through space, through narrated places which function as both repository and constructive agent of the character's, and her society's, identity. In other words, it may be viewed as the kind of space that Soja describes as *real-and-imagined* (*Thirdspace*, p. 11), as often mimetic but always metaphorical as well, social as well as aesthetic constructs.[41] Commenting on

---

[40] The *Concise Oxford Dictionary of Literary Terms* (1990) defines the novel as having 'at least one character, and preferably several characters shown in processes of change and social relationship' (p. 152).

[41] Patricia Yaeger observes in her introduction to *The Geography of Identity* that 'even though literature may not be valuable for its straightforward geography, it is extraordinarily useful in its constant, uncanny rendering of laborious space', by which she means the space where characters 'work and produce' (pp. 27–8). Lutwack, in *The Role of Place in Literature*, also privileges the non-mimetic value of literary space: 'it is difficult to avoid the proposition

Walter Benjamin's literary evocation of Paris and Berlin in *One-Way Street*, Keith and Pile build on Soja's earlier work and anticipate his configuration of 'thirdspace' when they note that Benjamin's written cities 'were not only simultaneously real and metaphorical worlds, they were also acts of representation that were consciously, cognitively and politically marked rather than the evocations of a purely aesthetic spatiality' (p. 33).[42] This may be said of all literary constructions of space, whether or not the author indicates an awareness of these implications. An imaginative reconstruction of social space necessarily draws on the political and social realities surrounding the text's composition, the artist's worldview, and the linguistic conventions that structure our retelling, our verbal architecture, of space.

Lefebvre warned of the dangers of applying spatial studies to literary texts, when he pointed out that 'The problem is that any search for space in literary texts will find it everywhere and in every guise: enclosed, described, projected, dreamt of, speculated about' (p. 15). This is true; it is impossible to conceive of a plot that does not happen somewhere, and as we have seen, spatial metaphors are so useful for the linguistic articulation of abstract concepts that creative writers rely on them heavily. Unlike Lefebvre, however, we as literary critics do not define this situation as a 'problem,' but see it rather as a reality that imposes special challenges for the application of spatial theory to a literary text. Careful differentiation is required in the analysis of different types of literary or textualized space, from the social to the mental; but both the social and the mental spaces must be read as metaphors, as artistic spaces which the author erects to contain, and to express, the identity and the development of her characters as well as to contain and articulate the reading of a world beyond the text.

The issue of writing geography has perhaps been most articulately analyzed by Denis Cosgrove and Mona Domosh. In 'Author and Authority,' they observe that the writing of geographers should never have been considered 'objective,' and they point to the need for a finely tuned examination of *all* mapped representations of space and place: 'The problems of writing in a post-Kuhnian world are not that it leaves us without any "objective" reality from which to base our work, but that it forces us to explicitly recognize our personal and cultural agendas, and the power that words give to these agendas' (p. 37). Their conclusions, central to the focus of the present study, referenced in part earlier in this introduction, here merit quoting in full:

that in the final analysis all places in literature are used for symbolical purposes even though in their descriptions they may be rooted in fact' (p. 31); 'All places, whether drawn from geographical reality or fantasy, from literature or actual life, serve figurative ends and thereby sacrifice part of their concreteness as they cater to some human desire or craving beyond present reality' (p. 32).

[42] Earlier in their study Keith and Pile had observed that the spaces of Benjamin's Paris and Berlin 'are not just a personal view but then they are not the true representation of city either. ... [T]hese spatialities are instead to be understood as a constitutive element of the social' (p. 9).

When we write our geographies, we are creating artifacts that impose meaning on the world. The moral claims implicit in our descriptions and explanations of landscapes and places are what have determined their choice as subject-matter, controlled the mode of study, produced the story we tell and structured the mode of its telling. Our stories add to a growing list of other stories, not listed in a logic of linearity to fit into a coherent body of knowledge, but as a series of cultural constructions, each representing a particular view of the world, to be consulted together to help us make sense of ourselves and our relation to the landscapes and places we inhabit and think about. These stories are to be read not as approximations to a reality, but as tales of how we have understood the world; to be judged not according to a theory of correspondence, but in terms of their internal consistency and their value as moral and political discourse.   (pp. 37–8)

Text is the product of creative imagination, but also the product of a material, social, and political context. In particular the writers included in this study, although they all choose to represent periods of the nineteenth or early twentieth century, nonetheless represent space in such a way as to reflect a contemporary reality, to explain today's women's places by first conceptualizing yesterday's. All five writers imply that, throughout the two centuries since national independence, women have continued to employ the same strategies for the negotiation of their movements and their identities. Place and movement have always been contested arenas for women, yet these texts imply that women have never settled into their assigned places. Rather, they continued to find ways to 'take their places,' to permeate boundaries and in the end, to claim their right to self-articulation.

A study of literary geography must confront the question of the spatial metaphors that pepper our theoretical and quotidian vocabulary. Foucault, Lefebvre, and Soja, among others, all address at some point the pervasiveness of spatial imagery in our discussions of authority (social 'positioning') as well as in our articulations of human mental processes (dream-space, the imaginary worlds, ideological space). While Foucault relies heavily on the use of the vocabulary of space to frame ideologies of social positionality, for example, Lefebvre argues for a separation of 'mental space' from social space, in order to preserve 'the social character of space' (*Production of Space*, p. 27) or, in Soja's words, 'the political concreteness of social spatiality' (*Thirdspace*, p. 146).[43] However, since all literary representations are symbolic as well as potentially mimetic, the question of the characters' spatial imaginary fuses with that of the authors themselves. Literature has always capitalized on the aesthetic effect of the spatial

---

[43] Further, Lefebvre argues that instead of assuming that the prevalence of spatial vocabulary reflects the human mind's need to think in spatial terms, in fact the space-based terminology is merely a linguistic convenience; and language, like space, is for him a social product. Thus our loose reliance on spatial marking to articulate abstract thought is further evidence of the pervasiveness of 'social space' rather than a true reflection of 'mental space' (*Production of Space*, p. 5).

metaphor, whether that metaphor describes a presumably external reality or the characters' inner worlds. Thus, for purposes of our discussion, those mental projections which take specifically geographical forms – for example, dreamscapes, topographical character descriptions, or 'flights of fancy' that take a character across imaginary landscapes – will be considered alongside descriptions of material reality, as representative of the work's geographical imaginary, and as representing a perspective on sociopolitical realities as well as tools of effective artistic imagery which create worlds for the text's reader.

Conclusion

Both novelists and academics – the latter category understood to include geographers as well as literary analysts – are cultural producers. In articulating the politics of place, Nigel Thrift asserts that 'the use of place in literature and the reading of literature in order to understand place is a [...] political decision' (p.21). Novels explore the ways in which spaces help to generate the identities of their protagonists; but these novels at the same time themselves generate ideas of place which shape the geographic vision and interpretation of their readers. In what Thrift calls a 'double-sided process of ascription-appropriation' (p. 21), literature creates place signification at the same time that it builds upon it, not just reflecting but producing place affects. Like space itself, literature is a social product, and as such it is 'both reflective and generative of the wider social contexts (including other texts) within which [it is] produced and received' (Jones et al., p. xxxii). But in the end, novelists write space – and academics study space – because of what it reveals about its inhabitants, both the empowered and the disenfranchised. The study of places is a study of community, of the relations among people and between the people and their (built and natural) surroundings. A spatially focused reading of literary works involves, as Friedman notes, a study of 'the figure in terms of the ground, describing character within and through cultural locations inscribed in spatial configurations' (pp. 137–8). Or, as the title character in John Fowles' 1977 novel *Daniel Martin* observes: 'For the first time in my life I realised how profoundly place is also people.'[44]

But additionally, the examination of literary space must also involve considerations of aesthetic structuring, of the ways in which a novelist evokes a sense of place within her work, thus generating as well as reflecting a particular ideological stance. For the power of the text, any text, lies in its power to convince, to open readers' eyes to new horizons, to alert its readers to the dynamics through which they and others navigate, in the negotiations of everyday life and the interplay between identity's pull towards homogeneity and its counter-assertion of essential difference.

[44] Quoted in Thrift, p. 19.

2

In the Commercial Pipelines:
Restrepo's *La novia oscura*

Introduction

Laura Restrepo's *La novia oscura*, when read as plot – as sequence of events – narrates a chapter in the life of Sayonara, a legendary prostitute who worked in Colombia's oil-rich interior sometime during the late 1940s. First-person reflections by the narrator/reporter frequently interrupt the narrative, as she quotes her sources and inserts her own comments on both Sayonara's mystique and the process of the novel's construction. However, a spatial reading allows for a clearer vision of the motors that drive both the surrounding society and the narrative itself. A geoliterary study exposes not the lives of two individual women, but a shifting power dialectic that involves the individual, the Church, culturally embedded issues of race and class, the state and its military, and the overarching presence of globalized capitalism in the form of the US-owned Tropical Oil Company.[1] The novel's geoplot thus focuses on one individual's attempt to negotiate her own path through and around the obstacles of these hegemonic structures.

This novel is Restrepo's fifth; however, both this work and others by Restrepo have remained curiously understudied by Latin American critics, until her recent receipt of the prestigious Premio Alfaguara for her subsequent novel, *Delirio* (2004) increased her international visibility significantly. The most insightful study of *La novia oscura* to date is that by Claire Lindsay, ' "Clear and Present Danger": Trauma, Memory and Laura Restrepo's *La novia oscura*' (2003), which explores the novel within the context of contemporary Colombian violence and the writing of trauma. Carlos Arturo Arboleda discusses her use of language in his 2001 article, and Montserrat Ordóñez examines the novel's treatment of sexuality and prostitution in her study of 'ángeles y prostitutas' in two novels by Restrepo (2000); but apart from these few analyses and several book reviews and interviews, the work remains largely unexplored by critics. Given the intricacy

---

[1]   In 1919, the Tropical Oil Company (a branch of Standard Oil Co., now Exxon) was granted a 30-year exclusive contract – the Mares Concession – to extract oil from the area now known as Barrancabermeja, in the department of North Santander. The effects of this presence on the surrounding towns, as well as its impact on Colombian national and international policy, are significant in current discussions of the Colombian oil industry as well as the history of the military's ascendancy in controlling local populations.

of its narrative style, which it manages to balance with popular appeal and read-ability, it is certainly a novel that merits further study.[2]

When the novel is read through its spatial polyhedron of intelligibility, the reporter's intercalated reflections become not an interruption to the narrative, but a strategic counter-positioning. Her parallel commentary gradually makes explicit the links between the love story (the legend of 'la puta y el petrolero' [p. 410]) and contemporary issues facing the Colombian nation. Identifying with certain aspects of her distant counterpart and delving into the heart of Sayo-nara's mystery, the narrator observes and evaluates the historical process that has produced 'ese país marcado por la violencia' (p. 247).

Unlike Sayonara, the reporter does not face restrictions of mobility. She travels across Colombia and to the United States tracking Sayonara's path. Nonetheless, her obsession with Sayonara – an obsession she shares with all who encountered the legendary prostitute – reflects the admiration that she feels towards a woman who appeared to carry her own power with her, and to negotiate boundaries with unconscious ease. The narrator's envious tone, echoing that of the many people she interviews in compiling her story, serves as evidence that the hegemons of gender- and sex-based norms have survived into the present.

The central plot is a simple one: a young girl, silent about her name and her origins, follows the Magdalena River to the village of Tora, seeking her secu-rity and fortune by the most secure route available to her – by entering the sex industry based in the *barrio* of La Catunga. She meets Sacramento, also an orphan making his living as an errand boy, who delivers her to the home of La Catunga's most famous madam, Todos los Santos. The matron takes the young girl under her wing, baptizing her with the exotic name of Sayonara, while Sacramento eventually leaves to 'become a man,' pursuing his own fortune in the oil fields of the Tropical Oil Company.[3] There, Sacramento meets another worker, el Payanés, who later visits and develops a relationship with Sayonara. While the prosti-tute in fact gives her heart to him, he does not return her affections. Meanwhile Sacramento, now the third point in the love triangle, repents of having delivered Sayonara to a life of prostitution, and he dreams of one day rescuing her from the life she chose. Eventually, because el Payanés breaks off his relationship with Sayonara, she marries Sacramento out of a sense of loyalty as well as to find a path to a new life. Although the couple travels together in a fruitless attempt to leave behind her past, she eventually succumbs to her continuing passion for el

---

2   Leila Guerriero has published an overview of the novelist's life and works, in her article 'Nómade por naturaleza,' which appeared in the *Suplemento Cultural* of Argentina's *La Nación* in 2004; however, this piece does not include discussion of Sayonara's own nomadic trajec-tory.

3   It is no coincidence that Sacramento's departure is narrated in the same chapter as Sayonara's initiation into sex work. Sacramento, like Sayonara, imagines his future in terms that link bodily maturation with economic advancement: 'Voy a meterme de petrolero para regresar tostado, peludo y con mucha plata' (p. 64).

Payanés and returns alone to La Catunga. In the story's ambiguous ending, she finally walks away, either with el Payanés or alone, into an untold future.

The story's reconstruction, through interviews with those who knew Sayonara and in the reporter's imaginative re-presentation of their memories, takes place where the original events did: in La Catunga, 'barrio de las mujeres' within the village of Tora. However, the site's constancy is undone by the passage of time: Sayonara is gone, the prostitutes are now aged, and the eyewitnesses' memories contradict each other as strongly as do their attitudes towards those memories. While the geographic locus of the narrative past and present remains the same, the place has changed entirely; but with Tora as the narrative headquarters, the reporter pursues her story across the country and even internationally, wherever the continuing threads of Sayonara's life lead her. The contrast in mobility between the work's two protagonists is mirrored by differences in terms of their awareness of social, political, and macro-economic conditions. The reporter's education and experience, and the benefit of historical perspective, expose the power network – the intertwined economic and sexual exploitation engineered by the triple threat of Church, government, and foreign oil interests – and the false idealism of sentiment, to which her story's focus, Sayonara, remains blind. Yet all of this knowledge, this clarity of vision that the modern woman storyteller appears to have acquired, meets its match as she attempts, ultimately unsuccessfully, to decipher Sayonara's motivations, her character, and the source of the power she exerts, seemingly effortlessly and unconsciously, on those around her.

The forces of social reproduction engendered by the Tropical Oil Company produce the social, religious, and political entities that appear to govern Tora and that delimit Sayonara's material and figurative autonomy. Our spatial reading will address the question 'Who was Sayonara?' as a set of geographic interrogations against this transnational superstructure: Where was she? Where did she want to be? How did she get there, or not, and against what obstacles? The answers to all of these questions lie in the local dialectic of power as erected and maintained by 'la Troco.'

Tropical Oil Company (la Troco) – 'ésta es la cara que tiene el progreso'

As an outspoken critic of global capitalism, Restrepo articulates a vision of spatial production very much in line with that presented by Lefebvre and grounded in Marxist social theory. The capitalist enterprise (Tropical Oil) constructs spaces which reflect and enhance its own productive ability (for example, the drilling complex and the all-male workers' barracks), and then uses those spaces to direct not just the work but the lives of its employees. Extending its reach to ensure continued productivity, Tropical Oil then promotes construction of La Catunga, the venue of female work, a *barrio* of prostitutes which exists primarily to service the oilfield workers. This structure of social reproduction, tolerated by the Church and regulated by national health officials, overlies and obliterates the pre-existing community structures of Tora. While some communities within the village may pre-date the arrival of the US oil conglomerate, these social groups have been redefined and reassembled by the new economic forces upon which Tora is now constructed. For example, the indigenous pipatona women have been socially re-cast under the capitalist class system which also foments racial prejudice; they now serve as prostitutes in La Copa Rota, La Catunga's worst dive. Based on the twin workplaces of production and reproduction (Tropical Oil and La Catunga), local conceptualizations of family, religion, health, the body, and social stature are manipulated through specific places: the health clinic, the church, the plaza. The capitalist enterprise erects or controls these structures in order to organize the society, classify it, stabilize it, and ultimately profit from it. These physical sites, then, serve both to represent and to exercise power over Tora's inhabitants.

The story's territory is the north central province of North Santander, Colombia, and specifically the oil fields of Mares, which were controlled by the US-based Tropical Oil Company between 1919 and 1951. Temporal designations are vague, the worker uprisings and violencia of the early 1950s providing the only temporal marker. We can assume that the narrative present is the 1990s,[4] and that perhaps some four decades have passed since Sayonara's time and La Catunga's heyday. The narrator represents Tropical Oil's hegemony in the form of a verbal landscape that reflects the refinery's dominating physical presence. In one of the novel's final chapters, the narrator's wide-angle lens creates a space of representation, demonstrating that the shaping force of 'la Troco' extends beyond its physical environs:

> Hasta que asomó en el cielo el último viernes de ese último mes del año y rozó primero las chimeneas de la refinería, luego las copas de los árboles más altos, enseguida los techos de las casas y por último las espaldas desnudas de las mujeres dormidas, para encontrar a Sayonara ya bañada y vestida y desayunada, de rodillas ante el Cristo de las barbas rubias. (p. 407)

The reporter sketches first and foremost the structures of the industrial plant. In telescoping fashion, the natural world, the domestic environment, and ultimately the lives of each individual – down to their most intimate geographies – are drawn, materially and symbolically, in the shadow of the corporate structure. The blond Christ testifies to the company's cultural influence, but the narrator reveals through the strands of her tale that the sex industry, as incarnated in La Catunga, is also an outgrowth of this industrial paradise. Brothel sex is supported by la Troco as long as it is good for business, and it is eliminated eventually when it no

---

4   The narrator/reporter is modeled closely on Restrepo herself, and the novel's publication date is 2000. Additionally, there are frequent references to Colombia's contemporary situation, as characterized by continued violence, drug trafficking, and kidnappings.

longer appears to serve la Troco's interest, that of maintaining a happy, relatively docile male workforce.

The workers' bodies also function as a space of representation for Restrepo. For example, while el Payanés (the oil worker whom Sayonara loves) does visit La Catunga and enjoy physical satisfaction there, he belongs wholly to la Troco. The ideal capitalist worker, el Payanés finds joy and fulfillment not only in the security of his paycheck but in the production process itself. The corporate ideology of profit and loyalty insinuates itself into his worldview to the point that he inscribes it into his flesh, in the form of a tattoo. This corporeal branding appears in the site normally reserved for a lover's name. He experiences love at first sight when he 'meets' la flaca Emilia, the oil drill of Camp 26:

> –Qué Emilia esta; nunca había visto una bestia tan formidable –dijo conmovido el Payanés, contemplándola con estupor y recelo como si fuera un templo pagano, acariciando con delicadeza la contundencia de sus fierros y haciéndole sin saberlo un juramento de fidelidad que habría de cumplir sin fisuras desde ese primer encuentro hasta el propio día de la muerte. ... La alianza entre ellos dos quedó pactada esa misma noche, cuando a él se le acercó un mercachifle errante que se daba mañas en el arte del tatuaje y le ofreció la inscripción indolora del nombre de la mujer amada en cualquier parte del cuerpo.
> –Escríbeme Emilia aquí, en el pecho.   (p. 129)

Sayonara builds her dreams around her own fantasy of sheltering herself forever in his sensuous chest. But el Payanés's one true love is a drill, a piece of la Troco's immense machinery, whose name is carved into his flesh, and with whom he appears to fuse himself, in a simulacrum of copulation, as the drill pumps fiercely (p. 219). He reveals late in the novel that he has left his wife and children behind, in his native region of Popayán, in order to merge his identity with that of the corporation; and while the novel's ending is ambiguous it is assumed that he leaves Sayonara behind for the same reason, to pursue the 'American' dream. While his marriage to industry may seem voluntary, a vision of the way power works through physical spaces and corporeal surfaces reveals that el Payanés has been purchased, body and soul, by la Troco.[5]

Oil, then, is the modern territory's defining cultural element. Oil overtakes national identities, constructs its own laws and imposes a new and distinct cultural identity on all those whom it absorbs. Oil is connected to, and delineated by, a network of pipelines circulating among a myriad of workers and a single set of allegiances, rumors, legends, and reconstructed history. Sayonara's fame as a mysterious and sensuous prostitute, for example, extends far beyond the limited geographical region in which she travels. The pipelines serve as communicative

---

5   El Payanés's personal attachment to *la flaca Emilia* causes him to abandon the workers' strike in order to protect her (p. 264). Thus la Troco succeeds in its domination of this proto-typical worker.

veins; 'su gloria se extendía doquiera que corrían los tubos petroleros' (p. 96). The pipelines carry not only stories but their very characters. El Payanés eventually disappears into this network, a replacement 'homeland' of transients whose patriotism reflects only the values of production: 'un petrolero trashumante, como llaman a quienes van acompañando el tubo en su recorrido desde las selvas del Catatumbo hasta los desiertos de Siria, ida y vuelta y otra vez ida' (p. 219). This industrial superstructure, with its US-destined profits, its devastating ecological footprint, and its self-serving structures of social engineering, wields a network of influence that mirrors its network of underground pipelines. La Troco thus restructures the political and cultural systems of each society it envelopes, stripping workers of their regional and cultural ideologies and replacing them with the illusion that they are worthwhile and fulfilled contributors to the capitalist enterprise. They are now citizens of the borderless 'tierras petroleras' (p. 97).

The State – 'el Estado proxeneta'

La Troco could not occupy its territory, or its position of authority, without the consent and the protection of the Colombian state, its government and, most visibly, its military.[6] From the outset the oil company appears as a fortress, complete with armed guards. Company and government are bedfellows, as is confirmed during the *huelga de arroz*, when the workers' rebellion is put down by General Del Valle's national army (p. 303). The government's position involves apparent subservience to la Troco as well as manipulations of the US corporation so as to guarantee financial gain and the perpetuation of their own regime. Both entities, la Troco and its 'deputy' the Colombian state (p. 23), milk the prostitution industry as a way to satisfy the perceived needs of their other two local workforces, the refinery laborers and the soldiers.

Spatially, the government imposes itself in La Catunga primarily through the healthcare clinic. State-employed physicians examine the prostitutes for disease and then issue health cards to legitimize – and brand – the women as prostitutes. The system in effect makes them government-sanctioned employees. The clinic exists not to ensure the prostitutes' health or the clients', but functions rather as a mechanism of vigilance and control, a Foucauldian panopticon. The doctors 'de dudoso diploma' (p. 78) treat the women as prisoners, ordering their submission and the removal of their clothing with obscenities, rough gestures, and threats. Profit is part of the doctors' motivation; they demand bribes, primarily of a monetary nature. As Todos los Santos points out, 'a la que esté enferma no la curan sino que le cobran el doble por el visto bueno' (p. 76).

---

6   For a thorough and useful summary of theories of capitalist reproduction, which involve the collusion of the economic, social, and political spheres (including the state's role to protect and stabilize the capitalist enterprise in moments of crisis), see Jennifer Wolch and Michael Dear's introduction to *The Power of Geography: How Territory Shapes Social Life* (1989).

As a conclusion to this chapter about the medical clinic, the narrator/reporter explicitly links the mutual support networks of la Troco and the Colombian state. La Machuca, another prostitute, tells the reporter about a French investigator who revealed 'que las prostitutas de Tora le pagábamos más al Estado en controles de salud y en multas, que la Tropical Oil Company en regalías' (p. 83). This reference explicitly places the prostitutes alongside the oil workers as an exploited labor force. The whores, not unlike el Payanés, believe that they are choosing their own path, pursuing their dreams of prosperity and security. But in many respects the international enterprise is pimping the Colombian nation just as it does the women of La Catunga.

However, the power of these officials is not limited to currency; they also make clear their direct control over the women's bodies. When Sayonara protests at the rough treatment of her *madrina*, the doctor responds with a reminder of his complete authority: '–Déjela que insulte, doña –dijo el médico con voz tan brusca que las de afuera alcanzaron a escuchar–. La próxima vez esta mocosa va a tener que chupármela para que le haga el favor de expedirle el carné' (p. 79). The vulgarity of the doctor's threat is intended to keep Sayonara in her place, by reminding her of the dual oppression of class and gender. Masculinity grants him as much power as does his status as a government official, and both of these identities take precedence over his role as physician.

Nonetheless, the medical clinic of La Catunga does not retain its dominant position. As Lefebvre notes in *The Production of Space*, '[space] escapes in part from those who would make use of it. The social and political (state) forces which engendered this space now seek, but fail, to master it completely' (p. 26). Sayonara succeeds in transforming the medical clinic into a site of resistance, when her newness to the degradation, combined with the sense of untouchability that will become her trademark, leads her to organize an uprising that culminates in the torching of the clinic. The narrator records Todos los Santos's memory of the event, which places Sayonara in a different kind of space: 'vio a su niña avanzar serenamente, como Cristo sobre las olas, por un estrecho camino abierto entre las llamas, bailarina de vértigo al borde del desastre, y me jura que vio también cómo las bocanadas de humo le mecían el pelo con delicadeza y cómo el fuego se acercaba, manso, a besarle el vestido y a lamerle los pies' (p. 82). The clinic is eventually replaced by a new medical center, operated by a doctor who brings humane care to the prostitutes. The shift in power relations is signified in the novel by architectural replacement: the new clinic is constructed over the ruins of the federal structure, representing Sayonara's victory over the space of the pimp state's authority. The destruction of the government's space of representation, and Sayonara's successful rejection of the controlling and condemning federal gaze, foreshadows the rest of her story. As she moves unspoiled through the streets of La Catunga and through the hands of her customers, she retains this powerful aura, despite the degradation implied by her chosen profession.

Sayonara as negative space – 'una casa vacía'; 'espacios abiertos'

Asked about *La novia oscura*'s genesis, Laura Restrepo has explained that, while conducting on-site research for an article on gasoline cartels in this region of Colombia, she came across a photograph of a dark and mysterious young woman,[7] and was drawn to follow that story line rather than the one that had brought her there. Within the novel, the reporter follows the same path; mesmerized by the image, she seeks out the photographer, who echoes her own sentiments about the woman's captivating presence. The investigative reporter-turned-narrator then begins to track Sayonara's footsteps, as well as to chronicle her own physical and philosophical journey of discovery, in order to decipher the mysteries of the prostitute's universal and captivating appeal. These mysteries are repeatedly articulated in spatial terms.

In her initial attempt to convert this photograph into words, the narrator reaches for a geographic reference point, describing the image as that of a mestiza girl 'que respiraba un vaho de selvas vírgenes y al mismo tiempo de bajos fondos, que de verdad perturbaba' (p. 143). The novel is an attempt to 'enfocar este caleidoscopio quebradizo y volátil' (p. 229) into a verbal portrait that carries more dimensions than the photograph, without losing that essence which el Tigre Ortiz, the photographer, succeeded in capturing with the camera's eye, and which first attracted her to Sayonara's story.

The reporter is mesmerized by the impression, captured in the photo and echoed by those who knew her, that Sayonara walks within a solitary space, holding at bay her lovers, her fellow prostitutes, and her friends. While she has 'ojos de niña que ha visto demasiado' (p. 143), she at the same time appears completely aloof, uncontaminated, pure amidst hundreds of lovers. In order to convey this characterization, the narrator constructs her verbal portrait around spatial metaphors of separateness. For example, focalizing through el Payanés as he sees Sayonara for the first time, dancing in the brothel, the narrator writes: 'Perdida en sí misma como si ondulara en sueños, Sayonara flotaba en el chorro de luz. En medio del ruido y la condensación humana, el espacio donde se hallaba aparecía aislado como un sagrario, inasible e inviolable, anegado en aire de otro mundo como un paisaje lunar' (pp. 139–40). She walks surrounded by a 'fulgor de soledad' which attracts him – like all other men – irresistibly (p. 228); when he first recognizes his own longing for her, he thinks aloud, imagining the gulf between her and her lovers in spatial terms: 'Hasta la soledad de esa mujer no se abre camino nadie' (p. 140). But instead of falling in love, Sayonara fills herself with 'espacios abiertos' (p. 271); in another passage in which the reporter reflects on her untouchable air, she compares her to an empty house: 'Como corriente de aire en una casa vacía, soplaba en su nuca el aliento de muchos extraños' (p. 278). Again, reinforcing this image of spiritual isolation coincident with the

---

[7] This is the photograph that appears on the cover of the novel, in both the Spanish (Anagrama) and the English (HarperCollins) editions.

most extreme physical proximity, the narrator describes her as 'tan entregada a los hombres como olvidadiza de ellos, detenida en la carrera circular de su propio tiempo y sin tender puentes sólidos hacia el mundo exterior' (p. 247). All of these concrete images are articulated by different characters, who converge in their attempts to verbalize the intangible through spatial imagery, as they note the perceived distance between Sayonara and her physical environs. They function to represent her as the authority over her own created space, which protects her from the grasping hands of those who desire her. Her legendary desirability is ironically rooted in this very ability to define and take her place, and to hold them at a distance.

Yet while her reputation creates a global circle of admirers,[8] she remains lonely in her space, untouched by their possessive gazes. Instead, she exhibits what Claire Lindsay terms 'dissociative disorder' ('Clear and Present Danger,' p. 48).[9] A notable example of this retreating into herself occurs during one of her conversations with the doctor Antonio María, during which she, in a moment of confidence, confesses her solitude: 'a veces creo, doc, que no hay lugar para mí en el amor de los hombres' (p. 226). As she turns her back on him to wash her hands, oblivious to his hunger for her, he devours her with the possessive male gaze of erotic desire, figuratively taking control of her body as the physical surface between his desires and her inner self:

> mientras ella seguía haciendo lo suyo con los movimientos honestos de quien no sospecha que es observado, la miró como nunca antes se había permitido mirarla, valga decir, con ojos que buscan poseer aquello sobre lo cual se posan, y repasó con la dolorosa tensión del deseo esas manos de largos dedos y uñas almendradas. ... Luego, despacio, sorbo a sorbo, persiguió la suave línea del antebrazo hasta verla esconderse entre la manga corta, y pasó enseguida al caracol de la oreja, que le ofreció la fascinación de un pequeño laberinto carnal, y enseguida al reluciente prodigio de esa melena que se negaba a quedarse atrás aunque ella la espantara sacudiendo la cabeza, y que volvía a deslizarse sobre los hombros, viva e indómita, para caer hacia delante e inmiscuirse en el salpicar del agua. ... sus ojos tomaron minuciosa nota de la inquietante vibración que a las nalgas de la muchacha le imprimían los movimientos enérgicos de las manos mientras se enjuagaban. (p. 227)[10]

---

[8] 'Sayonara se había convertido, en tierras petroleras, en la inspiración de todo hombre digno de llamarse así' (p. 97).

[9] Claire Lindsay's illuminating study discusses Sayonara's self-isolation as the consequence of trauma; similar symptoms are exhibited by Aurora in Allende's *Retrato en sepia*, as the result of similar events involving the eruption of violence during childhood.

[10] It should be noted that this is one of the novel's most erotic passages. More intimate physical encounters, such as Sayonara's sexual initiation with the elderly Manrique (p. 69) or her first physical encounter with el Payanés (p. 153) are left tantalizingly unnarrated, making this imaginary scene of contact more tangible than Sayonara's recognized sexual transactions.

The narrator emphasizes the significance of this passing encounter by making it its own chapter in the novel, an unusually brief chapter of less than three pages, representing the blaze of desire that Sayonara can kindle instantly and that smolders forever in the memories of the men who desired her. But this hungry gaze has no effect on Sayonara, and the reporter hypothesizes that therein lies the secret of her power and, at the same time, her tragedy. Impervious to men's touch and insentient to their arousal, she remains isolated.[11] Thus, while her body is temporarily purchased by the men who visit the brothel, and by the imaginations of all the men she encounters, she succeeds in defending a geography even closer in, a territory to which they cannot lay claim. To depict all of this mystery, Restrepo harnesses the connotations of space and movement to represent the negotiation of power.

At the novel's opening, the young girl has seemed to appear from nowhere;[12] years later, at the novel's end, she disappears into the same kind of oblivion. While the efforts of the investigative reporter eventually do uncover her geographic origins, she never succeeds in learning where Sayonara's next stop was, after her departure from La Catunga. Her roles as prostitute and as wife no longer tolerable, Sayonara waits by the river, hoping that el Payanés will come to escort her to their future together. Yet in a masterfully ambiguous passage, the narrator writes both that they go off together, and that she leaves alone. In the words of Todos los Santos, those who thought they saw the pair disappear together in fact saw only 'espejismos, que no son más que reverberaciones del deseo' (p. 411). Todos los Santos's desire was to see the two lovers finally free from the oppressive pulls of the 'American' dream, so that they could create their own future together – once more articulated in terms of geographic exploration: 'el uno en pos del otro y el otro en pos del uno y ambos siguiéndole el rastro a la vida … abriéndose camino hacia un futuro incierto' (p. 411). However, the inherent contradiction, which only the now-blind Todos los Santos sees, is that this image of shared space does not fit the restless and solitary spirit of Sayonara.

Instead, Sayonara disappears into an unknowable future. Instead of settling into a prescribed social role, she opts to prolong her identity play, taking on new exteriors in an attempt to protect her innermost space. Thus she makes her final pilgrimage, alone, into a no-place which might allow her to construct herself. As she traveled with Sacramento she had sought invisibility, anonymity, 'ese país sin recuerdos que es tierra de nunca jamás' (p. 335), but she cannot find it as long as she travels with him, with his judgmental gaze and the burden of his accusatory memories. If indeed she does disappear alone into the future, following the river towards true oblivion, then she succeeds in her quest; for even the resources

---

[11] As Sayonara herself points out to the doctor, being possessed by many is like not being possessed at all, because she is incapable of holding, or being held in, the love of one man (p. 226).

[12] Sacramento recalls that 'no supo cuándo ella, liviana como un recuerdo, se encaramó a la zorra' (p. 16).

available to the investigative reporter, combined with her consuming obsession for uncovering the eventual fate of Sayonara, yield no trace of the woman who now pursues her 'tránsito por territorios de la nada' (p. 350). She has successfully disappeared from the landscape, and has taken her place somewhere else.

El río Magdalena and liminal space – 'al Magdalena lo alimentan los efluvios de la naturaleza y los humores de los hombres'; 'una masa de oscuridad que invitaba a caminar sobre ella'

The Magdalena River contrasts with the built environment, as a constant and a symbolic presence that connects the entire country (p. 158), and that serves as the key feature of the novel's natural landscape. It not only marks a material feature of the Mares region, influencing the initial placement of la Troco's facilities, but it also plays an important symbolic role in the story, as a liminal space. Winchester, McGuirk and Everett's analysis of the spatial practices of boarding schools presents significant conclusions about the importance of liminal places in the formation of identity. They discuss these spatially separate areas as sites for development, for the shedding of one identity and the adoption of another, for example during adolescence or at other stages of maturation; they mention as an example the Gold Coast of Australia as a 'place of desire and pilgrimage where boundaries are crossed, and identities and states are in transition … a location where transitions are possible' (p. 63). In that article they also mention that the spaces where liminality occurs tend to be 'on the margins, whether physical, political, or cultural margins' (p. 60). The Magdalena River, running past the edge of the village of Tora and functioning as a system of orientation and navigation for the entire region, serves precisely this function, as the site of fluid identity formation for the novel's main character.

Sayonara first appears by the river, having allowed it to lead her from her place of origin (Ambalema) to her new identity in Tora. The threshold to her new life is marked by her encounter with Sacramento, who waits by a dock in order to earn his living transporting people and their goods to the town. The narrator pauses in the telling of her story, to emphasize the role of the river as a heterotopic site of social confluence: 'El río flotaba en un sopor de cocodrilos mensos y el champán que traía viajeros y buscavidas, tagüeros y caucheros, avivatos y muertos de hambre de todos los puertos del Magdalena, se demoraba más que otros días en llegar' (p. 16). The young girl does not arrive on the raft, but rather appears as if from nowhere, as if evoked by his own wandering thoughts or by the flow of the water itself (p. 16). The now-aged Sacramento interrupts the reporter's retelling of this meeting, in order to mark Sayonara's emergence from the river as an identity threshold. He tells her that the person who appeared so suddenly was not yet Sayonara, but 'la niña que se convertiría en Sayonara y que después dejaría de ser Sayonara para ser otra mujer' (p. 16). As she passes across these various thresholds in her life's journey, she returns each time to the river, which serves as both a connecting thread and a 'location where transitions are possible' (Winchester et al., p. 63).

It is no accident that Sayonara's first sexual encounter with el Payanés also occurs along the riverbank (p. 150). During the passage to this site, el Payanés and Sayonara sit watching the river, and el Payanés begins to identify her with the river itself, noting that her skin caressed his 'con la misma indulgencia con que el fondo del champán iba lamiendo la superficie del agua' (p. 152). Their conversation constitutes a verbal foreplay that draws them closer together, while at the same time revealing Sayonara's deep identification with the Magdalena. Finally, she makes explicit her ties to the river, ending the conversation with a partial confiding of her own origins: 'Yo también soy de este río. Pero de otro pueblo, que está más arriba' (p. 152), and the narrator concludes the section by noting that forever after, el Payanés would associate her with the Magdalena River.

Their encounter, which might be seen as a second deflowering because of its distinctness from her many other corporeal transactions, takes place beside the river; but in the narrator's imagined reconstruction, the 'episodio ordinario' pales alongside the arousal of the river passage itself (p. 155). As the lovers separate, they make a vow to continue their encounters not in the café but at the riverbank, on the last Friday of every month. Sayonara gives el Payanés an amulet by which to remember her, but he turns the river into an even stronger thread that will link them, overcoming the potential dislocations that their nomadic futures might bring:

> –Nunca sabes adónde te ha de empujar tanta guerra. Si abandonas Tora, digo, y te aquietas en cualquier otro rincón, tú esperas a que llegue nuestra fecha, caminas en línea recta hasta topar con el Magdalena y me esperas a la orilla.
> –Este río es muy largo –objetó ella–. Atraviesa de parte a parte el país …
> –Tú busca el río, que yo sabré buscarte a ti.   (p. 158)

Furthering its significance as a site of transitions, the river is the place that marks the end of Sayonara's and el Payanés's relationship. Again, the river serves not only as backdrop to this transitional scene, but as a symbolic marker, as the place where the innocent verbal images created between the two lovers during their first encounter have now been washed away: 'El río Magdalena, que un día había incendiado sus aguas para recibirlos, convertido en hoguera que consumía y no quemaba, ahora les pasaba por enfrente menso y aburrido, testigo apático de su desencuentro, sin sacar a relucir lavanderas, ni tortugas, ni ocho cuartos, ni músicos viejos, ni nada parecido a piaras de cerdos que bajaran a calmar la sed' (p. 315).

The river then serves as a site of purification, as Sayonara remains there alone all night, allowing her tears to flow into the river's water. The narrator dedicates several of the novel's most lyrical paragraphs to the girl's physical and symbolic fusion with the river that night ('lluvia, savia, leche, sangre, nieve, sudor y lágrimas, al Magdalena lo alimentan los efluvios de la naturaleza y los humores de los hombres' [p. 323]), to her identification with the dead bodies that she imagines were washing past her in the darkness, to her own thoughts of throwing herself into the river as a way of passing to another existence, in a way that the cemetery forbids and in a way that she longs for, anticipating the novel's end: 'Por eso no se dejan enterrar … Por eso buscan el río, porque bajo tierra, solos y quietos, se mueren, mientras que en la corriente viajan, pueden mirar a sus anchas el cielo y visitar a los vivos …' (p. 324). And when she returns home the next morning, Todos los Santos notes that like a snake, Sayonara has shed her own skin by the side of the river, leaving behind her adolescence and entering the next phase of her life (p. 325).

The river marked the arrival of Sayonara, her awakening to love with el Payanés, and her loss of innocence. It should thus come as no surprise that the river serves as the site of the character's final transition, her ambiguous disappearance either alone or with el Payanés. Faithful to her vow to him, and trusting in the rumors that – la flaca Emilia having been dismantled – he is seeking new employment via the network of oil pipelines (p. 406), she waits by the river on the month's final Friday, for him to escort her off to their new future (p. 411). The audience that watches this final performance, momentarily blinded by the sunset's reflection on the waters, remains uncertain of whether el Payanés did appear or not; the only certainty is that Sayonara herself, 'la niña de los adioses' (p. 324), does displace herself, following the course of the river, shedding yet another skin to reinvent herself, passing into the liminal space and thence to the mobility of body and of identity that she had sought.[13]

'El amor del café' – 'reinas y señoras del lugar'; 'aquél era otro mundo'

A space-focused study of La Catunga must take into account the context of the sex industry as presented in Restrepo's novel. The activity ostensibly viewed as both primitive and destabilizing by the controlling forces of Church and state is nonetheless tolerated as long as it is useful; and it is regarded in a much more natural way by the prostitutes themselves, as they retrospectively explain their vocation to the reporter. The reporter's accompanying reflections provide further commentary on the potential benefits and joys of this apparently free social structure, and on the mechanics of its marginalization.

The pleasure principle is the basis of the justification for the prostitutes' activity. Throughout the many conversations on the topic, throughout the novel,

---

[13] As observed in the introductory chapter of this study, women often opt for remaining in a state of liminality rather than passing through the threshold to assume a permanent identity; Teather, citing studies by Schouten and Turner, notes that 'without culturally prescribed and shared rites of passage … people cannot move smoothly from one role to another. … [O]ne option that these "liminoids" have is to undertake the construction of new identities alone' (p. 14).

economic need is seldom articulated as a basis for the lifestyle these women have chosen. While some acknowledge that they initially sought refuge in La Catunga after being expelled from other social spheres, they relish their identity as 'reinas y señoras del lugar' (p. 200). Their sovereignty is based both on the admission of female sexual pleasure and on the sensations of diversion, beauty, and autonomy in which they flourish within their world.

The prostitute Machuca, nicknamed 'la Gustosa,' for example, represents in most detail the idea of prostitution 'por vocación' rather than 'por obligación' (p. 188). Years later, after the eradication of La Catunga, the elderly Machuca – now a clerk and thus officially on the government payroll – recalls with unrepentant nostalgia the days when 'la cama fue mi altar' (p. 269):

> Yo no me metí de puta por huir de la miseria ... ni porque me violaron, o me trajeran al oficio arrastrada o engañada, sino por soberano placer y deleite. Para qué le voy a mentir, siempre supe disfrutar del jolgorio, del dinero, del aguardiente, del tabaco y por encima de todos los bienes terrenales, del olor a varón. El calor de hombre, ¿me comprende? ... ojalá haya un Dios en alguna parte para que el día del Juicio pueda gritarle a la cara que hice lo que hice porque sí, en honor a la lujuria y porque me dio la gana. (p. 269)

Her admission breaks down traditional gender barriers, as she lays claim to the same pleasures Tora's male residents take for granted, from the social freedoms to the indulgence in erotic pleasure. Within La Catunga, the 'muchacha de la vida' (p. 75) is not seen as selling her body, but as owning it.

Nonetheless, while the prostitutes celebrate their transgression and the reporter/narrator envies their apparent freedom, La Catunga remains in the shadow of la Troco, as a structure of its engineered social reproduction. North American feminist bell hooks has defined oppression as 'the absence of choices' (*Feminist Theory: From Margin to Center*, p. 5). When Sayonara arrived in Tora, young, female, and penniless, she demanded to be taken to the town's best brothel, but only because this was the most ambitious option within a very limited range of possibilities. There is no social structure outside the corporate enterprise, and within it she is forced to offer her body as the only commodity she possesses. The power she later exerts, as the legendary queen of her position, should still be viewed as limited – she rules only the space which was allotted to her. For this reason, her eventual rejection of the role should be seen as a spatial transgression, a crossing of the river, that represents a declaration of independence from the society that la Troco had built.

While la Troco tacitly fosters the prostitution enterprise as a constitutive element to a happy workforce, the medical clinic (mentioned above) and the Church serve as the controlling sites, which unite in their desire to contain the disorder implied by free sexuality. Of the two, the Church is of course more powerful, since it wields the constant vigilance of the eye of a condemning God. For example, as a boy Sacramento, guilt-ridden about his illegitimate birth to an anonymous prostitute, is interned in a religious boarding school, and recalls the unrelenting gaze of a supernatural authority, 'un Dios Padre que todo lo ve porque es un gran ojo hinchado, un ojo voyerista y furibundo y triangular que solo habrá de parpadear con benevolencia ante quienes logren ser modelo de castidad, de humildad y sacrificio' (p. 163). One visible manifestation of this spiritual judgment comes in the form of the ubiquitous statues of saints, 'ojones … con unos ojos de vidrio que despedían miradas verdaderas' (p. 164). But this glassy gaze simply mirrors the condemning perspective of the society surrounding La Catunga: 'Puta la madre, puta la hija, puta la manta que las cobija – comentaban los pudorosos al verlas pasar' (p. 86).

In spite of their apparent defiance of Church-imposed norms of conduct, the prostitutes also feel shame when they view themselves through this Eye which robs them of their power over their own space: 'las prostitutas eran reinas y señoras del lugar, pero eso no quería decir que en el fondo no tuvieran una fuerte conciencia de vivir en pecado' (p. 200). Thus despite their flagrant transgressions, they expose themselves willingly to the condemnation of Church society by participating in the penance rituals of Holy Week; barefoot and penitent, they make their own pilgrimage – not to the church building from which they have been banned, but to the movie theater, where Jesus of Nazareth, a film in Technicolor, is being shown for their exclusive viewing and edification. Their access to the celluloid savior, a Hollywood film with Spanish subtitles, is granted by the state, in no less than the Cine Patria. This place, theirs for a day, functions as a counter-site to the Church, one which demands penitence yet keeps the prostitutes from contaminating the space of the pious. As spectators of a film rather than participants in a religious rite, the penitent prostitutes weep before 'la pantalla del [Cine] Patria' in a ritual of purification and then depart, 'preparadas para soportar otro año de vida sin lamentarse ni protestar' (pp. 85–6). The state-sponsored and Church-condoned ritual provides emotional cleansing, but its most significant lesson is resignation; the prostitutes should continue working, but submissively and with relative invisibility, not in a way that challenges the dominant order.

The narrator blames the Church for the sense of shame that delimits the prostitutes' social position, when she observes through doctor Antonio María Flórez that the body/soul dualism preached by Christianity does not affect *las pipatonas*, the prostitutes of indigenous cultural identity. These sex workers (marginalized by multiple factors as women, indigenous, lower-class, prostitutes) share none of the internalizations or the bodily dissociations that underlie the mestizo prostitutes' schizophrenic worldview. While Sayonara and her colleagues struggle with the social and spiritual implications of their way of life, the non-Westernized *pipatonas* openly admit that they simply work to earn a living, 'sin hacer tanto nudo en la cabeza' (p. 202):

> Lo bueno, para ellas, era mantenerse con vida, y morirse era lo malo; no tenían una ética sexual más complicada que ésa, o mejor, no obedecían tanto a una ética como a una suerte de determinación biológica, según la cual mujer era

mujer, prostituta o no, y hombre era hombre, fuera el que fuera. Me hizo gracia saber que para ellas el cuerpo masculino estaba compuesto por cabeza, brazos, piernas, tronco y tronquito, y el femenino por cabeza, brazos, piernas, tronco y para-el-tronquito.   (p. 203)

The symmetry of the male and female body provides the basis for the moral code, and the overlay of moral codes and condemnations is absent. These women live so far beneath the gaze of la Troco and its reproductive structure that they are undamaged by its power to control and compartmentalize. The *pipatonas* do not hesitate to admit the reality of their own female bodies. Based on his observations of both groups of prostitutes, the doctor clarifies to the reporter that the culprit is 'the Christian upbringing' (p. 202) that is an arm of capitalist production systems.[14]

La Catunga – 'la zona de tolerancia más prestigiosa del planeta'

Alongside the world of la Troco, with its North American work ethic and ties to a controlled and productive lifestyle, the story paints La Catunga, the *barrio* of distinctly Colombian fare. From the outset, this settlement within Tora is set apart, in terms of both class and lifestyle; while its inhabitants are forbidden to enter the church[15] or to be buried in its graveyard, they have constructed their own gynocentric social order within the confines of their *barrio*.

Their society is built around the heterotopic café, the central domestic image. Indeed, the café takes the place that the domestic home represents in the dominant culture. Clearly, the characters' identity is inseparable from the places that shelter their intimate encounters. Yet in this society of such differently constructed values, into which the women do not land by choice but by the exclusion of other options, the women of the cafés do not accept secondary status. Instead, they value their freedom, their easy access to men and affection, the prosperity that comes from their indirect dealings with the Tropical Oil Company, and the festive weekend atmosphere. For these reasons, upon her arrival the young girl who will become Sayonara demands to be taken to 'el mejor café de este pueblo,' despite Sacramento's attempts to deter her from her chosen path:

–¿Sabes quiénes trabajan allá? –le preguntó–. Las mujeres de la vida. De la vida mala.

---

[14] Feminist philosopher Elizabeth Grosz explores at length the Western culture's artificial separation of body and soul, carnality and conscience, in her study *Volatile Bodies: Toward a Corporeal Feminism* (1994); like Restrepo's doctor figure, she too correlates this way of conceiving – and censuring – sexuality with the teachings of the Christian tradition (p. 5).

[15] The church is named Santo Ecce Homo, '*behold the man*'; while this is the name of a Catholic mission church in Colombia and also of a holy site in Jerusalem, its name still may be read as symbolic here, as the label of a church dedicated to the patriarchal image.

–Ya lo sé.

–Quiero decir de la vida muy, muy mala. De la peor. ¿Estás segura de que quieres ir?

–Segura –dijo ella con una certeza sin atenuantes–. Voy a ser puta.   (p. 17)

Her early assertion of agency bears significance in terms of the overall representation of prostitution. La Catunga appears as the refuge for abused and abandoned women, a safe haven which offers not only financial security but also protection from the hostile forces of the larger Colombian society. La Catunga's matriarch appears, in turn, as a woman who chose her own path and who now, even with the prosperity that life as a madam affords, enjoys 'un buen retiro que no dudaba en romper de tanto en tanto, cada vez que el alma volvía a exigirle contento y las entrañas calor' (p. 23). In a society that cannot offer shelter to the unfortunate – particularly if they are female – La Catunga, 'la zona de tolerancia más prestigiosa del planeta' (p. 19), becomes a safe haven, and Todos los Santos a 'defensora de los derechos de las muchachas contra la Troco y su lugarteniente el Estado colombiano' (p. 23).

La Catunga has its own palpable atmosphere, in this town where the Troco headquarters, military personnel, the officially sanctioned class systems, and the whores, live side by side, albeit in distinctly zoned areas. At first sight, the *barrio* is a poor but clean neighborhood, where doors remain open, houses stand 'sin misterio ni secreto' (p. 19), and men are conspicuously absent. Inhabitants are listed, in order, as animals, boys who dream of working in the oil industry, girls who dream of being teachers, and women in house slippers. As the young girl and her guide approach La Catunga, a difference in the air, the *barrio*'s mysterious but palpable distinctiveness, soon becomes apparent to the young girl:

> Un barrio pobre, como cualquier otro. Salvo las bombillas de colores, ahora apagadas e invisibles, que pendían sobre las fachadas como único signo de la diferencia. De la grande, insondable diferencia. Apenas la niña quiso dar un paso adelante, el corrientazo brutal que le azotó las piernas le hizo comprender, de una vez para siempre, que La Catunga estaba encerrada dentro de un cordón imaginario que quemaba como golpe de látigo.
>
> –Una vez adentro no vuelves a salir. –Oyó que la voz de Sacramento le advertía, y por un instante su corazón resuelto conoció la duda.   (pp. 19–20)

Restrepo thus symbolically erects boundaries around La Catunga. The invisible wall contains a refuge, but also serves to entrap the prostitutes. Of course, the wall is maintained not by the women themselves but by the forces of social reproduction – in this case the condemnation of Church and society – that allow the women entrance but not exit. This geographic zone of alternative lifestyles, clearly useful to the external society which can thus maintain the surface appearance of propriety, is represented as 'ese territorio marcado con hierro al rojo donde tenía cabida lo que afuera era execrable, donde la vida se mostraba por el envés y el amor reñía con los mandatos de Dios' (p. 20). At the same time, the zone of social inversion exists under state-sponsored guidelines in the form of identity cards, tolerated by the Church and by the dominant society who forms its client base, as well as surviving on the (indirect) support of la Troco.

Late in the novel, the reporter describes a sewage ditch that runs behind Todos los Santos's house; the redolent stream carries with it all the dregs of modern society: 'Arrastra material orgánica descompuesta, juguetes inservibles, toallas higiénicas usadas, jeringas, tapas de recipientes, algodón que tal vez limpió infecciones, restos de un colchón, plásticos azules, periódico de ayer: la vida, en fin, en la intimidad de sus residuos y de sus suciedades' (p. 361). This plumbing system pollutes the air of La Catunga, but notably, the waste that it carries comes from all of Tora. La Catunga is in fact the landing place for all those whom society would consider its 'dregs,' from orphans to prostitutes, from the indigenous woman (p. 236) to the transvestite young man (p. 237). Referring to the sewage behind her house but parabolically also to La Catunga in general, Todos los Santos attributes the existence of the barrio itself to the town's two authorities, federal and economic: 'en este pueblo chapoteamos entre nuestra propia mierda porque ni las autoridades ni la empresa petrolera han sido capaces de construir alcantarillado' (p. 362). Yet in spite of its function as a repository for society's waste, La Catunga retains its energy and freedom as a site of social contact freed from preoccupations about any individual's past or future.

The centers of La Catunga are the cafés, the permissive spaces where prostitutes meet, flirt with, drink and dance with, and lie with their customers. The prostitutes move up and down this social ladder, according to the stature which their professional success brings them. La Machuca describes as follows the descent which precedes the end of many a prostitute's career: 'Toda chica de la vida sabe que siempre habrá un bar más barato … y otro más y otro más a medida que te alejas del centro, la cuesta apenas inclinada para que la caída no sea aparatosa, y se consuela pensando que son varios los años y los peldaños por los que puede ir rodando antes del llegar al fondo, a lo que propiamente se dice el fondo del fondo' (p. 321). While many cafés are associated with La Catunga, the novel offers a clear portrait of only two of them, representing the extremes of the social hierarchy: Dancing Miramar, a 'café de categoría' (p. 235), and La Copa Rota, 'el fondo del fondo' (p. 321), the home of those to whom all other doors have been closed.

Dancing Miramar – 'universo entero y triple, como la Trinidad, de nacimiento, amor y muerte')

The very name of the Dancing Miramar communicates its stature among Tora's cafés. The exotic English 'dancing' adds the appeal of Tropical Oil's higher class culture, and 'Miramar' implies altitude, a privileged positioning. Both are of course false, since few Americans are in attendance and the ocean is nowhere to be seen. The salon itself is in fact located 'al fondo de aquel pasaje, contra la malla de la Troco' (p. 20); but the label is more important than the reality. As noted above, the actual physical location lies behind the headquarters of la

Troco; but within, la Negra Florecida, the proprietor, has created a 'salón versallesco' (p. 114).

As la Negra Florecida explains to the prostitute, all of the phases of life are contained within this one microcosm, for she has rooms especially designed for birth, for making love, and for dying. Significantly, the same space doubles as a funeral parlor, replacing the cathedral as the venue for wakes and funeral services; superstition demands that the walls be washed between a funeral and a night of festivity, but other than that and a change of lighting, the space lends itself equally to both activities, 'el culto del amor y el culto de la muerte' (p. 114). Within the figurative walls of La Catunga, the women have thus constructed a physical space which suits the flow of their social structure. Juxtapositions which would be unthinkable in the 'outside world' occur with naturalness here, as the space seeks to reflect rather than to impose an alternative societal structure.

This is the café to which the as-yet-unnamed Sayonara demands to be taken when she arrives seeking 'el mejor café de este pueblo' (p. 17); had she not insisted, and had she not found Sacramento, her more natural landing site would have been La Copa Rota, the café of the indigenous *pipatona* prostitutes and the other societal castaways.

La Copa Rota – 'el ombligo del mundo'; 'lugar último y límite'
With its name degraded as much as the Dancing Miramar is elevated, La Copa Rota is home to La Fideo, a skinny and violent prostitute, to Enrique Ladrón de Guevara y Vernantes, the albino dwarf painter, and to others who have reached the bottom of the social scale. Status is conveyed inversely by one's distance from the town center, and La Copa Rota lies on the margin, both geographic and social: 'Quedaba a la orilla de un camino de herradura a media hora del pueblo, a la propia sombra de la espesura, donde ya alcanzaban a sentirse el acoso del tigre y el aliento verde de la gran humedad' (pp. 235–6). In contrast to the velvets and satins of the Dancing Miramar, La Copa Rota consists of 'una tienda de grano con techo de paja y suelo de tierra pisada que durante el día era expendio de alimentos y que en las noches se transformaba en burdel, con media caneca en un rincón por todo baño y alumbrado con mecheros a falta de electricidad' (p. 235). There, 'ubicado al margen de toda humana vanidad,' the truly hopeless exiles find each other: 'inaceptables especímenes de su respectivo universo, cada cual a su dolida manera' (p. 236).

Unlike the festive environment of Dancing Miramar, of boyfriends and lovers, promises of fidelity and broken hearts, La Copa Rota contains only the essentials of a brothel, aimed at those who cannot afford luxury with their love: 'llegaban cansados y muertos de hambre de mujer, iban a lo que iban y enseguida se quedaban dormidos sobre los bultos de cereal, o se retiraban y no volvían, o volvían cuando ya las mujeres les habían perdido la fe' (p. 237). This clientele consists not of the raucous petroleros on furlough, but rather of the true labor class, 'la clientela más zarrapastrosa de Tora, los llamados de pata al suelo, una población migrante compuesta por cazadores, leñateros, tagüeros y demás rebuscadores pobres de la selva, que regresaban de sus andanzas exhaustos, palúdicos y engusanados a buscar consuelo entre las primeras piernas que los quisieran acoger' (p. 236). The prostitutes in turn correspond to their clients' level; the *pipatona* women dress in 'unos apretujes de tela barata que las volvían pesadas e informes como tonelitos, y en unos zapatos de tacón coneto que les amorataban los dedos de los pies' (p. 236), and appear unaware of the transgressive nature of their sexuality. They do not derive power or stature from their profession, but rather, as doctor Antonio María Flórez had observed, they view the sex trade as their means of making a living, without worrying about issues like shame, sin, or fidelity.

While the prostitutes of Dancing Miramar seek the spotlight, La Copa Rota offers invisibility to its residents and clients (p. 274), 'según las leyes centrífugas de la marginalidad' (p. 236). Yet in this 'ombligo del mundo' (p. 239) the albino dwarf is metamorphosed as 'don Enrique,' while the unappealing la Fideo becomes attractive: 'ella se desnuda, recibe un trago y eleva los brazos, entorna los ojos y hace ondular su cintura de alambre, otro trago y su cuerpo oscuro – casi soplo, apenas sombra – se dora en reflejos de candelas' (p. 234).

The reporter observes that Sayonara's arrival – young, penniless, and innocent – and dark skin predestined her more for La Copa Rota than for Dancing Miramar. How she averted that destiny, steering her own course, and how she acquired power from the advantageous positioning that Todos los Santos's patronage afforded her, is in fact the focus of the entire novel. The reporter realizes this approximately halfway through her story: 'en buena medida el meollo de esta historia consiste en el periplo que debió dar ella para eludir esa fatalidad' (p. 239). In other words, the distance between Dancing Miramar and La Copa Rota represents the distance between triumph and surrender, between a locus of privileged empowerment and one of submission and survival. The theory of Todos los Santos, expressed in the novel's first pages, is that 'las criaturas voluntariosas como ella [Sayonara] chalanean el porvenir y lo amañan a su antojo' (p. 18), and that the force of Sayonara's own will allowed her to bypass La Copa Rota and ascend to the heights not only of Dancing Miramar but of a fame unsurpassed by any of the prostitutes of the global petroleum-based network. The contemplative reporter, rendering explicit the symbolism of her real-and-imagined spatial imagery, theorizes that La Copa Rota, representing naked truth, lies at the heart of Dancing Miramar, and indeed at the heart of all human activity; but daily life, like the Dancing Miramar, is more or less covered over by velvet disguises (p. 239). Finally, however, the reporter gives in to the mystery of Sayonara's destiny versus her will, opting simply to tell the story as she has reconstructed it, and concluding: 'las cosas, suavemente, se explican por sí solas y … no hace falta ponerse a divagar' (p. 239).

El Barrio Staff – 'Ese es el otro mundo'; 'un voluntario campo de concentración'

One of the most humorous episodes also contains the most scathing representation of space, as it reflects the distance between US culture and this occupied Colombian territory. It is also a comment about the power dynamic that links both together in the Magdalena River region. Todos los Santos takes young Sayonara and her four little sisters, as part of their education, to a fence that divides Tora from the sheltered North American-style community in which the Troco staff lives. Their observations of foreign customs expose the hypocrisy not only of this Barrio Staff, from which foreign bosses determine the will of thousands of industrial workers 'desde la piscina con reflejos azules de su barrio enjaulado' (p. 251), but of North American mores as well.

Barrio Staff's very existence, a microcosm designed to replicate a North American suburb, conveys the invisible yet unbreachable gulf that separates la Troco and Tora. The divide extends as well between the de-cultured working class, housed in barracks and harnessed to the machines' rhythm, and the culture-bound executives and engineers that control the company operation:

> era una réplica reducida a escala del american way of life, como si a un confortable vecindario de Fort Wayne, Indiana, o de Phoenix, Arizona, le hubieran sacado una tajada para transplantarla a la mitad de la selva tropical con todo y sus jardines y piscinas, sus prados bien cuidados, sus buzones de correo como casitas de pájaros, la cancha de golf, la de tenis y tres docenas de viviendas blancas, espaciadas, idénticas entre sí, íntegramente importadas desde los muebles de alcoba hasta la primera teja y el último tornillo.   (pp. 212–13)

Barrio Staff effectively sterilizes itself against any intrusion of Colombian lifestyles, to the point that the children peering through the fences see nothing that they can understand, nothing that fits their worldview. They note, for example, that there is no one outdoors: '¿Aquí no vive nadie, madrina?' (p. 213), and wonder at the exotica of cutting the grass, washing the dog, playing at sports, pointless pursuits that serve merely 'para mantenerse ocupados y para matar el rato mientras pueden regresar a su país' (p. 215). In ironic inverted interpretations, the children suppose that the purpose of door and window screens is to keep people caged in, that American dogs must smell worse than theirs if they need such frequent washing, and that Americans must be cold-blooded like lizards if they need to sunbathe. But alongside such satirical comments, Restrepo utilizes these naïve observations to expose the equally absurd economic and cultural imperialism. Children ask why oil is taken from the land, and therefore whether it is good business to 'vender terreno sin petróleo' (p. 214), since they cannot conceive of any other reason for a nation to cede its own wealth to privileged foreigners. Their innocence exposes Restrepo's view of her country's absurdity, in allowing itself to be pimped by North American capitalism.

Barrio Staff thus exists as a space of representation for the 'American way of life.' La Troco implicitly theorizes that the order and docility of US workers is, at least in part, generated and stabilized by their housing structures, and that by reproducing and transplanting those structures wholesale the corporation can homogenize its international enterprise and avoid potentially destabilizing contact with the occupied territory.

The strongest critical inversion of this conversation between Todos los Santos and her protégées occurs at the outset, when one of the children asks why the residents are locked in and the adoptive mother explains:

> –Los encerrados somos nosotros, los de afuera, porque ellos pueden salir y en cambio a nosotros no nos dejan entrar.
> –¿Y por qué no nos dejan entrar?
> –Porque nos tienen miedo.
> –¿Y por qué nos tienen miedo?
> –Porque somos pobres y morenos y no hablamos el inglés.   (pp. 213–14)

The protective barriers erected between Barrio Staff and the local residents do represent the foreigners' fear of the native population. During the rice strike, the Golf Club is revealed to have been constructed as a fortress, a safe haven disguised as a recreational complex, 'una auténtica fortaleza de concreto diseñada para estas eventualidades, aunque la hubieran camuflado bajo el cálido colorido de las bugambilias' (p. 254). This is but one of many instances where Restrepo implies a parallel between la Troco and an occupying military force. The industrial conglomerate invades with a strategy, and leaves a wake of devastation, occupying territory and erecting defensive boundaries to mark it. In addition, expecting a violent defensive rebellion to erupt at any time, it stations armed guards along its 'borders' and it exerts tremendous physical and psychological control over the occupied communities.

La Troco and the erasure of La Catunga – 'las mejoras'

Throughout the novel, the reporter reveals that the ties between the petroleum industry and La Catunga are more complex than would at first be assumed. The obvious connection is economic, as we have seen: la Troco's all-male community, specifically 'Campo 26,' descends onto La Catunga monthly and feeds the local economy with their hunger for the food, drink, and sex of which they have been deprived. At early points, the characters seem to be exercising their own will. Work in the oil camps is highly coveted as a ticket to prosperity, and the women of La Catunga enjoy the autonomy of their weeks and the festive atmosphere of the paydays. Additionally, there are the oil workers' furloughs to look forward to, the customers' monthly descent to Tora. However, as the novel continues and relations between the workers and la Troco deteriorate, the narrator gradually exposes the degree to which La Catunga's existence has been engineered by the US corporation.

As Lefebvre noted in *The Production of Space*, hegemonic structures continually erase and rebuild the physical environment as a way of consolidating power. After the workers' strike, la Troco alters its social plan for the area. Rather than maintaining the all-male barracks, they decide instead to promote the social institutions of marriage and family, using the army as well as the Church to further this social engineering, in the hopes that it will lead to greater stability – read docility – for the workers. This new campaign is an ideological version of the 'Barrio Staff,' a North American transplant which will further homogenize the transnational workforce of la Troco. The corporation naturally employs both the army and the Church as allies, using a concurrent outbreak of syphilis as the justification for the new social plan. Replicating on a smaller scale the design of North American suburbia, they offer a physical symbol, a house, as a lure to each of the striking workers, knowing that this new spatial arrangement will bring with it domestic coupling, stability, indebtedness; in short, a social structure modeled more closely on the North American image. The new architecture will both reflect and promote the new ideology, thus maximizing productivity:

> Cayó en cuenta de que tener hombres desarraigados y hacinados en barracas, con una hamaca y una muda de ropa por toda pertenencia y con una puta por único amor, o sea con mucho por ganar y nada por perder, era echarse encima enemigos encarnizados e imposibles de manejar. En cambio un hombre con casa, esposa e hijos, al que la empresa le ayudara a sostener esa desmedida carga, se la piensa dos veces antes de arriesgar su trabajo para lanzarse a luchar. A menos eso pensó la Tropical Oil Company: que ya era hora de modernizar su estructura para mejor controlar al personal indómito que mantenía enjaulado en los campos petroleros.   (p. 302)[16]

Sacramento buys into the scheme immediately. After all, it fits a plan of control of his own: he will use his house to domesticate Sayonara, separating her from the other prostitutes and 'redeeming' her. He will then own her exclusively. Thus the idea of capitalist hegemony is translated to the individual level, and class oppression translated to gender-based oppression. He will buy Sayonara with the promise of home and hearth, just as la Troco plans to buy its workers' loyalty. His plan fails, however, when Sayonara comes to realize what Todos los Santos tells the reporter: that marriage and entrance into respectable society is a 'gilded cage,' 'porque ahorca con la soga más fina, que está hecha de cariño y que aprieta el cuello como collar de perlas' (p. 338). In the end, Sayonara abandons the home

---

16 Lefebvre mentions the replacement of dwellings by homogeneous, economical, and orderly 'housing,' as a central element of social reproduction under capitalism (p. 287). He notes that these housing plans involve seeking the lowest threshold of tolerability rather than any kind of individual satisfaction (p. 316); see also Keith and Pile, p. 24; Hayden, p. 19.

that Sacramento offers to (trap) her; she instead opts for the peripatetic life of the liminoid, following the real or imagined figure of el Payanés into oblivion at the novel's end.

La Troco's new plan erases La Catunga. 'The improvements' include its renaming, into a respectable *barrio* called La Constancia (p. 391). Analogous to the razing of the buildings, the army also forcibly shaves the prostitutes' heads, stripping them of the physical beauty which is their pride's weapon against their shame, and leaving them defenseless, 'con una opacidad de rabia estéril en la mirada' (p. 327). Again the authorities thus brand the bodies of their subjects, inscribing identity by forcibly marking their corporeal surfaces. This generation of prostitutes is in a sense fired by la Troco, and the women who knew Sayonara now live their lives on a subsistence basis, spending much of their time recalling the festive heyday of their youth. Machuca, for example, the most openly transgressive of the prostitutes, becomes a copy clerk for the mayor's office, thus legitimizing her identity as an employee of the State.

However, the sex industry itself, minus its spaces of celebration, survives, albeit under a cloak of greater secrecy and in spaces of greater marginalization. As Sayonara/Amanda makes her way back to Tora, she encounters huts where the new generation of prostitutes, degraded and unmasked, wait next to their cots for secretive and efficient johns:

> las viajeras se toparon con la primera enramada. A la vera del camino, así sin más, cubierta con chamizos y plásticos, con tres latones por paredes y hacia la parte del frente un costal por cortina; de un metro escaso de altura de tal manera que una persona cabía sólo acostada. Al lado de la enramada, sentada sobre una piedra, esperando, había una mujer muy pobre con los senos al aire y los labios pintarrajeados. (p. 379)

With the demolition of La Catunga comes destruction of the solidarity that once existed among the women; the prostitute described above shoos away Sayonara from the area, 'antes de que me espanten a la clientela' (p. 380). At the next hut, exposed to the view of passers-by, an oil truck driver buys the services of a prostitute while his assistant waits his turn. The capitalist ideology of profit and competition now completely dominates the sex industry, as it has been reconstructed by la Troco, and the replacement of the carnivalesque cafés with these utilitarian shacks converts the prostitutes into wage slaves, waiting to service their customers. As la Fideo later observes, even La Copa Rota, the most degraded of the brothels of La Catunga, was 'un palacio' compared with the new venues of prostitution (p. 384).

Interspersed with these shelters, along the Troco-constructed highway, are new billboards warning of the hazards of illicit love and promising the rewards of stable matrimony, as summarized in an amused tone by the reporter: 'Hombre sin hogar, aseguraba la sabiduría en forma de letrero, es como santo sin manto, como ave sin nido, como nido sin ave, como casa sin techo, como techo sin casa, como testa sin sombrero o vice-versa: todas cosas desamparadas, indeseables e incompletas' (p. 380). The juxtaposition of the shelters and the billboards – both maintained by la Troco – underscores the hypocrisy of the structures sanctioned by Church and state, a hypocrisy which had been explicitly repudiated by the prostitutes in the earlier days of the celebratory La Catunga.

Imagined spaces – 'El gran mundo queda leeeeejos, allá, más allá, donde sólo llegan los aviones'

The characters in *La novia oscura* have very different levels of geographic mobility. While Sacramento and el Payanés travel via the pipelines of la Troco, the prostitutes remain largely stationary, both trapped in and comfortable in their created world of La Catunga. Sayonara, from an itinerant past and towards an itinerant future, in fact remains in one place throughout the majority of the story's primary time frame; the world appears to orbit around her. Nonetheless, one recurring set of objects in her life opens doors – or at least windows – onto the rest of the planet. Sacramento, roaming to seek his fortune but anxious to maintain his physical presence in Sayonara's world, sends her numerous post-cards, which she seizes and venerates as glimpses of other places and as keys to access a virtual mobility.

Significantly, the postcards do not depict the locations around Colombia to which Sacramento travels. Rather, they represent a bricolage of images across time and space, images which substitute for a reality that neither Sacramento nor Sayonara will ever see. The narrator verbally reproduces twelve of these post-cards, at different moments in the novel, collapsing them into their captions: for example, *Fachada del Palacio Panchayat en Katmandú capital de Nepal* (p. 99), *Lagarteranas en traje típico elaborando Encaje tradicional de la Región* (p. 99), *Plato y legumbrera en Porcelana blanda de Sèvres* (p. 99), *Rincón de los Jardines de Luxemburgo* (p. 100), *Urna Fúnebre cultura Muisca* (p. 120 11), and *Jarrón de porcelana Dinastía Ming siglo XIV* (p. 120). Most of these postcards repro-duce created rather than natural objects – works of art or architecture, artifacts of other civilizations, rather than landscapes. They represent an alternative ethos of production, one which emphasized art and beauty over industry and profit. The temporal and geographic range of the images, so distant from the territories that Sacramento actually traverses, allows Sayonara to create an imaginary and self-ordered universe to which she can escape at will. She creates an 'espacio sagrado' on the wall of her bedroom. At this altar, this virtual window, she care-fully arranges the postcards in a constellation around the figurine of the 'Cristo rojo,' 'formando un rombo, un círculo, un amago de mariposa u otras figures a veces geométricas, a veces antojadizas, que se impregnaban de los reflejos bermejos de la veladora y de alguna impía manera se integraban a la fascinación y al pánico que le inspiraba aquel espacio sagrado' (p. 99). The contemplation of these fragments of the world becomes her preferred space of escape from the ordinary world that surrounds and encloses her, and the arrival of each new post-card allows her to revise and reconstruct her imaginary universe:

> Cada vez que le llegaba un postal nueva, Sayonara entraba en desacuerdo con el lugar que le correspondía en el muro según el viejo diseño. Entonces las desclavaba todas, aprovechaba para volverlas a leer, las barajaba y mezclaba y las volvía a colocar, una por una, dejándose guiar por corazonadas o caprichos … indefinidamente, en un orden variable y cabalístico que ni ella ni nadie sabía interpretar pero que parecía ir prefigurando el curso de los acontecimientos de su vida. (pp. 99–100)

The intuitive and random ordering of this physical space, representing the exercising of control over an alternative universe, recalls la Maga's intention-ally casual and accidental wandering of the streets of Paris in Julio Cortázar's *Rayuela*. In that novel, the female protagonist believed that she could penetrate the mysteries of the universe only by stumbling onto them rather than through a planned and ordered quest. Here, Sayonara also seeks a transcendent vision as she shuffles the images she receives, and then studies them to wrest a personal meaning from them. Through this device she is once again, and in a different way, 'a queen and señora of position.'[17]

Her use of these postcards should be contrasted with Sacramento's. While his missives vary so widely in their representation of cultures and epochs – he appar-ently purchases them with little attention to the images that adorn the front side – his brief messages to Sayonara, scrawled on the back, are always of a consistent tenor, and filled with gerunds to connote a feeling of immediacy:

> *Pensándolas y Recordándolas, sin más por el momento, Sacramento. … Todo marchando correctamente esperando que igualmente para Ud. cariñoso recuerdo para Ud. y similarmente para la señora Todos los Santos … Esperando y deseando volver a verla pronto, suyo con respeto Sacramento.* (p. 99)

For Sacramento, the postcards are a device of control, a method of inserting himself into Sayonara's world while he is physically distant.[18] However, judging from what the narrator tells us, Sayonara does not read his messages again and again; nor do the postcards serve to evoke his presence; rather, it is the insights into other worlds that draw her. By pinning the cards to the wall, she opts for the exotic visual image over the possessive written message.

---

[17] *reinas y señoras del lugar* (p. 200), as cited earlier in this chapter.

[18] 'un destino chacotero … lo obligaba a enviarle misivas a quien sin saberlo adoraba, y lo forzaba a perseguir por el laberinto de los caminos justamente aquello que había dejado en casa' (p. 99).

The significance of the postcards is underscored by the fact that they reappear near the story's end, constituting the novel's penultimate image. The narrator concludes with the anecdote that the elderly Sacramento continues to write post-cards to the vanished Sayonara/Amanda. He does so both for himself and for her; for himself to feel her presence, and for her because 'ella apreciaba recibirlas,' and because he recognized that she valued the postcards much more than she loved him, although he never understood why: 'Con todo lo demás, incluyendo el matrimonio, no logré sino importunarla, pero mis postales le alegraban el genio según ella mismo me dijo' (pp. 411–12). Their roles have been reversed; Sacramento is now fixed in space, while Sayonara wanders through untraceable territories. In marked and ironic contrast to the designs on the wall that Sayonara created with the images of her youth, these unsendable postcards lie jumbled in a shoebox, as a kind of bait for her to return to the sender.[19]

The real-and-imagined spaces of the narrator

We have noted earlier in this discussion that *La novia oscura* in fact paints portraits of two protagonists: Sayonara, and the investigative reporter. The latter obviously shares close biographical parallels with the author herself, a reporter in present-day Colombia who, upon discovering a mysterious and attractive photograph, reconstructs a fascinating story by tracing the origins and following the trail of that image.[20] However, the narrator of *La novia oscura* does far more than simply reconstruct the story of Sayonara. She also narrates the history of her own investigative process; she ponders the unsolved questions and offers various hypotheses; she juxtaposes the differing recollections and interpretations of Sayonara's friends and colleagues, intercalated with her own prompts and responses. Most significantly, through the narrative medium of self-referentiality she carries the focus of the camera lens in three other spatial directions which serve to flesh out Sayonara's own story. First, we travel with her to the various sites she visits in tracking those who knew Sayonara: to Vermont where she speaks with Frank Brasco, to Ambalema where she teases the young girl's story from an elderly innkeeper, and to other towns across Colombia, where she travels 'rast-reando' (p. 174). Second, through the narrator the text repeatedly draws parallels to contemporary Colombia, and to the history of violence and exploitation that led to current social and political problems. And finally, the narrator allows us to

---

[19] Other images of photographs used as imagined spatial transcendence include the pornographic photos consumed by the eager eyes of the boys in the Catholic boarding school, serving as gateways to a 'país sin culpas de los sueños' (p. 167); the family pictures obses-sively reviewed by the oil worker significantly nicknamed Nostalgia (p. 208); and by extension even the photograph of Sayonara uncovered by the narrator herself, reflected on the novel's front cover, which opens a door onto a fascinating and compelling story.

[20] For the narrator's own summary of the discovery process, see p. 142.

participate in her own imagined journey, as she identifies with Sayonara, speculates about the prostitute's life, and interrogates the gender- and class-based assumptions that marginalize women such as those of La Catunga.

In her discussion of this novel, Claire Lindsay identifies the mosaic narrative structure as a verbal imaging of the novel's focus on trauma and memory. As she observes:

> insofar as the text is made up of different and often competing narratives or versions of 'reality,' based on the diverse accounts of the journalist's respondents, Restrepo's novel could be read also as a 'dialogized text.' In this regard, *La novia oscura* is therefore not only a novel 'of' or about trauma and memory, but also a novel as memory, in that it represents both in form and content the 'communal fictionalising, idealising, monumentalising impulses' mentioned ... by Jonathan Crewe. (p. 49)[21]

Lindsay's observations shed light on the formal intricacy that distinguishes this novel. Roaming indeed provides the narrative kinesis, on both the stylistic and the thematic level. At the same time that the narrative fragmentation reflects the processes of confronting repressed trauma, it also allows for the covering of extensive geographic territory, in an exploration of the distant and transnational causes of local and personal events.

The narrator's travels
In contrast to her protagonist, the reporter appears to have unlimited resources of time, money, and opportunity to go where her story takes her. The range of her journeys reflects the fact that while Sayonara's own mobility was quite limited, the effects of her life extend across many miles. Significantly, while many conversations between the reporter and her interlocutors are recorded, the most important encounter never does occur: a meeting between the reporter and Sayonara herself. The elusive figure remains unlocatable and thus uninterrogated. While the reporter is limited to second-hand accounts, through her investigative efforts and her narrative decision to include conflicting memories and opinions verbatim, she attempts to overcome this limitation as much as possible. In the end, while she still does not actually know or understand Sayonara, it could be argued that, having assimilated so many perspectives, so many fragments of the kaleidoscope, she now knows her more profoundly than do those who lived with

---

[21] Here Lindsay references two other studies that provide further illumination on the question of novelized trauma: Carolyn Pinet, 'Retrieving the Disappeared Text: Women, Chaos and Change in Argentina and Chile after the Dirty Wars,' *Hispanic Journal*, 18, 1 (1997), 80–108, from whom Lindsay borrows the term 'dialogized text'; and Jonathan Crewe, 'Recalling Adamastor: Literature as Cultural Memory in "White" South Africa,' in Mieke Bal et al. (eds.), *Acts of Memory: Cultural Recall in the Present* (Hanover: University Press of New England, 1999), pp. 75–86.

her and slept with her. The roving eye and body of the reporter stand in sharp
contrast to Sayonara's geographic fixity, but also demonstrate that even this
myriad of resources available to the modern woman reporter cannot penetrate to
resolve the mysteries around the dark bride.

The national space

Sayonara appears to have little awareness of herself as Colombian; but in contrast,
the narrator is extremely aware of the larger social issues around the 1950s
setting of her story and also the present, the turn of the twenty-first century, from
which she narrates. She explicitly mentions *la violencia* of approximately 1948–
58 (p. 223),[22] the period of military oppression and censorship which followed
the assassination of popular leader Jorge Eliécer Gaitán and which claimed over
200,000 lives, as the specific national backdrop to Sayonara's story. Additionally,
her frequent references to the army's omnipotence as well as to the economic
and ecological impact of the North American oil companies – including the
cycle of workers' strikes and the violent military response – are firmly grounded
in national history. She describes, for example, the contemporary vista of the
Magdalena River, which as we have seen played a key symbolic role in Sayonara's lifecourse, and which, as young Sacramento had observed in the novel's
first pages, tasted already of gasoline ('Ya se jodió el mundo –comentó–. Hasta el
agua sabe a gasolina' [p. 17]); decades later, the narrator writes: 'El otrora Gran
Río de la Magdalena se me aparecía como una larga ausencia: lenta, negra, recar-
gada de dragas ... y de otros aparatos metálicos y ortopédicos que la convertían
en una prolongación de la refinería, que se extendía en la orilla opuesta oxidando
el cielo nocturno con la combustión perpetua de sus altas chimeneas' (p. 123).
Such imagery forms a realistic backdrop of contemporary Colombia, against
which is juxtaposed the literary re-creation of Sayonara's personal history. In
other words, the Magdalena River is for Restrepo a real-and-imagined place
– a feature of the region's topography, a resource harnessed by the transnational
conglomerate, but also a symbolic space, intricately connected to Sayonara's
spatial and spiritual trajectories.

Most significantly, the narrator draws frequent parallels between the specificity
of Sayonara's time and place (the 1950s), and the national present of Colombia
(the 1990s). On several occasions she refers to the violence around Sayonara
as a cyclical constant for her country, analogous to the change of seasons in
other regions and accepted with a similar sense of fatalism (p. 250). Explicitly identifying herself as Colombian and therefore subject to the same storms
which besiege Tora on a regular basis, she creates a narrative parenthesis in order

---

[22] Restrepo does not include the specific dates, but the reference is clear to those familiar
with Colombia's history, when she writes, 'Decían que como la violencia mataba a los adultos,
muchos niños como ella [Sayonara] quedaban huérfanos y realengos, viviendo solos en cuevas'
(pp. 223–4).

to bring the national space into focus. There she articulates a perspective that contextualizes and generalizes the story of Sayonara, and that for its national referents as well as its dramatic intensity merits quoting in full:

> Como colombiana que soy sé que registro un mundo que permanece en combustión, siempre al borde del desplome definitivo y que pese a todo se las arregla, sólo Dios sabe cómo, para agarrarse con uñas y dientes del borde, alumbrando con sus últimos, arrebatados destellos como si no fuera a haber mañana, y sin embargo en el cielo amanece y aquí abajo el delirio cobra nuevos bríos, escatológico, imposible, y el nuevo día transita por un filo de angustia hacia un fin más que predecible y anunciado con estrépito por hombres y mujeres que golpean sus ollas vacías con cucharas. Y sin embargo a media noche, contra toda evidencia, nuestro peculiar apocalipsis queda de nuevo aplazado. Tal vez por eso estamos tan muertos, y al mismo tiempo tan vivos: porque cada anochecer nos aniquila, y nos redime el alba. (p. 282)

Tora in 1950 thus becomes a space of representation for the Colombian nation throughout the century. The same power networks continue to perpetuate themselves on the backs of the residents, who struggle to adapt and survive, or who seek ways to resist the battering of these shifting tides.

The narrator also considers the sex industry of Tora in light of this specific national context, implying that while prostitution may be a universal phenomenon, in *La novia oscura* it carries a particular worldview that reflects the national circumstance. In another self-referential passage which discloses the breadth of her work as a journalist beyond the confines of this narrative, she compares the prostitutes to other sectors of the Colombian population – including by extension her own – who for lack of options must accept the danger that threatens them on a regular basis:

> Me he dado cuenta de que la prostitución conlleva inclinaciones y fijaciones similares a las que en otras oportunidades he observado en los sicarios de las comunas de Medellín, los choferes de camión que deben atravesar zonas de violencia, los expendedores de bazuco de la calle del Cartucho de Bogotá, los apartamenteros, los mafiosos, los jueces, los testigos, los toreros, los guerrilleros, los comandos antiguerrilla y tantos otros colombianos que se juegan la vida por cuestión de rutina. ... Al igual que ellos, las mujeres de La Catunga saben que quien abraza su profesión arriesga el pellejo. (pp. 54–5)

In one of the several self-reflective moments that offer a glimpse into the heart of her story, the narrator contextualizes Sayonara's story as one that is typical of 'ese país marcado por la violencia' (p. 247), when she postulates that great personal tragedy has two possible outcomes, 'o las dos a la vez: o se carboniza o se ilumina. Si se carboniza queda reducido a media persona, pero si se ilumina puede ensancharse y crecer hasta convertirse en persona y media' (pp. 247–8). These are the two roads that lie before Sayonara, and the great mystery of the novel's ending involves not knowing which road she chooses. If she yields to her dreams of constructing a home with el Payanés (p. 371), this may be read as positive or negative – either she becomes his appendage as he follows the labyrinthine oil pipelines, or, as Olga hopes, 'ha sido feliz por todas nosotras' (p. 411): either 'half a person' or 'a person and a half.' Alternatively, if she leaves alone, this may also be either positive or negative: either she wanders away after dreams that are only 'espejismos' (p. 411), or she moves off into a future where she will take her own place: again, either 'half a person' or 'a person and a half.' While the narrator presents all of these options, she carefully maintains her own objectivity, giving the reader no hint as to which option is more likely. Instead, the final lens of the camera returns to the very spot where the reporter sits with Todos los Santos, as the aged puta reminds her, confidently, that 'ya volverá mi niña tarde o temprano, porque las vueltas que da su rumbo siempre pasan por mi casa' (p. 412). This final spatial image returns us to Colombia's cyclical history, elevating the story of one vanished prostitute to the level of national metaphor.

The narrator's virtual journey

One of the most intriguing aspects of *La novia oscura* is the relationship between the women we may consider as the two protagonists, Sayonara and the unnamed investigative reporter. As the above discussion has demonstrated, the reporter feels connected to her reconstructed character, in that both are Colombian, and thus face similar daily dangers and uncertainties. However, a more fascinating dimension of their relationship lies in the attraction that the reporter feels not towards Sayonara herself but towards the life of a sex worker.

Little is known about the reporter herself. She does not privilege the reader with information about her personal history, her age, or her marital status. However, we do know that her career lies outside La Catunga, for she explores through the pages of her narrative a world previously unknown to her, and which she finds surprisingly fascinating. For this reason, she frequently probes the aged prostitutes in order to step into their skin, to imagine trading places with them, to live vicariously in their world of alternative values and sensations.

The novel is comprised of forty-eight untitled and unnumbered 'chapters,'[23] and the central section, the twenty-ninth chapter, is dedicated to the narrator's most extended self-projection into the world of the prostitute. This chapter constitutes a narrative pause, at the center of the novel, a parenthesis where the narrator fuses her two diegetic realms, at least in her imagination. She opens the chapter with a long and lyrical paragraph that paints a peaceful domestic scene ('Sobre la tierra caía la noche tan suavemente, que parte de sus oscuridades se deshacían en espuma antes de llegar' [p. 265]), in which eight women of La Catunga knit, rock, stargaze, and exchange stories; two pages later, the narrator inserts herself into a parallel scene, from which Sayonara has disappeared but she herself has been added, observing and participating.

---

[23] In the English edition the chapters are numbered.

On that earlier night, the prostitute Machuca entertained the younger girls with the story of a mythical realm, a kingdom 'donde todas las mujeres, sin excepción de rango ni de edad, debían acudir una vez en su vida al templo de la diosa a entregarse al primer extraño que solicitara su amor, sin negársele a ninguno' (p. 266). This imagined realm inverts the social order of Tora; in Machuca's words, 'Todas las cosas eran muy distintas, porque las mujeres mandaban' (p. 267): in this realm as Machuca re-creates it, where the goddesses pre-date the male God, there are no taboos, no violations of norms, no sexual guilt.

Similarly, in the parallel scene many years later, the reporter studies with curiosity and some envy the alternative world of the prostitutes. She is filled with questions, some of which she voices to the women around her ('¿Es difícil tener tan cerca a un hombre que desconoces?' [p. 268]; '¿Y el cuerpo … no siente ningún deseo, ningún placer?' [p. 268]; '¿Pero no se da el caso de que alguna goce?' [p. 269]), and some of which are self-reflective, shared only with the reader: '… yo trato de descifrar el sentido de ese misterio que es el contacto con la piel de un extraño. ¿No negarse a un desconocido? Entregarse a lo desconocido, dejarse llevar, ¿será hundirse o será salvarse? ¿Qué dimensiones escondidas se abrirán, de pavor y de placer, de hallazgo y de pérdida?' (pp. 267–8). Her linking of the terms 'un desconocido' and 'lo desconocido' exposes the true object of her desire, which may not be precisely to lie with a stranger, but rather to venture into the world of the unknown, which she longs to experience from the inside rather than just as an outside observer.

This scene allows the greatest interpenetration between the two protagonists. The moment of open questioning allows the reporter to close the time gap that separates her from the object of her inquiry, to step into her skin and imagine the touch of a stranger, and to view the stars from the perspective of a woman who loves for money. It is significant that this narrative moment closes with the defiant and celebratory response of Machuca, as she shakes a fist at God and his guardians of morality and social order, and proclaims that she loves by vocation rather than by obligation, 'por soberano placer y deleite,' and 'porque sí, en honor a la lujuria y porque me dio la gana' (p. 269). This affirmation of strength and passion, alongside Machuca's earlier evocation of a mythical gynocentric space free from the sexual prejudices of contemporary society, affords the reporter a new insight into the lifecourse of her reconstructed protagonist, and sets the stage for the second half of the story's telling.

Conclusion

La novia oscura is the story of to what degree the Tropical Oil Company will permit transgression. The story of the prostitutes is analogous to that of the male workers, as both are labor forces put into place and then kept in place by the hegemony of the international enterprise. The narrator, as an investigative reporter, attempts to locate the provocative protagonist as the site of confluence of these various flows of power, which create her and then, in an ambiguous ending, either destroy her or are forced to turn her loose. If the story offers any potential for autonomous establishment of identity, it lies in reaching a territory beyond that owned by the Tropical Oil Company; and Sayonara's disappearance into the sunset offers that tantalizing possibility. If the questions 'Who is she?' and 'Where is she?' are linked, then the fact that we lose track of her may mean that she is who she wants to be, instead of who she is made to be. In this sense she shakes off the shaping forces of the capitalist enterprise, and finds an alternative place. Against this erasure, the narrator finds another kind of locatedness, as through the mosaic of her textual reconstruction she fixes permanently one segment of Sayonara's life: 'únicamente perdura lo que alcanzo a atrapar y a atravesar con un alfiler para dejarlo clavado en estas páginas' (p. 230).

3

Captured on Film: Allende's *Retrato en sepia*

Introduction

Isabel Allende achieved instant star status with her first novel, *La casa de los espíritus* (1982), and her two most recent novels – *Hija de la fortuna* (1999) and *Retrato en sepia* – are designed as prequels to that story.[1] They trace the lineage of the del Valle family (the family at the center of *La casa de los espíritus*) as well as a parallel family line, that of Eliza Sommers (protagonist of *Hija de la fortuna*) and her granddaughter Aurora (*Retrato*'s main character). At the same time, these later novels continue Allende's autobiographical bent by exploring the history of cultural and commercial interaction between the author's two home cities, Santiago in Chile and San Francisco, California. While *Hija de la fortuna* is conceived primarily around the motif of travel and adventure,[2] *Retrato en sepia* involves a more symbolic quest, the classic search for origins. The narration begins with Aurora's birth, but then travels backward to pick up where *Hija de la fortuna* left off – with Eliza Sommers' marriage to the Chinese physician Tao Chi'en. After chronicling the birth of Eliza's daughter Lynn and then her grand-daughter Aurora, the narration elides the first five years of Aurora's life; Aurora spends the next fifteen years and the rest of the novel attempting to recover the repressed memories of those first five years and, concomitantly, her lost roots in San Francisco's Chinatown.

As we discussed in the introductory chapter of this study, the question 'Who am I?' is closely connected with the question 'Where am I?' In *Retrato en sepia*, the critical geographical question of identity is not 'Where am I?' but 'Where am I from?' Aurora's inability to answer this question throughout her childhood, adolescence, and early adulthood leads to her sense of disorientation. She is constrained by her lack of roots and her consequent feeling of not belonging anywhere. The narrative engine is fueled by Aurora's having been put in a false place, and by her struggle to find a more authentic place, within and ultimately beyond the constraints of race, class, and gender.

The story's ellipsis of Aurora's roots reflects the black hole at the center of her

---

[1] Of course, Allende had a prolific publishing career during the intervening years, producing numerous novels, autobiographical works, children's fiction, and other works.

[2] Young Eliza Sommers travels to California in search of her lover Joaquín Andieta, who has left to search for gold. She dresses as a young man in order to track him; along the way she is befriended by the Chinese healer (*zhong-yi*) Tao Chi'en. Ultimately giving up her search, she returns to acknowledge her love for Tao Chi'en, and they take up their lives together in Chinatown, defying racial barriers as they work to free enslaved Chinese prostitutes.

memories and her psyche – her five years as a Chinese American, ending abruptly with the witnessing of Tao Chi'en's violent murder. Aurora is adopted by her paternal grandmother, Paulina del Valle, who works to erase Aurora's memory for two reasons: purportedly to erase the trauma of her violent uprooting, but in fact to expunge the Chinese and lower-class aspects of Aurora's heritage. The novel focuses on the intersection between these issues of gender, class, and race, as Paulina del Valle – an upper-class Chilean transplanted to the US – attempts to re-create Aurora in her own image, as a wealthy woman of European heritage. The question 'Where am I?' leads to the question 'Who put me here?' and the answer is not simply the patriarchal system, but the women who accede to it.

On the surface, the novel seems filled with positive female role models. Aurora has two grandmothers who have demonstrated autonomy, industry, and rebellion, both within this novel and throughout the earlier *Hija de la fortuna*.[3] Additionally, Paulina's cousin Nívea del Valle is a defiant character who fights in Chile for women's suffrage. However, when examined from a locational perspective, it is obvious that all of these women sacrifice their potential autonomy in order to maintain their gender-assigned roles as wives, and all three characters conform in general to the expectations of their social class. These women know their place, and ultimately keep to it – and they keep other women in their places as well. Thus they become perpetuating agents of a patriarchal system: Eliza walks two paces behind her husband and 'existe apenas' (p. 30), Nívea is constrained by the obligations of wifehood and maternity (freed in part only because her money allows her to employ a staff of nameless and faceless nannies), and Paulina relentlessly bedecks and bejewels herself (and Aurora) in order to maintain the façade required by her social position.

The fact that all three women make these sacrifices willingly becomes irrelevant, as these women deny themselves the mobility that their independent spirits demanded earlier in their lives. As long as Aurora attempts to locate herself within such spaces, she is out of place, and tormented by the nightmares of her repressed memories. At the end of the novel she – and also her grandmother Eliza, finally liberated by widowhood – does walk away from stasis, in order to become a successful nomadic figure, one that travels alone and without a destination.

In this novel, nomadic status is only possible once all shackles of female 'duty' are left behind, as well as all desires for stability and security. However, the nomadic figures who might have served as models for Aurora – all peripheral

---

[3]   In *Hija de la fortuna*, Eliza leaves home alone and pregnant; she defies gender norms by traveling as a male; and she breaks all barriers of race and class by marrying a Chinese man. Paulina del Valle, in the earlier novel, flees from a convent school in order to marry Feliciano, a man of inferior social class and dubious origins; she then becomes a very successful businesswoman. However, at the outset of *Retrato en sepia* both women have settled into their wifely roles, yielding to their husbands' decisions. Paulina in particular has in many respects imitated the haughty father against whom she had rebelled, as she flaunts her social class and looks down on those of inferior social position.

to the novel's main storyline – do not surface until late in the narrative and in Aurora's maturation process. The novel does present, eventually, three nomadic figures, who are only allowed to appear after Paulina's old age and eventual death lower the barriers which have kept them at bay. One is Amanda Lowell, the Californian prostitute who flouted the incest as well as the sexual taboo when she slept both with Paulina's husband Feliciano and with his son Matías (Aurora's biological father). Amanda disappears with Matías before Aurora is born, and does not reappear until she brings him home to die some fifteen years later. As we shall see, Amanda Lowell, 'pájaro que no vive en el cautiverio' (p. 217), rejects not only gender-based norms but also capitalism, the system so embraced by Paulina del Valle; instead, she constructs her own, more mobile value system (p. 216). The second transgressive woman is the widowed Eliza Sommers, who sidelined her nomadic spirit in order to serve as wife, mother, grandmother, and then nurse to her adopted mother Miss Rose;[4] once those to whom she is obligated are dead, she is finally free to resume her earlier course as a nomad, and eventually to carry Aurora on journeys of self-discovery with her. And the third autonomous woman – a more minor character – is one of Aurora's governesses, la señorita Matilde Pineda, who is banned by Paulina but then reappears with her lover Pedro Tey after the matriarch's death. These three figures, and eventually Aurora, transcend the confining spaces assigned to upper-class women, and find identity through movement; they thus embody the ethos of the symbolically geographic poem by Pablo Neruda, that Allende cites as the novel's epigraph:

> Por eso tengo que volver
> a tantos sitios venideros
> para encontrarme conmigo
> y examinarme sin cesar …
> sin más tarea que existir,
> sin más familia que el camino.

The trajectory of the nomadic Aurora is only alluded to in general terms, in the novel's final pages; the majority of the novel focuses rather on the character's progressive dislocations on three continents and, primarily, against the backdrop of the political and social changes of late nineteenth-century Chile. As was the case with Laura Restrepo's protagonist Sayonara in *La novia oscura*, the novel climaxes with the launching of the character into unmapped territory.

As Feal and Miller note in the Foreword to their collection of essays, discussion of *La casa de los espíritus* has in some senses eclipsed serious study of Allende's more recent novels.[5] Their collection, as well as Linda Gould Levine's recent *Isabel Allende* published by Twayne, admirably fill this analytical void.

---

4   After Eliza buries Tao Chi'en in Hong Kong, she feels obligated to reside in England during Miss Rose's last days; thus her duties as an (adopted) daughter replace her duty as wife.

5   See the concluding essay in Feal and Miller's collection, Beth Jorgensen's overview of

Feal and Miller's anthology includes three excellent studies of *Retrato en sepia*, articles which continue to stand as the major critical commentary to date on this novel. Most relevant for the current discussion is the contribution by María Inés Lagos, who studies Allende's current geographical situation in California, and her awareness of her own process of partial acculturation, as the key to her narrative perspective; according to Lagos, the author 'shows a world from the perspective of an insider who positions herself as an outsider' (p. 112) and therefore can create characters that fluidly cross borders, trying on and shedding identities along their way.[6]

As we shall see, Aurora's passport through space, and simultaneously the narrative's organizing device, is the camera. Photography plays a multifaceted role in terms of identity. First, the reconstruction of Aurora's past – the recovery of lost memories – takes place around photographs and postcards, found either in family albums or in souvenir shops in San Francisco. Thus the visual images serve to restore the physical configuration of her past, primarily as faces and bodies rather than landscapes.

Second, with the camera around her neck Aurora gains a kind of invisibility, which lends her access to spaces she otherwise either would not or could not visit. The camera makes her faceless, thus erasing the fear that she has been taught to feel when mixing with people of a different race or class from her own. On another level, the camera gives her a more acute eye, so that she is able to see and to capture the true 'rostro multifacético y atormentado de Chile' (p. 220). Finally, the camera not only sharpens her own perspective, but grants her power over the way that others see. Only the true rebel character, Amanda, understands and verbalizes this potential of the camera; she points out to Aurora that 'tú puedes ver el mundo y obligar a los demás a verlo a tu manera' (p. 242). The camera, then, grants not only geographical mobility but sovereignty over places, as Aurora is finally able, camera in hand, to map her own world.[7]

Retrato en sepia explores questions of national 'belonging' as well as individual identity. Several characters live abroad for many years, but a recurrent theme in the novel is the eventual longing for the homeland.[8] This sentiment

criticism on Allende: '"Un puñado de críticos": Navigating the Critical Readings of Isabel Allende's Work' (pp. 128–46).

6   Two other essays in this collection also constitute significant contributions to discussion of *Retrato en sepia*: María Claudia André, 'Breaking through the Maze: Feminist Configurations of the Heroic Quest in Isabel Allende's *Daughter of Fortune* and *Portrait in Sepia*'; and Eliana Rivero, 'Of Trilogies and Genealogies: *Daughter of Fortune* and *Portrait in Sepia*'. All three essays also appear in *Latin American Literary Review*, in a special issue dedicated to Allende (30:60 [2002]).

7   Writing is developed as a talent parallel to photography. Aurora first learns to photograph, then to describe, landscapes and portrait for her sight-impaired photography teacher, and finally to write; the novel should thus be seen as Aurora's written photograph of her own and her family's trajectory.

8   The homeland continues to serve as a magnet for almost all of the travelers. For example, Miss Rose Sommers, an Englishwoman who lived for many years in Chile, expresses her desire

certainly reflects the author's own sense of estrangement from Chile, after so many years in California.[9] As a narrative device, this intercontinental stage allows for a more complex vision of race, class, and gender. The San Francisco of the late nineteenth century is depicted as a heterotopia, a border town that both juxtaposes and maintains separate the Chinese, Hispanic, and Anglo populations. Class issues are complicated by the fact that wealth and race do not necessarily correspond with each other; for example, the powerful Paulina del Valle, from her mansion on Nob Hill, is still marked by her Hispanism – her 'acento de cocinera' (p. 144).[10] Eliza, purportedly Chilean, marries a Chinese man but operates an English-style tea house in the Anglo section of town. Tao Chi'en, a healer, has achieved international fame as an expert on acupuncture but is still barred from practicing in Anglo hospitals within San Francisco. The novel thus reflects a mixture of races and classes, but never a blending – instead, borders are explored, interrogated, and renegotiated throughout Aurora's lifescape. Interestingly, issues of gender are less complex; there is little distinction between the role of (upper-class) women in Chinatown, in Anglo San Francisco, and in Santiago, as patriarchal bourgeois norms rule all three locales.

The European continent, and the voyage there and back, functions as a liminal narrative device, and in that arena Paulina exerts her strongest shaping force on her granddaughter's identity. The novel narrates two trips to Europe: the first occurs as Paulina erases Aurora's memory of Chinatown and shapes her into a Chilean *señorita*, and the second when the protagonist is readied for her debut as an eligible *señora*-in-waiting. Aurora returns from both voyages changed, further distanced from her own roots, as the European heritage is privileged over the Chinese, North American, and indigenous Chilean genetics.[11] While in

---

to 'envejecer en tierra propia' (p. 24); Tao Chi'en, Americanized in citizenship and in attire, nonetheless 'siempre se siente extranjero' (p. 63) and wishes to be buried in Hong Kong; Eliza Sommers is recorded as thinking of Chile as 'ese lejano país donde no había puesto los pies en más de treinta años, pero seguía considerando su patria' (p. 86); Paulina calls patriotism an 'estupidez' (p. 30) but later recognizes that 'estaba envejeciendo sola, lejos de sus hijos, sus parientes, su idioma y su tierra' (p. 154); Aurora herself belies her nomadic status by stating about herself and her lover that even though their cohabitation might cause less scandal in the US, 'los dos sabemos que no podríamos vivir en otra parte, sólo en este Chile de cataclismos geológicos y pequeñeces humanas' (p. 113).

9   Allende left Chile during the Pinochet coup of the early 1970s, going into voluntary exile in Venezuela. In 1988, while giving a lecture in San Francisco, she met the man who would become her second husband, Willie Gordon, and since that time has resided in California.

10   The intertwined issues of race and class are contested in San Francisco, in both directions. While her Hispanic background restricts her social ascendancy in California, Paulina reinforces class prejudice by asserting the superiority of her own European pedigree: 'Paulina y Feliciano hicieron fortuna. Se colocaron en la cumbre de la sociedad de San Francisco, a pesar del obstáculo casi insalvable de su acento hispano. "En California son todos nuevos ricos y mal nacidos, en cambio nuestro árbol genealógico se remonta a las Cruzadas," mascullaba Paulina entonces, antes de darse por vencida y regresar a Chile' (p. 18).

11   Aurora's biological heritage is pieced together by a reading of both *Hija de la fortuna*

some senses the boat serves as a heterotope,[12] it is more accurately understood as interstitial, as the site of separation which traditionally marks developmental transitions.[13]

The various sites of the novel's plot establish spaces where characters struggle for ascendancy. Major political and economic forces of hegemony, such as Tropical Oil in Laura Restrepo's novel, do not play such a direct role in *Retrato en sepia*. Revolutions and wars occasionally involve certain characters, but little seems to change in the overall social hierarchy. Instead, this novel focuses on the effects of capitalist accumulation on an individual level. The novel's archetypal capitalist character, interestingly, is female. Paulina del Valle establishes herself as a force for globalization, when she realizes the potential of shipping fruit from Chile to California, and white flour from California back to Chile.[14] She delimits her own autonomy in order to fit into the capitalist power structure, using frontmen to navigate the spaces of business transactions that lead to her accumulation of wealth; but she exerts power on those around her as well. She thus functions as the nexus of power flows and the novel's chief hegemonic agent. Our discussion will focus on the shaping influence of power through various specific sites of the novel. The North American stage involves three locations in San Francisco: Nob Hill, Chinatown, and Eliza's tea house at the cultural and physical borderland. With a European voyage as transition, the novel next focuses on Santiago; our discussion will analyze the places of Paulina's mansion, the role of the nameless servants, and the charitable Club de Damas, which attempts to bridge that gap. Finally, following another European parenthesis, the narration locates itself in rural Chile, in Aurora's marital home of Caleufú, where tradition and Catholicism govern the assignment of gender- and class-specific spaces. Our discussion of these sites, as well as the leap towards nomadism at the novel's end, will expose the novel's geoplot, the mechanisms of power which shape identity through space, and the navigational skills exercised by the protagonist in her search for her own place. As mentioned earlier, Aurora opens her narrative around the question 'Where am I from?' But one of the nomadic models, Matilde Pineda, alters the central question when she says, 'no importa de dónde uno viene en esta vida, sino adónde uno va' (p. 177). This locational focus is resisted by Aurora at the time Matilde offers it, but the novel's end reflects that Aurora

and *Retrato en sepia*. Her father, Matías del Valle, is Chilean, of Spanish descent. On the maternal side, her grandfather is Chinese; her grandmother Eliza has an English father (John Sommers) and an anonymous indigenous mother; but she was raised in Chile, by English immigrants (the sister and brother of John Sommers).

[12] It should be noted that the boat was one of the principal heterotopic devices signaled by Foucault in his definition of the term; as we shall see, the intercontinental voyage does involve a juxtaposition of social classes, but very little intermingling.

[13] See the discussion of liminal states, in the Introduction to this study.

[14] The ill effects of this trade for flour production in Chile are noted by the narrator: 'así arruinaron a varios agricultores chilenos, incluso al padre de Paulina, el temible Agustín del Valle, a quien se le agusanó el trigo en las bodegas porque no pudo competir con la blanquísima harina de los yanquis' (p. 17).

eventually adopts this spatial vision, as she transgresses all of the borders that her race, class, and gender would assign her.

San Francisco - 'en California, tierra sin tradición, había espacio para todos'

Throughout *Hija de la fortuna* and from the outset of *Retrato en sepia*, San Francisco in its newness is presented as a contrast to the time-honored, Catholic-ordered social structures of Chile. Both novels contain numerous verbal cacophonies of peoples, sounds, smells, and sights; at first glance, San Francisco is heterotopic, 'todo revuelto, como si hubiera sido levantado deprisa' (p. 29). For example, upon Severo del Valle's arrival from Chile, he is met with a visual bricolage of races and classes: 'Entre el tráfico ruidoso de animales y coches se abría paso una muchedumbre cosmopolita: americanos, hispanos, franceses, irlandeses, italianos, alemanes, algunos indios y antiguos esclavos negros, ahora libres, pero siempre rechazados y pobres' (p. 29). However, as the final phrase of the description indicates, a rigid hierarchy of race and class lies just beneath that heterotopic surface. While the Chinese population is numerous, it is powerless, segregated in terms of influence as well as residence: 'la población china era entonces casi invisible, nacía, vivía y moría al margen del acontecer americano' (p. 153). While lower-class women may have moved about more freely in marketplaces and other public spaces, the novel focuses on upper-class women, who carefully maintain their social respectability by restricting their public appearances only to certain geographical arenas.

There are certain benefits to the invisibility offered by San Francisco's diversity. Eliza, half-indigenous and half-British, marries Tao Chi'en and takes up residence in Chinatown; but she adapts herself to the restrictive gender norms of that cultural arena. And when her daughter Lynn becomes pregnant out of wedlock, social convention here does not demand that the pregnancy be hidden: 'En China o en Chile su hija estaría perdida, la sociedad no tendría perdón para ella, pero en California, tierra sin tradición, había espacio para todos. ... la compasión para su hija contaba más que el honor familiar' (pp. 85–6). Nonetheless, when the novel's three primary Californian places are examined closely, it becomes apparent that rigid norms operate within the various territories of San Francisco, and borders are not so easily transcended. In other words, while San Francisco has some superficial attributes of a transgressive frontier town, the spaces mapped most closely by the novel – Chinatown and Nob Hill – house mechanisms that continue to constrain their options.

Chinatown – 'en la calle bullía la vida salvaje del barrio chino'
From the outset, Allende's representation of Chinatown is paradoxical. On the one hand, she depicts narrow, crime-filled streets, opium dens, and roving gangs (*tongs*) that rule by terror and brutality. The inhabitants are numerous ('su muchedumbre inagotable de abejas humanas yendo y viniendo deprisa' [p. 13]) and exotic ('el tráfico de carretones y los ladridos tristes de los perros en sus jaulas esperando el cuchillo del cocinero' [p. 13]). Primary occupations include cooking, laundering, traffic in sex slaves, and selling drugs.[15] On the other hand, Tao Chi'en and his home stand apart from this messy, noisy crowd. An island of peace and wisdom within Chinatown, the home of Tao Chi'en is elegant and cultured: 'La familia de Eliza Sommers y Tao Chi'en residía en una casa espaciosa y confortable, más sólida y de mejor factura que las demás de Chinatown' (p. 63). His medical clinic (the first floor of his home) is a clean, well-lighted place, in contrast to the crowded chaos that surrounds it. His character and his physical bearing correspond to that abode. He strides through the street with the dignity of his status as a *zhong-yi* (healer), the legal protection of his US citizenship, and his Americanized dress.[16]

Nonetheless, the community does not share his willingness to transgress racial and gender boundaries, in his marriage to the Anglo-Hispanic Eliza Sommers. The couple shares an idyllic space in their matrimonial bed,[17] but in the streets they conform to social norms: 'En el transcurso de los años esa pequeña mujer blanca y aquel chino alto llegaron a ser una visión familiar en Chinatown, pero nunca fueron totalmente aceptados. Aprendieron a no tocarse en público, a sentarse separados en el teatro y a caminar en la calle con varios pasos de distancia' (pp. 62–3). Furthermore, they raise their daughter Lynn in voluntary compliance with the limitations of Chinatown's spatial gender assignments: 'Nunca le permitieron jugar en la calle, como hacía su hermano Lucky, porque en Chinatown las mujeres y las niñas de familias pudientes vivían totalmente recluidas. En las escasas ocasiones en que andaba por el barrio, iba de la mano de su padre y con la vista clavada en el suelo, para no provocar a la muchedumbre casi enteramente masculina' (p. 65).

The bodies of Lynn and her brother Lucky determine their place in Chinatown. Lucky looks typically Chinese and carries the status of maleness, but Lynn, 'el producto afortunado de razas mezcladas' (p. 56), can pass as white: 'poco tenía Lynn de su padre, salvo los huesos largos y los ojos orientales' (p. 64). Furthermore, Eliza distances Lynn from Chinatown, giving both children Amer-

---

[15] In a voyage into the inferno of the opium dens, Severo del Valle and the butler Frederick Williams descend into Chinatown to rescue Matías del Valle, who has overdosed on opium (pp. 49–51).

[16] 'Tao Chi'en había renunciado hacía años a la típica coleta de los suyos y andaba con el pelo corto engominado hacia atrás, de impecable traje negro, camisa de cuello laminado y sombrero de copa' (p. 65).

[17] 'Desde esa primera noche de amor durmieron en apretado nudo, respirando el mismo aliento y soñando los mismo sueños' (p. 62).

ican names[18] and educating Lynn outside the borders of the society in which she herself has chosen to live: 'Fuera de Chinatown ... Lynn circulaba plenamente libre, como cualquier muchacha blanca. Se educó en una escuela presbiteriana' (p. 65). The mother teaches Lynn to confine their Chinese cultural practices to within the walls of their home, speaking English to each other and dressing in the American rather than the Chinese style (p. 64). Eliza consciously takes all of these steps, with Tao Chi'en's approval, in order that their daughter might later escape the confines of Chinatown. In other words, the place cannot be changed; the only hope for some degree of autonomy is flight from that place, and this is Eliza's goal: 'deseaba que [sus hijos] se integraran por completo en los Estados Unidos y vivieran sin las limitaciones impuestas a los chinos o a los hispanos. Con Lynn lo consiguió, pero con Lucky sus planes fracasaron, porque el muchacho estaba orgulloso de su origen y no pretendía salir de Chinatown' (p. 64).

Thus Tao Chi'en and Eliza are limited as transgressive characters. Their ambivalence about their situatedness in Chinatown leads to an internalized self-hatred on the part of their daughter Lynn ('se avergonzaba de su raza' [p. 64]).[19] This cultural schism induces Lynn to fall in love with the man most distinct from her father that she can find: the effete and decadent Matías del Valle, who impregnates and then abandons her. Lynn's misfortunes may be directly attributed to the contradictions of her upbringing, her parents' imperfect attempts to raise her above her assigned station in life, and their failure to acknowledge their own internalization of prejudices toward the limiting horizons of Chinatown.

Tao Chi'en's granddaughter Aurora starts out on a better footing. She too is born into Chinatown, but her mother Lynn dies in childbirth, and Eliza, grieving, turns the child's upbringing entirely over to Tao Chi'en. More maternal than paternal, Tao Chi'en raises her with respect for the Chinese heritage, symbolized by her consistent appearance in Chinese garb and the retention of her Chinese name, Lai-Ming. He also plans to challenge gender norms on her behalf, dreaming of making her his true cultural heir and the first female *zhong-yi* (p. 327). Even so, Tao Chi'en and Eliza repeat the cultural translocation that they had unsuccessfully attempted with Lynn:

> era necesario sacar a la criatura de Chinatown algunas horas al día para americanizarla. En ese punto al menos, los abuelos estaban de acuerdo, Lai-Ming debía pertenecer al mundo de los blancos, donde sin duda tendría más oportunidades que entre chinos. Tenían a su favor que la chiquilla carecía de rasgos asiáticos, había salido tan española de aspecto como la familia de su padre. (p. 327).

18 Lynn 'debió llamarse Lin Chi'en, pero sus padres decidieron anglicanizar los nombres de sus hijos y darles el apellido de su madre, Sommers, para facilitarles la existencia en los Estados Unidos, donde los chinos eran tratados como perros' (p. 56).

19 Eliza, for example, insists to Tao Chi'en that Lynn will not marry within her father's race: 'Estamos en América y no se casará con un chino ... creo que Lynn se casará con un blanco' (p. 67).

Again the image of internalized racial inferiority, or of the desire to relocate one's cultural heritage, can be read into this passage. Prosperity in the United States requires the distancing from one set of cultural practices and assimilation into the other realm, one which offers more options for autonomy.

Tao Chi'en's pride in his Chinese heritage might have allowed Aurora to succeed with one foot in each world; but his influence over her ends abruptly with his murder, when she is five years old.[20] Immediately, Eliza reverts to the attitude of cultural preference that she had shown with Lynn. Using as an excuse her duty to carry her husband's body back to Hong Kong, she delivers the young Aurora to the home of Matías's mother, Paulina del Valle, where the girl will have all of the advantages of growing up white.[21] This erasure of racial and cultural heritage leads to the repression at the heart of Aurora's search for identity; as we shall see, only upon discovering her roots and revisiting Chinatown can Aurora make her own way in the world.

Thus Chinatown exerts power over its residents, both the native Chinese and any other immigrants to this sector of San Francisco. Allende's protagonists from *Hija de la fortuna*, Tao Chi'en and Eliza Sommers, are represented by the narrator as noble in spirit and open to cultural difference; but an analysis of the geoplot complicates this interpretation. The characters' conformance to the limitations of their territories, and the failure of their attempts at transcending those limitations, point to a stronger hegemonic influence than even these admirable individuals can thwart. As the place where the Anglo US has confined its undesirables, Chinatown functions in the novel to communicate to its inhabitants the need to know and keep to one's place, in order to survive.

Nob Hill - 'donde sus habitantes se sentían extranjeros'

Paulina del Valle's forty-five-room mansion on Nob Hill functions as the location of the capitalist enterprise. As mentioned earlier, from there she directs her husband Feliciano, her butler Frederick Williams, and an army of lawyers and servants, in her quest to accumulate wealth, power, and most importantly, social standing. In both temperament and body, she is presented as a devouring figure, consuming both food and profit at a frenetic pace. As San Francisco is heterotopic, Paulina's home too contains a random juxtaposition of objects acquired for the purpose of ostentation.[22] The example which opens the novel is that of Paulina's ornate Florentine bed, imported in the midst of the US Civil War and

---

[20] The *tongs* murder Tao Chi'en because of his own cultural transgression, in appealing to Anglo religious and legal authorities in order to bring an end to the trade of sex slavery: 'la regla de oro [para sobrevivir en Chinatown] consistía en no mezclarse con los blancos ... y resolver todo, en especial los crímenes, entre compatriotas' (p. 331).

[21] Eliza says to Paulina: 'Usted puede ofrecer a mi nieta una vida mucho mejor de la que yo puedo darle. ... Soy extranjera en todas partes, pero deseo que Lai-Ming tenga raíces, una familia y buena educación' (p. 146).

[22] For example, 'Existían dos salones de música con finos instrumentos italianos, aunque en esa familia nadie sabía usarlos y a Paulina la música le daba dolor de cabeza' (p. 43).

paraded through the streets of San Francisco purely as an example of opulence, privilege, and power.[23] The architecture of the house itself reflects the same hunger for accumulation: 'se construyeron una disparatada mansión, una de las más opulentas de la ciudad, que resultó un delirio de varios arquitectos rivales contratados y despedidos cada dos por tres' (p. 17).

As we have noted, Paulina's youthful rebellion against societal restrictions, narrated in *Hija de la fortuna*, are left behind in this novel. Instead, she vests her mercantilist aspirations in feminine garb, limiting herself to acting behind the scenes, ordering her husband, her butler, and her nephew Severo to carry out her ingenious schemes for acquiring wealth: 'Tú callas, observas, escuchas y me cuentas. Luego haces lo que yo te diga sin hacer muchas preguntas, ¿estamos claros?' (pp. 44–5). A pure capitalist, she acquires money not for what it can buy but for its own sake, for the thrill of outmaneuvering her opponents (pp. 42–3). She profits from war, for example, increasing her investments in sugar during Chile's war with Perú and Bolivia because 'en tiempos malos la gente come más dulce' (p. 81).[24]

In her 'guerras mercantiles' (p. 28) Paulina learns well the elitist lessons of both the US and Chile. In spite of the fact that her Hispanic heritage, her inescapable Spanish 'acento de cocinera,' bars her from true membership in the Anglo upper class, her drive for acceptance among the residents of Nob Hill leads her to perpetuate discrimination against other races and classes. Most notably this occurs in her attitude towards Tao Chi'en, whose name she never remembers; she refers to him only as 'ese chino' (pp. 90, 103).

Capitalism links the upper class of San Francisco with that of Chile. The same set of governing values operates in both arenas, in terms of class prejudice. As Paulina notes, 'El dinero y la posición social cuentan mucho aquí y en Chile' (p. 101). As we shall see in our discussion of Santiago, Paulina displays the same attitudes towards her indigenous servants there as she does toward the Chinese and lower-class populations of San Francisco. Her own sense of superiority is grounded in demonstrating her ascendancy over those around her, and that ascendancy is guaranteed only by the accumulation of wealth.

This material success comes at significant cost. The devouring Paulina develops a body 'perfectamente adecuada al tamaño y suntuosidad de su mansión' (p. 148), obese and falsified. The narrator repeatedly emphasizes her false teeth, her wigs and dyed hair, her elaborate clothing, jewels, and perfumes. All of this emphasis on her packaging is intended to mask her corpulence, the consequence of obsessive accumulation. However, the socially imposed expectations of feminine beauty, the required subjugation of the body, result in self-hatred on the part of Paulina. Convinced that she is no longer desirable, she first requires her

---

[23] The ultimate goal of this display was to humiliate her husband Feliciano and his lover, Amanda Lowell (p. 15). Wealth and acquisition thus function as direct tools of power.

[24] She also anticipates the route of the transcontinental railroad and buys land at low prices, in order to sell at a profit when towns are eventually constructed.

husband to make love to her in the dark, and eventually she bans him from her
bed altogether. Their two bedrooms, at each end of a long hallway in the elaborate mansion (p. 21), represent spatially their emotional distancing, as mounds of
flesh and goods function to separate them. Ironically, the narrator points out that
these standards of beauty and consequent revulsions exist only on the part of the
woman; to Feliciano they would not have mattered (p. 23).[25] On the other hand,
Feliciano then conforms to the *machista* expectations of the Chilean and the US
society, turning to mistresses, and eventually to Paulina's hated rival Amanda
Lowell, for sexual satisfaction (p. 21). Thus, Paulina's capitalist urges drive her
husband into the arms of another woman, and herself into her private bedroom
where she pines for the lovemaking of her younger days (pp. 22–3). Capitalism
carries great cost for the female mercantile warrior, eventually confining her to
solitude.

In spite of the obstacle of her Hispanic heritage, wealth appears to allow
Paulina access to the upper crust of Nob Hill society. However, gender norms
turn out to be stronger than class affiliations. After her husband's death, Paulina
is invited nowhere; she learns that without the front-man, a woman – at least a
foreign-born one – cannot transcend social barriers: 'nadie la convidaba, ya no
era la primera en recibir invitación a las fiestas, no le pedían que inaugurara un
hospital o un monumento, su nombre dejó de mencionarse en las páginas sociales
y apenas la saludaban en la opera. Estaba excluida' (p. 144). Invisible in both the
social and the financial realms, without a husband she must admit defeat. This
fact plus the desire to raise her granddaughter in Chile combine to force her back
to her homeland, after some thirty years of absence. Ironically, Aurora's later
research through newspaper and document archives demonstrates that Paulina
had fallen victim to the same invisibility as the Chinese population she scorned:
'La orgullosa familia de mis abuelos paternos vivió en San Francisco por treinta
y seis años sin dejar mucho rastro. ... El palacete de Nob Hill es hoy un hotel
y nadie recuerda quiénes fueron sus primeros dueños' (p. 153). The space of a
Hispanic woman in San Francisco, while glorious for a time, proves ephemeral,
even at the upper-class level, and the power of patriarchy, whether in the Hispanic
or the Anglo world, continues to define the place of women.

*The Salón de Té – 'con un manual de instrucciones para armarla como un
juguete'*
Eliza's pastry and tea house, 'con una fragrancia deliciosa de azúcar y vain-
illa' (p. 30), plays a crucial spatial role in the novel, as a border site of contact
between races and classes. Its location in the central Plaza de la Unión implies
Eliza's escape – geographical, economic, social, and symbolic – from China-

---

[25] Later in the novel we see that Paulina learns nothing through her life experience; as a
much older woman and married to Frederick Williams, she isolates herself during her illness
because she is certain that he will not love her if she does not correspond to a feminine corporeal ideal (p. 236).

town. Separated from the gendered confinement and racist suspicions of Tao Chi'en's world, she operates her own business, with the purely capitalist goal of buying her children's way into Anglo society. Knowing that Tao Chi'en donates most of their income to his charitable work, she in contrast runs her own business 'para no atormentarlo con peticiones de dinero; necesitaba independencia para dar a sus hijos la mejor educación Americana, pues deseaba que se integraran por completo en los Estados Unidos y vivieran sin las limitaciones impuestas a los chinos o a los hispanos' (p. 64). Nonetheless, her little business does not challenge gender norms in the way that Paulina's involvement in global trade does; her goals are maternal, and her enterprise very feminine, full of delicious culinary aromas, fragility, lace and linen.

As with Paulina's Nob Hill mansion, the architecture of the Salón de Té carries symbolic value. The building arrived from England as a kit, complete with the 'manual de instrucciones para armarla como un juguete' (p. 30), like a prepackaged little piece of the Old World, transplanted to offer upper-class patrons a European refuge from San Francisco's surrounding dirt and noise. The Britishness of the site corresponds to Eliza's character; in spite of having been raised in Chile and having spent some thirty years in the United States, she still speaks English with the British accent learned from her adoptive parents (p. 31). Even though the British and the Chinese share a cultural bent towards tea, Eliza opts to capitalize on the European rather than the Asian heritage, to appeal to a more affluent customer base.[26] In the tea house, she is as artificially constructed and as transplanted as the building itself.

As a narrative device the Salón de Té functions effectively, as the only possible site of contact between the del Valle family and Eliza, who share an admiration for British culture. But even as Paulina continually re-emphasizes the class differences between herself and Eliza,[27] it should be noted that similar economic systems are in place at Nob Hill and in the tea house. Eliza employs Mexican waitresses, who imitate her mask of invisibility as they wait on her customers: 'Servían dos empleadas mexicanas de largas trenzas, albos delantales y cofias almidonadas, dirigidas telepáticamente por la pequeña señora Sommers' (p. 30). In this sense, Eliza has imported more than simply the architecture of her business; she imports the class hierarchies of Old World aristocracy, directing her servants with a nod or a look.

The tea house thus functions as the opposite of a heterotopia. It does allow for contact between social classes, but in this rarefied atmosphere that contact is anything but dangerous or destabilizing. Instead, interactions are rigidly controlled by class-based norms, and an artificial culture is created as a refuge for the rich against the hubbub that reigns in the Plaza de la Unión. In this

26 It should be noted that on the second floor Eliza does stock Chilean chocolates, specifically to cater to Paulina del Valle's preferences.
27 'La fortuna de la señora Del Valle y su sangre de aristócrata la colocaban muy por encima del nivel social de la otra' (p. 31).

liminal space, Eliza's daughter Lynn is allowed to immerse herself in the artificial romance of English novels. The fantasies constructed in this unreal environment isolate Lynn from reality, later leading her to fall in love with the wrong
man (Matías del Valle). Her adult character later reflects the superficiality of
the space in which she developed: 'Su languidez no era elegancia, sino pereza
y su melancolía no era misterio, sino vacuidad' (p. 69). The space in which her
dreams are spun is a false one, one that was constructed in order to launch her
into a particular social class, and from that environment she emerges ill equipped
to deal with the reality of San Francisco.

The ship to Europe – 'no hay que mirar para atrás'

The novel does not provide many details about the voyage to Europe, which lasts
one year, marking the transition between Aurora and Paulina's life in San Francisco and their new existence in Santiago. The lack of detail can be attributed in
part to the fact that the narrator, Aurora, was only five years old at the time, and in
part to the fact that the trip's purpose was to erase her memories. Images from the
ship demonstrate that the group – Paulina, her new husband (and former butler)
Frederick Williams, Aurora – traveled first-class, in 'una suite de tres habita-
ciones' for Paulina, another for Williams, and a separate room for Aurora and the
nanny. The rest of their staff – 'el peluquero … dos mucamas, un valet, un criado'
(p. 157) – remain invisible, keeping to their places somewhere below first-class.
The voyage functions as a crisis heterotopia, a place apart where the wild and
traumatized child can be refashioned into a young lady.[28] Notably, Paulina uses
this time not only to create new family legends for Aurora, but also to teach her
mathematical skills, so that her granddaughter will be able to contribute to her
empire by keeping the accounting books. Thus she passes to her granddaughter
the dual legacy of lineage and ambition.

In this 'floating piece of space, a place without a place' (Foucault, 'Of Other
Spaces,' p. 27), Frederick Williams also reinvents himself, transforming himself
from butler into aristocratic husband.[29] The impressionable Aurora spies from
corners as Frederick and Paulina by example teach her the art of creating identity. The result is a schism that plagues Aurora for many years, until her roots are
rediscovered: 'había un vacío negro en mi memoria, algo siempre presente y peli-
groso que no lograba precisar, algo desconocido que me aterrorizaba' (p. 159). In
terms of the narrative engine, the ship serves also as a transitional site, to shift
the focus of the novel from the United States to Chile.

---

[28] After Eliza leaves Aurora at the house on Nob Hill, the child escapes and returns to
Chinatown, where she is kidnapped and finally rescued; in part the boat trip is intended to
prevent future attempts at flight.

[29] The end of the novel reveals that this is not Williams's first reinvention of himself; he
had been a prisoner in Australia before vesting himself as the del Valle's manservant (p. 311).

Santiago – 'cada uno en su lugar y un lugar para cada uno'

In comparison with San Francisco, Chile's capital city presents superficial geographical differences but underlying similarities in the social assignment of space. When Severo arrives in San Francisco from Chile, and again when Paulina returns to Santiago, the narrator highlights differences – the hubbub, the diversity, the color and originality of the frontier city contraposed to the staid, aristocratic atmosphere of Santiago.[30] But both cities share the Western hierarchies of class and gender separation, from a spatial and a behavioral perspective, and Paulina del Valle, in Santiago as in San Francisco, perpetuates these structures at the same time that she is herself constrained by them.[31]

When Severo first left Chile for San Francisco, he idealized the United States as 'un soplo de aire fresco' in comparison with the rigidity of class structures and Catholic repression of his native country; 'deseaba cambiar a Chile, darle vuelta por completo, purificarlo' (p. 35). He speaks in these terms because, in his youthful idealism, he focalizes from the vantage point of the newly discovered middle class, which was agitating for change. However, when Paulina del Valle later sweeps into Santiago, she adjusts her horizons immediately to the class structures she had inherited from her own patriarch. She locates her newly created family in a mansion similar in ostentation to the Nob Hill home. She extravagantly displays her wealth, buying space in the theater and in the streets (p. 173), but always with class in mind: 'tan pronto abrió las puertas de su mansión pasó a encabezar la vida social de Santiago, porque lo hizo con gran

[30] Contrast, for examples, the following panoramas of San Francisco (cited above, in part) and of Santiago:

> San Francisco había deslumbrado a Severo al atisbarlo desde el barco. ... Acostumbrado al aspecto somnoliento del Puerto del Valparaíso, donde se había criado, el muchacho quedó aturdido ante la demencia de casas y edificios en variados estilos, lujo y pobreza, todo revuelto, como si hubiera sido levantado deprisa. ... Entre el tráfico ruidoso de animales y coches se abría paso una muchedumbre cosmopolita: americanos, hispanos, franceses, irlandeses, italianos, alemanes, algunos indios y antiguos esclavos negros, ahora libres, pero siempre rechazados y pobres.   (p. 29)

> Santiago era una ciudad hermosa situada en un valle fértil ... ciudad tranquila, somnolienta y olorosa a una mezcla de jardines floridos y bosta de caballo. Tenía un aire afrancesado, con sus árboles añosos, sus plazas, fuentes morunas, portales y pasajes, sus mujeres elegantes, sus tiendas exquisitas donde vendían lo más fino traído de Europa y del Oriente, sus alamedas y paseos donde los ricos lucían sus coches y estupendos caballos .... Era una ciudad señorial, muy diferente a San Francisco con su sello inconfundible de lugar fronterizo y su aire cosmopolita y colorido.   (p. 163)

[31] In her discussion of Allende's recent novels, María Claudia André interprets the recurrent absence of mothers as freeing: '[the] daughter escapes the anxiety of having to mirror the maternal figure or to differentiate her own image from that of her progenitor' (p. 78). She is correct in noting that the maternal absence places greater weight on the influence of the surrounding community, in offering the daughter various options for constructing her own identity. Nonetheless, it should be noted that in this novel, Paulina del Valle fully assumes the constricting maternal role, attempting to shape her granddaughter into a younger version of herself – a woman who will follow in her path, in every way.

clase y buen tino, conocedora de cómo odian en Chile a los ricos y mucho más si son presumidos … para que no la acusaran de siútica o nueva rica, el peor epíteto posible' (pp. 172–3). Paulina affects an air of progressive cosmopolitanism, serving international dishes and dressing in the latest British styles, but beneath this façade her classist attitudes remain intact.

Paulina's house becomes a public as well as a private arena; Aurora remembers it as a gathering place for young artists, for the free exchange of radical ideas, including the notion of accepting women as equals in the art world (p. 173). In this way as in business, Paulina attempts to create new spaces for women. But in the business and the political arenas she is not at liberty to choose her own place. She continues to utilize her second husband as she used the first, as her front-man for business dealings; he joins the all-male Club de la Unión, to serve as her eyes and ears for speculation and deal-making.[32] Her niece Nívea agitates for women's suffrage, but Paulina, content with her secondary role for herself and her granddaughter, takes a reactionary position: 'algunas de nosotras reinamos tras el trono. … Yo no necesito el sufragio para hacer lo que me dé la gana' (p. 212). She does what she wishes, but she does not wish to do anything radical enough to threaten the structures that undergird her position of privilege. She maximizes her power in the space that she is assigned. Additionally, she demonstrates her lack of solidarity with other women and her lack of confidence in their potential for autonomy, when she warns Nívea that women, if granted suffrage, 'votarán por quien les ordene el marido o el cura, las mujeres son mucho más tontas de lo que te imaginas' (p. 212). Paulina's rebellions have all been for her personal benefit, but she does not see them as changes to the overall hegemonic structures. Instead, she reinforces those structures by exerting power over the women around her – in particular, the servant class.

Whether on Nob Hill or in the mansion of Ejército Liberador, numerous servants are referred to and taken for granted, but none of the maids or nannies has a name or a face within the narration. Through this discursive strategy, Allende emphasizes that they are granted no place – whether out of guilt or preference, the employer class prefers to make them invisible. The servants are depicted in terms of their functions rather than as a physical presence in society. For example, Aurora narrates that during the overland portion of their return from Europe, they lost some servants, but fortunately were able to replace them without undue difficulty: 'Por el camino habíamos perdido a la niñera, que se enamoró de un argentino y prefirió quedarse, y una criada a quien la derrotó el tifus, pero mi tío Frederick se las arreglaba para contratar ayuda doméstica en cada etapa de nuestro peregrinaje' (p. 162). The servants, largely female, give the primary characters both the time to pursue their business and social interests, and the luxuries of their upper-class lifestyle.

Even the liberal Nívea del Valle, whose radical enjoyment of sex brings her

---

[32] The Club de la Unión is not only all male, but all upper-class, 'hombres de bien' (p. 171).

too many children, relies on a faceless staff of nannies, in order that she can freely pursue her social activism. We note the irony of spatial distribution in the following paragraph, in which Aurora and her governess Matilde Pineda meet with Nívea to talk about creating new spaces for women: 'Cuando Nívea venía de visita, siempre encinta y con varios hijos pequeños en brazos de las respectivas niñeras, la señorita Matilde Pineda abandonaba la pizarra y mientras las empleadas se hacían cargo de la manada de criaturas, nosotras tomábamos el té y ellas dos se dedicaban a planear una sociedad más justa y noble' (p. 169). This new society, thus far, is only for the upper class; and the progress of the upper class is only possible on the backs of the women of the lower class, who must therefore keep to their place. The servants remain in the background, quite invisible to the women who plan the future of their supposed sisterhood.

This image of women's servitude is quite distinct from the idyllic portrait in Severo's mind, as in San Francisco he struggles to understand the servant hierarchies of Paulina's household. He recalls his own servants in Chile, as if they had been part of the family: 'Nunca vio que despidieran a una criada; esas mujeres entraban a trabajar en la casa en pubertad y se quedaban hasta la muerte' (p. 42). An alternative perspective is presented later in the novel, where Nívea's and Severo's own maids are seen more realistically, as essentially enslaved by Chile's economic system:

> adolescentes reclutadas en el campo y destinadas a servir por el resto de su existencia, a menos que quedaran encintas o se casaran, lo cual era poco probable. Esas doncellas abnegadas crecían, se secaban y morían en la casa, dormían en cuartos mugrientos y sin ventanas y comían las sobras de la mesa principal. … cuando las hijas de la familia se casaban se las llevaban consigo como parte del ajuar, para que siguieran sirviendo a la segunda generación.   (pp. 197–8)

This is the novel's only glimpse into the rooms that lie behind the ostentatious salons of Santiago's upper crust. It is notable that the poor in Santiago seem hidden – or else invisible to the privileged gaze – in contrast to San Francisco's open heterotopia of rich and poor (see note 30, above). In Chile, Nívea may work to subvert gender norms, but class attitudes seem much more difficult to restructure.

As a counter-space to the all-male Club de la Unión, the novel presents the women's arena of social action, the Club de Damas. In its traditional form, the Club de Damas looks like benevolence, but it is in fact a social stepping-stool for women: 'socorrer a los indigentes es tarea obligatoria de las mujeres de buen pasar. Mientras más se sacrifican por los pobres recorriendo hospitales, asilos, orfelinatos y conventillos, más alto se colocan en la estima general, por lo mismo pregonan sus limosnas a todo viento' (p. 165). Aurora describes the discomfort of occasional gift-bearing trips to the poor neighborhoods, as the women showed off their generosity 'en nuestro lujoso coche,' inspiring not gratitude but resentment on the part of the recipients of their charity: 'nos daban las gracias con grandes muestras de humildad, pero con el odio vivo brillando en sus pupilas'

(p. 165). However, this vehicle for social advancement does undergo a significant evolution: Aurora's liberal governess, Matilde Pineda, suggests that the Club offer small-business loans to the poor women rather than giving them their cast-off clothing and leftover food.[33] The loans are designed specifically for women because, as Matilde points out, the men are eligible for government aid, but the national structures ignore women and children. The idea appeals to Paulina's capitalist bent, and because this is still, ostensibly, charity work, it is legitimate business for the upper-class women as well. The lower-class women then turn 'women's work' into profitable but still gender-appropriate enterprises, using the loans to finance 'un gallinero, un taller de costura, unas bateas para lavar ropa ajena, una carretela para hacer transporte' (p. 169).

Matilde Pineda, a relatively minor character in the overall Sommers/del Valle family saga, emerges as the only woman who truly changes women's space in Santiago. She is tangential to the plot but a protagonist of the geoplot. The unmarried Matilde Pineda is the figure who offers Aurora an alternative to the repressive convent schools in which Paulina repeatedly enrolls her; instead, she educates Aurora in public places, by taking her to museums and libraries, by hiking and by reading the newspaper with her – and in exploring these places, she teaches the young girl to interrogate Chilean hierarchies of race, class, and gender (p. 175). Her innovations in the Club de Damas become national policy after the Revolution, making lower-class women visible for the first time to the agents of national development (p. 253). Matilde's subversion of female space is symbolically summarized by her installation of a clandestine printing press in a back room of Paulina's own home during the Revolution of 1891 (pp. 184–5). Most notably, Matilde is one of only two women in the novel (the other being the concubine Amanda Lowell) who remain free of the mobility-ending bonds of matrimony. When she reappears after Paulina's death, it is revealed that she has carried on a long-time extramarital affair with the bookstore owner Pedro Tey, with whom she now lives openly (p. 309).[34] She has thus constructed her life on her own terms, escaping the hegemonic and normalizing gaze, flouting traditional roles about the place of women, and leading other women – even the reactionary Paulina – to change their ways of seeing gender and class. Nonetheless, while her role as mentor is remembered gratefully by the adult Aurora, she does not have any immediate impact on Aurora's development, because Paulina's influence dominates the space in which the young girl matures.

[33] As Matilde points out, 'La gente no quiere regalos, quiere ganarse la vida con dignidad' (p. 169).
[34] This relationship was hinted at earlier in the novel, when Pedro Tey, tortured during the Revolution, reveals that he only endured the torture for Matilde Pineda's sake; until that point their relationship had been seen as purely platonic and intellectual (p. 196).

The Grand Tour – 'la sólida telaraña que mi abuela ... tejió en torno a nosotros'; 'el mercado matrimonial'

Aurora's second voyage to Europe with Paulina serves again as transition between the arena of her maturation – Santiago – and her marital home of Caleufú. In part the trip is motivated by Paulina's need for medical treatment in London, and in part, from her desire to learn about wines for her next budding enterprise; but Paulina also considers the Tour necessary in order to mold Aurora into a younger version of herself, 'porque yo [Aurora] ya tenía dieciséis años y estaba en edad de adquirir un barniz cosmopolita y un ajuar matrimonial, como dijo [Paulina]' (p. 227). During this voyage, Aurora's exterior self is refashioned into marriage-able material, and she is launched into the social circles to which her class enti-tles her. And indeed, at a dance in Paris she meets the man Paulina decides she will marry, Diego Domínguez, 'hijo de gente conocida' (p. 243), as well as the man who will be her future lover, the doctor Iván Radovic. These two figures henceforth replace Paulina as the pillars of Aurora's identity, the first by assimi-lating her into his world, and the second by entering hers.

The boat itself is described in much more detail than was the case on the first voyage; now, with Aurora seeing it through the camera's eye, it does approxi-mate much more closely Foucault's heterotopic model. As a photographic artist, Aurora finds little to attract her in first class, where everything is too neat. But in the decks beneath, she comes into close proximity, for the first time, with the freer environment of the middle and lower economic classes. She uses her camera as a passport to enter this other space, from which she had been barred in Chile, and she discovers a new kind of existence:

> Yo bajaba a menudo a las cubiertas inferiores para tomar retratos, sobre todo de los viajeros de la última clase, que iban hacinados en la barriga del barco: trabajadores e inmigrantes rumbo a América a tentar fortuna, rusos, alemanes, italianos, judíos, gente que viajaba con muy poco en los bolsillos, pero con el corazón rebosante de esperanzas. Me pareció que a pesar de la incomodidad y la falta de recursos, lo pasaban mejor que los pasajeros de la clase superior, donde todo resultaba estirado, ceremonioso y aburrido. Entre los emigrantes había una camaradería fácil ... por las tardes salían a relucir las guitarras, los acordeones, las flautas y los violines, se armaban alegres fiestas con canto, baile y cerveza.   (pp. 247–8)

As Foucault has theorized, the contact between heterogeneous groups in this kind of counter-site can be dangerously destabilizing ('Of Other Spaces,' pp. 25–7). Below decks, away from Paulina's controlling gaze, Aurora discovers her vocation: photographing this other world and sharing the images she captures. Furthermore, there she establishes her relationship with Iván, the counter-suitor, who offers an alternative to Paulina's driving capitalism; when she offers to invest in a private medical clinic on his behalf, he reproaches her: 'Creo que la medicina no es un negocio, sino un derecho, señora' (p. 249). Like the alternative world of the second-class travelers, Iván's worldview opens up new horizons for Aurora, showing her the world just before she submerges herself into the restrictive space of married life, at the rural patriarchal home of Caleufú. After her marriage ends, Aurora will return both to her vocation and to Iván, thus returning to the liminal space just outside classifiable society.

Caleufú – 'un paraíso doméstico que no era para mí'; 'nadie más sospechaba por esos lados el tamaño del mundo'; 'la fresca casa de adobe y tejas que su padre estaba construyendo para nosotros ... tal como antes había hecho una para su hermano ... y tal como haría para su hermana. ... Por generaciones los Domínguez habían vivido siempre juntos'

The repressive space of Diego and Aurora's rural home is identified with the still-strong influence of the Catholic Church beyond the capital's confines. The elaborate daily and holiday rituals are part of the same hegemonic structure that put women in their traditional Western place, as abnegated servants of their families.[35] The figure who incarnates that image is Diego's mother Elvira, 'esa mujer suave y discreta, totalmente dependiente de su marido, sin ideas propias, incapaz de lidiar con los esfuerzos mínimos de la existencia, pero que compensaba su falta de luces con una inmensa bondad' (pp. 286–7). The patriarchal home which absorbs Aurora into its generations-old structure – architectural and social – is the world of duty, where individual pleasure has no place. Instead, roles and movements are rehearsed, inherited, uncontested. Diego and his father construct the house in advance of her arrival, dictating the places that she will spend her days, 'en la propiedad, tal como antes había hecho una para su hermano Eduardo ... y tal como haría para su hermana Adela cuando ella se casara. Por generaciones los Domínguez habían vivido siempre juntos: el amor a Cristo, la unión entre hermanos, el respeto a los padres y el trabajo duro, decía, eran el fundamento de su familia' (p. 254). Duty to family and to faith blend in this Church-constructed world, where from the outset Aurora – after her tutelage by Matilde Pineda and her venture below decks on the ship from Europe – chafes at her confinement.

Three spatial refuges provide intervals of respite from the atmosphere of obligation in which Aurora is placed. One is the photographic lab, the room of her own, that she locates in a back room of the house (p. 263), although she frets at the lack of locks that therefore makes true privacy impossible (p. 266). The second is the countryside; this section of the novel contains several episodes of

---

[35] Throughout the novel, women are accomplices of the repressive Catholic Church; for example, they side with the priests against the liberal reforms which would have granted women more rights (p. 178). Nívea points out to Severo that 'la mayoría de los hombres, por católicos que fueran, ansiaban modernizar al país, pero las mujeres, mucho más religiosas, se volvían contra sus padres y esposos por defender a la iglesia. ... las mujeres de clase alta y el clero manipulaban las cuerdas del poder' (p. 87).

the 'green-world archetype' often used in literature as a woman's refuge from male hegemony.[36] In her gallops through the countryside, dressed in men's pants and with the wind blowing through her hair, Aurora sublimates her frustrated sexual desires, and enjoys physical and spiritual autonomy, if only temporarily.[37] She also photographs these places (p. 265) in order to recapture the sensation of freedom back in her darkroom. Finally, respite from the confinement of marital duty is found during the Christmas celebrations at the ranch, when the arrival of the neighboring *pehuenche* tribe turns Caleufú temporarily into a heterotopia (pp. 284–6). The scene is idealized into a carnivalesque environment of celebration, with Aurora again crossing dangerous boundaries into alternative social realms, via the mask of her camera.

Aurora observes two social characteristics of the *pehuenche* which later prove significant, and which also turn out to be intertwined. One is a radical equality between the sexes; in contrast to the Catholic women of Caleufú, '[l]as mujeres nada tenían de tímidas, eran tan independientes como los varones' (p. 285). The other is nomadism: 'Cuando se agotaban los pastos o se aburrían del paisaje, arrancaban del suelo los palos que sostenían sus techos, enrollaban las telas de las tiendas y partían en busca de nuevos parajes' (p. 286). By the end of the novel Allende demonstrates that nomadism is essential to women's equality, as rootedness brings with it only obligations for the female. In the words of Gertrude Stein, 'It's great to have roots, as long as you can take them with you' (in Braidotti, *Nomadic Subjects*, p. 1).[38] Eventually Aurora will follow the path of Matilde Pineda, of Amanda Lowell, of Eliza and of the *pehuenche* women, rejecting the Western structures of home and hearth in order to create a different women's space, the energy of which comes from crossing boundaries and exploring new terrains.

The nomadic space: 'navegar a la deriva ... sin rumbo fijo'

As we have mentioned, *Retrato en sepia* is peppered with intermediate role models, but also with more rebellious female figures who reject all Western traditions about the woman's place. Miss Rose Sommers, Paulina del Valle, the married Eliza Sommers, and Nívea del Valle, as well as Nívea's teacher Sor María Escapularia,[39] function as partially liberated women. All of them find ways

---

[36] For a full exploration of this archetype, see Annis Pratt, *Archetypal Patterns in Women's Fiction* (Bloomington: Indiana University Press, 1981). It should be noted that this archetype reinforces the culture/nature dichotomy long used in the binary and oppositional representation of the sexes (see the Introduction to this study for further discussion).

[37] The green space is also the arena for Aurora's cathartic gallop through the rain, after discovering that her husband is having an affair with her sister-in-law Susana; in that space she can shout and cry alone, without violating the stability of the family unit (p. 299).

[38] Cited earlier, in our Introduction.

[39] This Catholic nun violated censorship regulations to pass books to her student Nívea,

to contest their assigned roles, but without overturning the hegemonic structures which make the system function; instead, they manipulate those structures to their own advantage. They negotiate for themselves a degree of autonomy, but still rely on either a male figure or the Church to protect their status, to shield them from the social and economic ostracism that true rebellion implies.

Other female figures risk more, and create a radical arena in which they can pursue their own agendas. La señorita Matilda Pineda, as mentioned above, defies social norms in two ways, collaborating with subversives during the Revolution and opting to live with the bookdealer Pedro Tey instead of marrying him; she alights for a while in the home of Paulina del Valle, as Aurora's governess, but this is clearly just another stop on a continuous journey. Amanda Lowell is an archetypal nomadic figure; with flamboyant red hair and her head held high, she occupies center stage wherever she is, and seems impervious to the attacks of 'society women' like Paulina del Valle. She appears in San Francisco, in Paris, and in Santiago, but does not remain in any of these places. As companion to the syphilitic Matías del Valle, she nurses him for a time, but eventually brings him to Santiago to die. During that time she expands the horizons of young Aurora, showing her an alternative way to perform as woman. She is held up as a contrast in every way to the avaricious Paulina:

> No podía concebirse dos mujeres más diferentes, la Lowell nada ambicionaba, vivía al día, desapegada, libre, sin miedo; no temía la pobreza, la soledad o la decrepitud, todo lo aceptaba de buen talante, la existencia era para ella un viaje divertido que conducía inevitablemente a la vejez y a la muerte; no había razón para acumular bienes, puesto que de todos modos a la tumba se iba en cueros, sostenía. (p. 216)

As in Laura Restrepo's *La novia oscura*, the forces of social reproduction enforce locational fixity in terms of behavior. Paulina, and other intermediate rebels, have not challenged the capitalist social agenda but merely carve a place for women within it. Amanda Lowell, on the other hand, rejects the structure entirely.[40]

Amanda shrugs aside all concepts of duty, even abandoning Matías before his death. Escape from the shackles of supposed moral obligation proves essential to the nomadic status. Following this model, Aurora eventually separates from her unfaithful husband, in spite of the grief this brings to her mother-in-law Elvira,

---

and encouraged her to study medicine as women in other countries were doing; she also reveals that she entered the convent not from vocation, but as an alternative to the confinement of marriage (pp. 37–8); the clear model for this character is the Mexican seventeenth-century nun Sor Juana Inés de la Cruz, who outlines similar ideas in her letters.

[40] André points out that the subplot of the enslaved prostitutes from China, the 'sing-song girls,' challenges the 'happy hooker' trope which, as she notes, has been 'so popular within the masculine tradition' (p. 81). Conversely, it must also be noted that the glamorized figure of the prostitute, representing erotic celebration, has been reborn recently in many novels by women, including Restrepo's *La novia oscura*, Sefchovich's *Mal de amores*, and this figure of Amanda Lowell in *Retrato en sepia*.

and instead strikes out on her own, establishing an occasional relationship with the counter-suitor Iván Radovic. Like her mentor Amanda, Aurora rises above the criticisms of society, rejects the prosperity that accompanies stability, and makes her own way.

Eliza Sommers follows a more complex route towards nomadism. As we are told in the prequel *Hija de la fortuna*, she was raised as a conservative child but then became an androgynous nomad, dressing in drag to pursue her vagabond lover Joaquín Andieta. She reverts to conservative norms when she marries Tao Chi'en, and by the time she reappears in *Retrato en sepia* she has, in her words, 'pasado veintitanto años de su vida cuidando a sus hijos Lucky y Lynn como una esclava' (p. 326), 'sin más horizonte que su hogar en Chinatown' (p. 321). Throughout her marriage she submits to the guidance of her husband, living in his space and under his spiritual tutelage. Even after Tao Chi'en's death she continues her duty-bound role, first taking his body to Hong Kong and then voluntarily submitting to further servitude in tending her aged aunt, Miss Rose Sommers, in London. Only after the death of the last person to whom she is obligated can she allow her nomadic spirit to reawaken: 'el germen plantado en esos años de nómada permaneció intacto en su espíritu, listo para brotar en el momento propicio' (p. 321). Her surrender of her granddaughter to Paulina, her honoring of the vow not to re-establish contact with Aurora, and her voluntary erasure of her personality in order to submit to the bonds of matrimony make her an ambivalent nomadic figure. But in her final appearance in the novel, she becomes Aurora's twin spirit, a truly free woman who negotiates her own place, ready to 'navegar a la deriva' and to 'viajar sin rumbo fijo' (p. 322).

All of these nomadic figures still find a way to keep a man in their lives. In one regard this reinforces traditional norms of heterosexuality and of woman's need for man; seen from another perspective, Allende is reaffirming the woman's right to celebrate her sexuality beyond the confines of marriage. Amanda is the only one of the female nomads who flouts monogamy, engaging in various relationships including the vaguely incestuous ones with Feliciano del Valle and his son Matías. The other women stand by their men – Matilde Pineda with Pedro Tey, and Eliza, even after death, with the spirit of Tao Chi'en.[41] Aurora, the novel's final nomad, leaves this matter open to further negotiation, opting for Amanda's model and living day by day: 'El segundo amor no fue una suave amistad que con el tiempo se convirtió en un romance probado, fue simplemente un impulso de pasión que nos tomó a ambos por sorpresa y de pura casualidad resultó bien … bueno, hasta ahora, quién sabe cómo será en el futuro' (p. 313). Most significantly, Aurora clarifies that this new architecture for a sexual relationship gives each of them a room of their own: 'El hecho de no estar casados nos facilita

---

[41] Widowhood does constrain Eliza's nomadic activities, since she does not consider herself complete without her husband: 'amor sólo puedo sentir por Tao. Sin él nada me importa demasiado; cada día que vivo es un día menos en la larga espera para reunirme con él de nuevo' (p. 337).

el buen amor, así cada uno puede dedicarse a lo suyo, disponemos de nuestro propio espacio y cuando estamos a punto de reventar siempre queda la salida de separarnos por unos días y volvernos a juntar cuando nos vence la nostalgia de los besos' (pp. 314–15). Thus she creates a space where she can exercise her freedom as a woman as well as an artist.

Intimate geographies: images of the body

The body is also a site of physical contestation, a surface on which power leaves its mark, at the same time that it can serve as the ultimate locus of self-expression. The latter is only rarely the case in Allende's novel, however, as the female object is generally shaped and used by the male gaze.

The strongest example of female commodification appears in the character of Lynn Sommers, the regrettably beautiful daughter of Eliza and Tao Chi'en. As stated earlier, she is represented as 'el producto afortunado de razas mezcladas' (p. 56). Her fortune lies not only in that she can pass for white, but in the fact that she has inherited only the 'best' features of her English, indigenous Chilean, and Chinese heritages. Of course, the ranking of features occurs entirely within Western paradigms. When a sculptor seeks a model for his statue 'La República,' he decides that the symbol of San Francisco needs to be of mixed race, and when he sees Lynn he knows that he has found the appropriate combination of racial features: 'alta, bien formada, de huesos perfectos, no sólo tenía la dignidad de una emperatriz y un rostro de facciones clásicas, también tenía el sello exótico que él deseaba. Había en ella algo más que armonía, algo singular, una mezcla de oriente y occidente, de sensualidad e inocencia, de fuerza y delicadeza, que lo sedujo por completo' (p. 68). Her beauty is only skin-deep, as she demonstrates no attractive spiritual or intellectual qualities throughout the novel, but those features are certainly less valuable than is this gift of Westernized beauty with a touch of the exotic. The sculptor carefully poses her, 'en la punta de los pies con los brazos en alto, en una postura imposible de mantener por más de unos minutos' (p. 71) and with intentional sex appeal, 'con una ligera túnica plisada que le colgaba de un hombro hasta las rodillas, revelando el cuerpo tanto como lo cubría' (pp. 70–1). The selection criteria of the sculptor, and then the sculpting of the model herself, reveal far more about white male ideas of beauty than they do about the female person. Lynn's lifecourse is determined entirely by the gift, or curse, of this beauty, an accident of genetics that resulted in a prized product. She is sought after and grasped at by nearly all men who meet her, and she opts to become putty in their hands.

Her allure and consequent vulnerability brings out the repressed Catholic Chilean heritage in her mother Eliza, who works as hard as any convent at controlling Lynn's sensuality, 'machucándole normas de modestia y enseñándole a caminar como soldado, sin mover los hombros ni las caderas' (p. 65); but Lynn's physicality exceeds her mother's reach, and eventually she does fall helplessly into the hands of the trifling Matías del Valle.[42] Conveniently for the narrative, she dies in childbirth, thus remaining the eternal symbol of idealized, youthful, exotic-and-Western beauty. As Matías himself later says on his deathbed, 'Una mujer demasiado bella no puede escapar del deseo que provoca' (p. 213).

A different example of female commodification occurs in the person of Paulina del Valle, whose self-image is determined entirely by how she imagines herself through male eyes. As we mentioned earlier, while her husband's feelings towards her never changed as she gained weight, she became ugly to herself, and thus denied her husband – and herself – access to her own sensuality. As she ages, or when she is ill, she loses value, and thus must deform herself in order to hide these out-of-control bodily changes. Her adornments – jewels, false teeth, corsets, dyed hair or wigs – are intended to mask her flesh, or to encase it in social superiority.[43] The narrator herself obliquely endorses the ideal of Western youth and thinness, with observations such as 'a pesar de su edad y su gordura, Paulina del Valle imponía la moda' (p. 173). While the sculpting is certainly required by the externally prescribed norms of female appearance, at the same time Paulina chooses to allow her body to be thus scripted, because it buys her what she wants – acceptance, social position, power. As we noted in the Introduction to this study, bodyscapes can be read as 'narratives of cultural identity' (Hayden, p. 13), and Paulina's falsified self encodes her self-determined identity.[44]

Perhaps regrettably, the novel presents a pattern wherein the intellectual women are described as relatively unattractive. Nívea is presented as very ordinary-looking: 'nada en su aspecto revelaba la fuerza de su carácter: de corta estatura, regordeta, con grandes ojos oscuros como único rasgo memorable, parecía insignificante hasta que abría la boca' (p. 36); and Matilde Pineda is equally deprecated: 'De aspecto la señorita Pineda no podía ser más chilena, esa mezcla de español e indio que produce mujeres bajas, anchas de caderas, con ojos y cabello oscuros, pómulos altos y una forma de caminar pesada, como si estuvieran clavadas en la tierra' (p. 175). The author may intend the reader to infer that their unprepossessing appearance made them less appealing in the marriage marketplace and thus allowed them to develop their intellects (both are voracious readers, for example); more likely, Allende harks back to a long narrative tradition in which the characters' minds shine all the more against the dullness of their bodies.

[42] The novel notes that 'Matías la admiró como otro de los muchos objetos de arte que coleccionaba' (p. 79).

[43] Paulina is unappealingly contrasted with the spare and natural Eliza del Valle (p. 31) and with the sensual concubine Amanda Lowell who so successfully markets her 'soberbias nalgas' (p. 19).

[44] This false equation of appearance with value is maintained by Paulina even after her own death; she decides to negotiate her way into the afterlife, in accordance with the apparent Catholic control over such matters, by having herself buried in a Carmelite habit. (Nívea and Aurora undermine this attempt by dressing her body in fancy undergarments, beneath the nun's habit.)

Of course, a central aspect of representation of the female body has to do with the experience and expression of sexuality. As in Laura Restrepo's *La novia oscura* and many other Hispanic novels, the narrator closely associates the Catholic Church with the repression of female sexuality. Aurora describes her convent education as exemplifying the linked virtues of 'la sumisión y la fealdad' (p. 66) and teaching the girls to be ashamed of their bodies: 'Las monjas debían comenzar por dominarnos el cuerpo, fuente de vanidad y de otros pecados. ... Nos bañábamos una vez al mes, cubiertas con largos camisones para no exponer nuestras vergüenzas ante el ojo de Dios, que está en todas partes' (p. 166). Since Aurora's marriage to Diego Domínguez takes place entirely within the Catholic value systems of his family, her sexual experience with him is devoid of pleasure, and linked to feelings of inadequacy on her part. On the other hand, three couples – four, including Aurora and her lover Iván at the novel's conclusion – model mutual sexual desire and pleasure. One is Severo del Valle and his wife Nívea, the only Catholic couple who permit themselves sexual freedoms. They began their explorations of each other's bodies in innocence, as children, innocent but at the same time 'aturdidos por el pudor y la culpa' (p. 36). Unable to resist their attraction to each other, the adolescents later thwart the vigilant and proscriptive eyes of spinster aunts, agents of the Church. Social class and Church-based repression are connected, as the following quotation demonstrates:

> Había mil ojos espiándolos. Las viejas criadas que los vieran nacer protegían esos inocentes amores, pero las tías solteras velaban como cuervos; nada escapaba a esos ojos secos cuya única función era registrar cada instante de la vida familiar, a esas lenguas crepusculares que divulgaban los secretos y aguzaban las querellas, aunque siempre en el seno del clan. Nada salía de las paredes de esas casas. El primer deber de todos era preservar el honor y buen nombre de la familia.   (p. 36)

As adults, their erotic explorations continue when Severo is injured during the war with Perú, and lies nearly immobilized in bed. His incapacitation necessitates the deferral of sexual initiative to his new wife Nívea, who delights fully in the role, and in thwarting the vigilance of the nun who dozes at his bedside (pp. 140–1). Her initiative and ingenuity are linked to two earlier transgressions of gender regulation: the surreptitious reading of Church-censored erotica, and guided by that reading, the exploration of her own body (p. 140).[45] This illicit self-knowledge and her husband's forced passivity create the basis for a gynocentric, lifelong relationship of desire, hampered only by the couple's irrepressible fertility (pp. 198, 252).

---

[45] Similarly, Aurora inherits from Eliza a trunk full of Miss Rose's pornographic manuscripts. This forms an interesting contrast to Allende's other novels in which women gain access to enlightening books about the world (in *La casa de los espíritus*), or about fantasy (such as the *Thousand and One Nights* in *Eva Luna*). Here, the forbidden texts expand personal boundaries, communicating gynocentric self-knowledge rather than exploring faraway worlds.

However, this is the only fulfilling sexual relationship that happens within the confines of Catholic marriage. The other relationships which allow for the experience of female pleasure are all extramarital (Tao Chi'en and Eliza, who never legally married [pp. 60–2], Diego and his sister-in-law Susana [pp. 293–5], Aurora and Iván [pp. 314–16]). Aurora opts not to narrate the details of her intimate life with Iván, but all of the other relationships are narrated in long, detailed passages that attempt to capture the mutual experience of carnal desire and orgasm. Many of these passages employ geographic metaphors to connote this most personal kind of exploration and occupation: Tao Chi'en knows Eliza's physical contours so well that 'fue como andar por sus suaves hondonadas y pequeñitas colinas con un mapa' (p. 60), and Susana guides Diego 'por la hermosa topografía de su cuerpo' (p. 295). Both references give primacy to the female experience, even though this experience occurs at the hands of the male lover. The body thus serves as the physical territory of the female self, a site that both gives and receives its due pleasure, and as a surface on which the lovers inscribe each other.

The motif of the camera, which plays an important role from the novel's title through the Epilogue, is intricately linked to conceptualizations of the body. As mentioned earlier, the camera lends Aurora access to social and political situations from which she would otherwise be barred for reasons of class or gender.[46] However, the images themselves also carry meaning in terms of Aurora's own power. By visually mapping the faces that society has opted not to see, she captures the imprints of their daily lives. For this reason she snaps shots that are unposed: Aurora speaks of her fascination for 'rostros curtidos por el esfuerzo y el sufrimiento' (p. 257) and for 'rostros curtidos por la intemperie y la pobreza' (p. 266).[47] The culture has inscribed itself onto the bodies of the lower classes, and Aurora, empowered by the camera, seeks to reflect those faces back to the upper-class viewer. Thus the photographed body becomes both the surface of power and an instrument of power.

This function of the camera, as Aurora's-eye-made-public, shifts from social and empathetic to openly political by the novel's end, when the narrator writes of her documentation of a workers' strike and their subsequent massacre: 'mis fotografías son el único documento irrebatible de que la matanza de Iquique ocurrió, porque la censura del gobierno borró de la faz de la historia los dos mil muertos que yo vi en la plaza' (p. 315).

Recurrent self-portraits also explore the link between the body and the camera. Aurora manipulates her self-image in front of the mirror, exteriorizes that by photographing it, and then studies the photos, in order to capture her self. In this

[46] Aurora lists the politically unstable sites to which the camera gives her access: 'las minas, las huelgas, los hospitales, las casuchas de los pobres, las míseras escuelitas, las pensiones de cuatro pesos, las plazas empolvadas donde languidecían los jubilados, los campos y las aldeas de pescadores' (p. 223).

[47] Aurora also observes: 'Al hacer un retrato se establece una relación con el modelo que si bien es muy breve, siempre es una conexión' (p. 223).

way she attempts to objectify her own body as her husband objectifies it, so that she can understand herself by studying the surface of her body: 'Me miraba en el espejo desnudo o apenas cubierta con las delicadas camisas de dormir de encaje que mi abuela había comprado en Francia y me preguntaba ansiosa si acaso él me encontraría bonita. Un lunar en el cuello o los pezones oscuros me parecían defectos terribles. ¿Me desearía como yo a él?' (p. 259).[48]

Finally, for Aurora, photographs of her deceased relatives keep their memories alive, and even in a sense reincarnate the people for her. Throughout the novel she documents her search for her roots by means of the recovery and re-examination of old photographs. The photographs counter the ephemeral nature of the body.[49] Aurora attempts to use photography against time, and in capturing the image of the body she attempts to capture the soul (p. 114).

The *chora* – 'una dimensión misteriosa donde el amor y la muerte son similares'

Because of certain plot and stylistic similarities between Nobel laureate Gabriel García Márquez and Allende, critics have equated Allende's depiction of the spirit realm with magical realism. However, when seen in the context of other women writers' configuration of space, this spirit-world is more accurately seen as a *chora*, that transcendent place-which-is-not-one that stands just beyond visible place. For Allende, the *chora* functions mostly as the repository for the spirits of the deceased; from there, they can continue to guide the actions of the living and to provide respite from solitude. The *chora* is clearly a privilege of women, in Allende's fiction; in *Retrato en sepia* the only male who accesses the *chora* in life (and also speaks from the *chora* in death) is Tao Chi'en, who as a trained healer is well versed in the powers of the unseen realm. His first wife Lin continues to accompany him from her *chora*-existence for the rest of his earthly existence. After his death, he and Lin maintain their connection to Eliza, a connection which is very nearly physical.[50] He is a rare male exception, but in this and in other respects he embodies many characteristics traditionally associated with women.[51]

---

48 This passage explains the cover photo of the novel as published by Plaza y Janés (2000) and HarperCollins (2001).

49 See for example the beginning of the Segunda Parte, where Aurora re-creates the physical presence of her grandparents by placing their photograph beside her bed (p. 110). See also the Epílogo, where the narrator speaks of the photographs as resuscitation of the dead (p. 343).

50 '[Eliza] No se sentía sola ni atemorizada ante el futuro, puesto que el espíritu protector de Tao Chi'en anda siempre con ella; en verdad están más juntos que antes, ya no se separan ni un solo instante. ... por las noches [ella] duerme en el lado izquierdo de la cama, para cederle el espacio de la derecha, como tenían costumbre' (pp. 320–1).

51 See for example the summary of his relationship to the young Aurora; in terms of traditional gender roles, he clearly replaces the dead mother rather than the absent father (p. 326).

In this novel as in several of Allende's other works, the principal function of the *chora* is to create a living matrilineage, through which women draw the strength to face their own struggles by availing themselves of contacts with strong women (or non-traditional men) who have gone before them. In her maturity, Aurora surrounds herself with the evoked presences of Tao Chi'en and Paulina, thus drawing the *chora* into direct confluence with her own physical space: '[Paulina] no desapareció en la inmensa negrura de una muerte definitiva, como me pareció al principio, una parte suya se quedó por estos lados y anda siempre rondándome junto a Tao Chi'en, dos espíritus muy diferentes que me acompañan y me ayudan, el primero para las cosas prácticas de la existencia y el segundo para resolver los asuntos sentimentales' (p. 306).[52] The confluence even becomes physical, as Aurora mentions that she both hears and smells the presence of Tao Chi'en around her (p. 318).

Apart from housing the presence of the dead, the *chora* serves other functions for the novel's female characters. In particular, Nívea appears to have on-demand access to the *chora*, using it to visit Severo as he lies delirious in the hospital (p. 129) and for occasional clairvoyance (p. 197).[53] In this way a strong female character transcends spatial limitations through sheer force of will.

In his study of the *chora* and liminal spaces, Scott Sharpe identifies childbirth as a moment when women have fleeting access to the 'between' space of the nonverbal realm. Nívea accesses this space, this threshold between life and death, during childbirth (p. 192), as does Lynn when giving birth to Aurora (pp. 96, 98). In these cases, as in Sharpe's study, childbirth is seen as the opening of one space into another, the bringing into existence of another being, an experience beyond bodily control, and thus a transitional space between bodily existence and transcendence. Eliza, watching her daughter Lynn give birth, articulates the *chora* concept in geographical terms:

> Eliza Sommers había pasado por la fatiga de dar a luz y sabía, como toda mujer, que ése era el umbral de la muerte. Conocía el viaje esforzado y misterioso en que el cuerpo se abre para dar paso a una vida; recordaba el momento en que se empieza a rodar sin frenos por una pendiente, pulsando y pujando fuera de control, el terror, el sufrimiento y el asombro inaudito cuando por fin se desprende el niño y aparece a la luz.   (p. 96)

Sexual climax, as an extreme physical sensation, offers the characters – male and female – another ephemeral access to the *chora*, or an alternative dimension described in Tao Chi'en and Eliza's case as 'ese extraordinario espacio,' and for

---

[52] Here again Tao Chi'en is associated with characteristics traditionally considered feminine: as the narrator summarizes, 'a los veinticuatro meses de criarla como una madre estaba completamente enamorado de su nieta' (p. 326).

[53] This novel, in its intentional development of the *chora* concept, more fully explains the source of the magical powers that Nívea and her descendants display in the earlier novel *La casa de los espíritus*.

Matías and Lynn as transcendence: 'durante un brevísimo instante se encontraron en otra dimensión, sin defensas, desnudos en cuerpo y espíritu' (pp. 79–80). This space is thus intimately connected to bodily sensation yet lies beyond it. Here, the sexual experience allows for a transitory union of identities that overcomes the boundaries of their two bodies.

The *chora* thus functions as a repository of power for women to access, and a dimension in which complete communication is possible. In this and other novels, the *chora* can be a spatial representation of what others would term the subconscious realm. In this sense, Aurora's persistent nightmares, the result of the repression of her childhood trauma, are seen as the unwelcome intrusion of the *chora* into the concrete world. The ominous children clad in black, the protagonists of the dream, are clearly located in the same realm as the spirits of the dead, since the narrator notes that the spirit of the deceased Paulina del Valle does battle with those creatures in order to protect Aurora (p. 312). In the end, the only impediment to the nightly demons is to 'dormir abrazada' (p. 112), implying that the two sleeping beings' subconscious is sufficient to hold the malevolent side of the *chora* at bay.

The links between photography and the *chora* are numerous, from the time that Aurora takes up the camera as a weapon against the nightmares (p. 114). She soon learns that photography can do more than capture the surface of an image; it can also capture a glimpse of the soul, which, like the moments described above, provides a fleeting contact with the other realm. Related to this is Aurora's feeling that she takes better photographs the morning after a nightmare, because she awakes 'alucinada y en carne viva, un estado óptimo para la creación' (p. 113). In this as in most senses, the *chora* is a space of possibility, and of a transcendent way of being that – for those aware enough to capture it – enriches the topographical realm of existence. Not only photography, but art in general proves an effective mechanism for the female protagonist to contact the *chora*, in an experience not unlike sexual orgasm: 'Algunas veces, al trabajar con una imagen en mi cuarto oscuro, aparece el alma de una persona, la emoción de un evento o la esencia vital de un objeto, entonces la gratitud me estalla en el pecho y suelto el llanto, no puedo evitarlo. A esa revelación apunta mi oficio' (p. 114).

Conclusion

The female protagonist of *Retrato en sepia* does not cover as much geographical territory as do the female nomads of some other novels. However, in terms of social position, she does adopt the nomadic worldview, as she moves freely and outside the boundaries prescribed by class and gender. In separating from her husband and navigating alone, or with an occasional lover, she at once loses her place and creates her own defiant place; in the face of social disapprobation, she responds: 'esos desaires no me quitan el sueño: no tengo que agradar a todo el mundo, solo a quienes en verdad me importan, que no son muchos' (p. 312). The character's trajectory is in one sense a circular one: before the age of five, her grandfather was raising her as one who would defy boundaries and create her own place, and eventually she is able to pick up her own journey where she had left off, and to take her own place as a woman and as an artist.

4

Grounded: Ferré's *Flight of the Swan*

Introduction

Rosario Ferré's third novel in English, *Flight of the Swan*, is a fictional embellishment of a real episode, Russian ballet dancer Anna Pavlova's brief stay in Puerto Rico during her 1917 Latin American tour. Borrowing the title – and much of the heroine's characterization – from a biography of Pavlova, published by dancer André Olivéroff in 1932,[1] Ferré uses Pavlova's fictionalized presence in Puerto Rico to consider questions of cultural identity, politics, and gender. The heterotopia she creates – juxtaposing Russian dancers and US political and economic forces against traditional Puerto Rican types – allows for a reading of the novel as a series of encounters between people with different histories and varying aspirations.

The ballet motif, in consonance with the book's title, establishes the central image of women who manage to soar above the constraints of daily life. The main character – referred to primarily as 'Madame'[2] – reigns as queen of a gynocentric universe, within which dedication to artistic transcendence is the law of the land. A surface reading of the novel might imply that Madame takes her places with her, as the territory of the stage allows her to re-create herself in identical ways across many countries and continents. On the ballet stage, women occupy the spotlight; as Ferré notes, the men play secondary roles, serving principally to elevate and launch the women dancers. Madame is the star, the swan, who guides her own flight towards the immortality that artistic superiority can offer. She appears in this way to have overcome the locating, immobilizing forces of hegemony.

However, when we ask the questions central to our study – not only where she is, but who put her there and whether her location is alterable – we arrive at quite a different reading. In fact, Madame's itinerary reflects another kind of flight, as she attempts to evade both the political and the economic problems that nip at her heels. Her path is mapped by her husband and manager, Victor Dandré, for whom ballet is not art but pure business.[3] He not only uses her and her troupe for his own material advancement, but he is just unscrupulous enough to create enemies among his creditors, from whom they all must then flee. His initial flight from

---

[1]   André Olivéroff, *Flight of the Swan: A Memory of Anna Pavlova* (1932).
[2]   This appellation is taken directly from Olivéroff's memoir.
[3]   See for example the opening sentence of chapter 4: 'For Mr Dandré ballet was a business venture like any other' (p. 21).

Russia – into which he lures Madame with promises of wealth and adventure – is occasioned not by the turmoil of the Revolution but by the need to escape from the scandal of his embezzlement. After touring Europe and the US, they do not fly but flee to Puerto Rico, in an attempt to accumulate quick cash so that they can continue their wanderings.[4]

Additionally, the tantalizing possibilities of a gynocentric universe are undone by the realities of that universe's governing principles. Ostensibly freed from the imposition of masculine norms, Madame becomes as dictatorial as any government or any patriarch. She establishes and maintains hierarchies among the girls of the troupe, as status is conferred by social origin and body type, as well as by level of allegiance to her guidance. The girls are all her servants, the nymphs to the sacred goddess, and she maintains her stronghold by taking advantage of their devotion both to her and to ballet, and by threatening them with exile from her mobile but rule-fixed world if they fight her dictates. In an interesting parallel to Western male hegemony, her rules have to do with sex and the body. The girls are instructed to dominate both the hunger and the lust to which lesser female bodies are tempted, so that they can sublimate all desires of the flesh to the goal of artistic transcendence. Seen in this light, the stage loses its appeal as an alternative female territory, and becomes merely a simulacrum of the exterior world, with women replacing men as the hegemons.

Flight of the Swan has been the subject of little critical commentary; apart from the initial reviews, only two substantive studies of the novel have appeared: Antonio Medina-Rivera's 'La aniquilación de las bellas artes y de la aristocracia en las obras de Rosario Ferré' (2003), which includes discussion of this novel through the lens of social class; and Patricia Vilches's insightful study, 'La violencia pública/íntima hacia la subjetividad del cuerpo femenino en Julia Alvarez y Rosario Ferré' (2003). In her discussion, Vilches draws attention to the ambiguity of both protagonists' representations, as they struggle against national and global constraints on the female body, and male and female limitations to women's mobility. Vilches assesses Masha's simultaneous 'subyugación/liberación' (p. 101) and her 'sumisa/rebelde' role (p. 111), vis-à-vis the violence that is regularly exerted on the female body, and posits, as will our analysis, that any transcendence that the ballet dancers achieve as women and as artists is only partial: 'si bien este desmantelamiento de la conceptualidad del ballet pareciera que acercara a la protagonista de *Vuelo del cisne* a un vuelo verdadero, ella no está verídicamente libre, sino que vive supeditada a la defamiliarización del arte que la ha mantenido al margen de la dependencia, solo para caer en manos del yugo patriarcal puertorriqueño' (p. 102).

---

4   It is notable that this characterization differs sharply from Dandré's role in Olivéroff's biography, in which the manager is portrayed as courteous, sensitive, and deferential to Madame's whims; for Olivéroff, Madame is the 'astute business woman' (p. 26) and Dandré 'watched over her like a guardian and waited upon her like a servant' (p. 37). In contrast, Ferré's fictionalization of the dancer places her squarely in the managing hands of the corrupt Dandré, and also complicates their personal relationship, as we shall see.

The novel's plot is structured around the temporary absence of Dandré, the alpha male figure, thus leaving Madame in a place where she might explore and perhaps renegotiate her own identity as a woman, as citizen of an apparently postnational world, and as a dancer. While her husband/manager is in New York (negotiating new tours, arranging for new passports, and taking up with new women[5]), Madame falls in love with Diamantino Márquez, a young stud who is also a rebel fighting for Puerto Rico's independence from the United States. Either because of her attraction to him or because she shares his goal of bringing about political change – her motivations are muddled in the novel – she first modifies her dance style, and then runs off with him. Essentially, she steps down from the stage and attempts to dance with and for the people. As a Russian émigré, she sympathizes with the poor of Puerto Rico, identifying their situation under US capitalist domination with the situation of the lower classes under Russia's czarist rule. At the same time, her proximity to Diamantino, combined with Dandré's absence, opens her body to new desires. Representing these dual awakenings, Madame ceases to dance the elitist *Dying Swan* of the Russian stage, replacing it with the more passionate *Bacchanale* – in her words, 'I want to dance about life from now on, not about death' (p. 177). Parallel to her dance we witness the negotiation of Puerto Rico's identity: the novel's most appealing characters – Diamantino, the poet Manuel Aljama, and the free-spirited Ronda Batistini – all articulate the need for Puerto Rico to free itself from US control, both political and economic.

But in terms of all of the questions outlined above, the novel ends in failure. Madame first ends up as a prisoner of the freedom-fighters, and then returns to Dandré's loveless embrace and mercenary control. Diamantino and Ronda are both killed, and Aljama silenced. Puerto Rico remains a colony of the United States, with a governor who does not speak Spanish. The narrator Masha, a dancer in the troupe, roots herself in Puerto Rico, endlessly re-creating the world of the *Dying Swan*. The failure of the swan's flight is iconically represented in the novel's last chapter, in Masha's description of a photo of Madame in the *New York Times*, 'standing at the top of the marble stairs in the lobby at the Waldorf-Astoria, looking as gaunt as a heron and holding on to Mr. Dandré's arm' (p. 260). With life wearing her down from soaring swan to ungainly heron, and still latched onto Dandré, Madame has yielded to the grounding forces that keep her in her place.

What is not clear is whether Ferré designed the novel as a tribute to the little-girl dreams that ballet can represent – and to the ambitions of a very young post-Spanish Puerto Rico – or whether she intended to create an ironic and ultimately pessimistic image of a woman's attempt at transcendence. Reviewers of the novel disagree on this question. In her online review, Barbara Lipkien Gershenbaum reaffirms the surface reading of the novel, asserting that Madame's story

---

[5]   See for example Madame's references to the probable existence of Dandré's girlfriend on pp. 105 and 137.

is the 'tale of a performer so devoted to her art that she emerges as a doomed heroine who sacrifices all for the dance' and who 'through her devotion to her art displayed a strong and vital character', in her concluding sentence Gershenbaum asserts that 'Anna Pavlova is a role model to us all.'[6] Other reviewers, such as Diana Postlethwaite and Maria DiBattista, rightly critique the sometimes unconvincing plot lines, but remain silent on the question of whether Madame is to be read as a role model or as a failure; DiBattista does, however, conclude her review with a reference to 'the "Swan's" aborted flight from the strict precepts of her own art.'[7]

The narrative structure does not assist in decoding the text. The story is narrated primarily by Masha, Madame's adoring maidservant and a dancer in the troupe. Her inconsistent narrative voice alternates between sophistication and naïveté. In personal terms, she either worships Madame or rages against the betrayal implied by her goddess's affair with Diamantino. On the political level, Masha speaks as the voice of the proletariat, the Bolshevik, the only character who understands the injustice of czarist Russia and of Puerto Rico's social stratification; in this sense she opposes her mistress's protected status and elitism. As Postlethwaite observes: 'it's never clear to what extent this narrator is meant to be reliable.'[8] Even in the novel's final chapter, the narrator's own stance vis-à-vis Madame's choices or lack thereof remains ambiguous.

My conclusion, against the backdrop of a spatial reading, is that Ferré did intend to chronicle her heroine's failure to achieve autonomy, but that she considers the sacrifice a necessary one for the sake of the higher goal, the preservation of her dance. Ferré might not see the capitalist side of the dance enterprise as hobbling the feet of the swan, but our geographic reading will reveal that it does.[9] For Ferré, Masha's eventual establishment of a Russian-style dance school in San Juan might not symbolize the dis-located perpetuation of empty illusions, but my considerations of her level of autonomy do in fact lead to that conclusion. Similarly, Ferré does portray the grassroots desire for Puerto Rico's cultural, economic and political independence, but she utilizes this plot line primarily for atmosphere or local color and not with real political intent – Ferré herself has favored statehood for Puerto Rico.[10] Thus, she may intend either Madame's Caribbean interlude or her novel's Puerto Rico to be read as images of adventure

6 www.bookreporter.com/reviews/0452283310.asp. This is the view that most closely corresponds to the portrayal of Pavlova in Olivéroff's 1932 biography.

7 http://www.counciloftheamericas.org/as/literature/br65ferre.html

8 *New York Times* Book Review, 29 July 2001.

9 Upon Dandré's return, Madame's elitist personality reasserts itself, thus demonstrating that her carnivalesque interlude did not alter her perspective of earned privilege: ' "To tell the truth, Masha, I was getting tired of sleeping on wire cots and having Spartan meals of codfish boiled with green plantain in small-town fondas. … It's wonderful to sleep in a bed again and eat in a real restaurant, with linen tablecloth and napkin" ' (p. 222).

10 Ferré's recent choice to write in English may also be seen as a decision not to insist on Puerto Rico's cultural difference from the United States.

rather than failure; but a postcolonial and spatial reading that exposes the unrelenting hand of hegemony points to the opposite conclusion: Madame's flights
are an illusion, which ends when the stage lights are turned off.

The space of the stage - 'the feeling of home evaporates; it doesn't exist at all. There's only the stage'

A discussion of this novel's geography must begin at center stage. The ballet
stage, at least until her arrival in Puerto Rico, is an environment of which
Madame is the architect, and a world that she can re-create in any political or
geographic context. In this sense it is an a-national space, within the bounds
of which Madame can be a citizen of any country. Yet this space carries with it
several ambiguities which complicate its function as a space of representation in
the novel.

While it is marketed – both by the character Dandré and by the novelist Ferré –
as an a-political space, Madame's stage carries with it the markers and the values
of czarist Russia. It is aristocratic, artificial, and resistant to change. The dancers
were trained in frivolity and indulgence, as they were the 'personal baubles' of
the Romanovs (p. 41). This training did sink in, as it produced a woman who
supposedly cares for the poor but who lives in an unreal world of white tulle and
sequins. A Puerto Rican reporter who fancies himself a Bolshevik sympathizer
dares to ask Madame a question central to our reading of the novel: whether
she considers her style of ballet 'an anachronism in a world of striking workers,
violent coups, and peasant massacres' (p. 84).[11] Madame throws him out of her
apartment, and Ferré too abandons the question – but it continues to lurk in the
wings of the stage space.

Within the safe and portable space of the stage, Madame orders and rules
over her own society, which is at several junctures compared to an imperial or
a military regime (pp. 31, 40).[12] The girls compete to get in and then to stay in
this world, in a competitive environment which rewards those who can sacrifice
the most. As dancers in training, they starve themselves in order to maintain
their lithe bodies, and work for a pittance or for nothing: 'most of us were used
to living on air, and we even paid our own expenses just to be able to dance on
the same stage as Madame' (p. 13). While the dancers comprise the wage slaves
of this female-centered society, Madame – known only by her reverent title –
plays the diva. She throws temper tantrums, boasts about never having danced

---

[11] See also the comment by Madame's mother regarding the elitism that lay at the essence
of czarist Russia's ballet: 'Sitting high up in the gallery I could see the audience in the orchestra
seats below, sumptuously dressed in lace and velvet and glistening with jewels. On stage the
dancers wore similar apparel and jewelry. ... The aristocrats were convinced they deserved
it all and were fascinated by their own spectacle. Meanwhile in the countryside the peasants
continued to starve' (p. 43).

[12] This image too may be traced to Olivéroff's biography of Pavlova (pp. ix, 54).

second to anyone, demands new costumes even when the troupe is penniless, and continues to insist that art trumps real life.

Repeatedly she insists on the a-political nature of the stage, using it as a screen between her and the division in her homeland. Dandré supports this claim, whenever it benefits his profit schemes; for example, when the Puerto Rican commissioner invalidates their Russian passports because 'Russia had ceased to exist' (p. 34), Dandré claims that she is above such national concerns: 'Madame only cares about her art. She doesn't get mixed up in politics!' (p. 35). Instead, she feigns transcendence. As Masha notes, evoking again the imagery of the swan:

> Many of our relatives in Russia perished during those years, when the White and Red Armies were grappling in mortal combat along a frontier thousands of miles long. . . . Those were anguished years, during which we, her followers, spent many sleepless nights worrying about the future. But Madame seemed to glide serenely over the troubled waters of her age: the Russian Revolution, the deaths of millions of her countrymen.   (p. 5)

Equally, the audiences who flock to the stage seek to block out reality by escaping into this false serenity: 'People needed to be happy and to forget about the Marne and Verdun, about the horrors of trench warfare and poison gas' (p. 10). These references to escapism undo Madame's frequent assertions of art for art's sake, of the transcendence that pure ballet represents. Instead, the stage becomes a constructed refuge from the horrors of the Russian Revolution and the World War, and Madame can be read as a woman who fled from the scene.

There is no question that Dandré seeks only his own economic comfort; however, Madame does occasionally allow political reality to invade the theatrical space. In Dandré's absence and once she has fallen in love with the rebel Diamantino, she begins to claim that she will dance for the people of Puerto Rico, in order to redress symbolically the wrongs done to Russia's lower classes: '"This time I'm not going to throw my lot in with the oppressors as I did in Russia, out of loyalty to the czar!" she cried, with no small measure of melodrama. She was going to help that zealot, Diamantino Márquez, bring justice to the world' (p. 147). However, these incursions into political activism, these attempts to bridge the gap between stage and reality, are unconvincing.[13] At the heart of the ambiguity, in terms of the stage as political space, is the conflation of Madame's dual motivations: she may experience some kind of limited social awakening, but this awareness is driven primarily by her carnal desire for Diamantino. Additionally, it must be noted that she is only enabled to alter the function of her stagespace in this superficial way because of Dandré's absence; once he returns, she again becomes the swan, gliding over – fleeing from – the storms that rage outside the theater.

---

[13] Madame lapses into sophisms such as the following impassioned defense of her art: 'The purpose of my dancing is to give joy to the people, and help create a better world' (p. 129).

The stage seems to offer possibilities, as a locus for female autonomy. On stage, the dancer has the power to re-create herself with each performance (p. 9). Furthermore, the stage's portability offers a vehicle within which women can safely travel; here once again the narrator employs the swan analogy: 'From the girls' point of view it was a magnificent opportunity to make their way in the world. To be free from all constraints of family! To fly around Europe like a flock of swans, in search of beauty, adventure, and romance, as Madame was able to do!' (p. 30). On the surface, this passage aligns itself with the thesis of female autonomy which this study traces: the woman can abandon the constraints of society and its attempts to fix her location, and instead can adopt the freedom of nomadism, of perpetual encounter and discovery. However, this novel does not sustain the premise. Madame is anything but free from the constraints of family, as she yields consistently to Dandré's mappings.[14] Furthermore, her stage is insulated against the possibilities of transculturation implied by the term 'encounter.' Madame rejects alternative styles and cultural influences, returning in the end to the either classic or tired *Dying Swan* dance with which the novel opened.

The stage functions as a symbolic space of representation, with the dances serving as manifestations of Madame's evolving – but ultimately unchanged – worldview. In spite of frequent assertions that the stage is beyond politics, the *Dying Swan* dance is presented by the narrator, Masha, as a political allegory, a 'prayer for peace': 'Our beloved St. Petersburg was the swan, torn by strife and civil war, its churches smoldering to heaven, its golden domes now sheltering atheists who murdered priests as they tended to the devout' (p. 21). Even though Masha frequently manifests her Bolshevik sympathies, this reading of the dance clearly demonstrates anti-Revolutionary sentiments, and the swan who tragically but gracefully dies is the murdered Russian aristocracy. In this sense, Madame dances the swan song of elitist, czarist Russia.[15]

Another favorite dance, *Les Sylphides*, may be read as the story of Madame's

[14] Pavlova appears to embody the nomadic ethos more closely in Olivéroff's biography than in Ferré's novel. In Olivéroff's depiction, she longs for the international adventures (pp. x–xi) and contrasts them frequently with the bondage of marriage and home, even to the point of advocating free love for the girls of her troupe: 'She must always have a lover. To be great artist [sic], you must have loved, you must know all about love ... you must suffer with love. But – listen to me, *galoupshik* – you must learn to do *without* it!' (p. 195). Indeed, in Ferré's novel the dancer does indulge in a lusty fling with Diamantino. But then Ferré returns her to the manipulating arms of Dandré and the stable bond(age) of her corporate marriage.

[15] Masha later interprets the dance more directly as the death of old Russia: 'Madame, in spite of being the daughter of a washer-woman, was identified with the nobility. She was a White Russian, and her solo *The Dying Swan* was the personification of the aristocrats' agony' (p. 111). Against this danced vestige of the czars, characters such as the independent-minded Doña Victoria criticize Madame's elitism as it is manifested onstage; Doña Victoria asserts that Madame should choreograph the fight for freedom, 'Stravinsky's *Firebird*, dressed in workers' overalls, instead of Saint-Saëns's *The Dying Swan* in musty, moth-eaten feathers. Art must be committed and denounce injustice if it's going to be any good' (p. 142). Madame ultimately rejects this idea of stage as counter-site.

relationship to Dandré. The heroine of the ballet is ethereal (her supernatural qualities denoted by a white tutu, delicate wings, and a predominance of toe dancing), but is destroyed by her love affair with a mortal man. A clear analogy may be drawn both to Madame's image of herself as transcendent and superior, and to Dandré's destructive harnessing of her talent for his own gain. Significantly, in the novel's final chapter Masha, having founded her own simulacrum of the Imperial Ballet School in San Juan, is preparing this same dance for her young students, thus perpetuating the destructive imagery.

The third ballet featured in the novel is Glazunov's *Bacchanale*, an obvious reference to Madame's attempt to break free of her ice castle and to experience carnal desire. Masha describes this dance as 'one of the few ballets I truly dislike, because it's so chaotic, asserting the supremacy of tumultuous passion over reason's wise counsel' (p. 92). Within the frame of this dance, Madame exchanges tulle and wings for a red tunic ('the whores' favorite color,' according to Masha [p. 147]). The frenzied ballet turns the stage into a dangerous countersite where lust rather than discipline governs the ballerina's body.

The space of representation merges with life in Madame's final performance of the *Bacchanale*. The ballet depicted Dionysus (now played by Diamantino) luring Ariadne (Madame) away from the isle of Naxos, against the opposition of the maenads, who eventually devour him. Since Madame's dancing troupe does see itself as Diamantino's rival for Madame's attention, and his open sensuality as a challenge to the dancers' gynocentric world, the girls move suddenly beyond the boundaries of simulacrum, and actually attack Diamantino/Dionysus (p. 180). This plot development is somewhat startling (and unconvincing), but clearly symbolic of the stage space fusing with extra-theatrical dynamics. The stage then becomes a physical link with the interior of the island, as Diamantino utilizes a trapdoor to disappear with Madame, leaving the dancers to conclude the play as they wish. This odd disappearance occurs in chapter 32, and Madame's whereabouts remain unknown until chapter 37, when Juan Anduce takes up the narration and locates her in the rebel stronghold of the island's interior. In this plot twist, then, the stage offers a frame of exit from the endless repetition of *The Dying Swan*, and the trapdoor constructs a pathway towards a new (albeit eventually empty) promise of self-definition. The cause of freedom, in Puerto Rican costume, thus 'takes' center stage.

However, as the novel later demonstrates, Madame finds the real world much less accommodating than the stage space, in terms of the possibility of creating herself anew.

Russia – 'our passports were now invalid, because Russia had ceased to exist'; 'we, as Russian citizens, are now pariahs without a country ... flotsam at the mercy of the waves'; 'a world that had been mercifully wiped out'

Madame's country of origin is only sketched in the novel through memory – that of Madame, of the narrator Masha, or of Madame's mother Lyubovna Fedorovna. While Madame restricts herself to nostalgic evocations of her glory days as the czar's 'bauble,'[16] Masha – of peasant origins – and Lyubovna Fedorovna – a laundress raped by the heir of an upper-class family – predictably paint a more critical picture of the homeland. Both focus on the rigid divisions of class and the economic and personal injustice that resulted from this system. Neither evinces a desire to return, although only Masha voices open support for the Bolshevik revolution. Drawing strength repeatedly from reminding herself of the difficulties she faced back home (pp. 178, 183), Masha carries her peasant identity with her, at one point even asserting that the Russia she and Madame had known had been 'mercifully wiped out' (p. 184). Still, all three characters, in spite of their differing evocations of the homeland, share the vision of Russia as a place that has been forever erased. Return is never contemplated. For her survival – that is, for continued earning potential – Madame must distance herself from her Russianness, within the larger Western stage. Thus she repeatedly asserts that politics do not interest her, and that while her art is Russian her talent has transcended national (political, if not sentimental) ties (pp. 36, 65).[17] Russianness becomes her costume, her trademark, but not her identity. Instead, she markets herself as the swan who soars beyond the war-torn strife of the world below, and whose talent serves as her passport.

In geographic and political terms, these characters who had fled from violence and toward the world's stages now accept their condition as permanent nomads. They may even be read as postnational characters, in the sense that they will now acquire arbitrary passports from whatever country will agree to issue them.[18] However, their nostalgic desire for stability, for 'home,' distinguishes these char-

---

[16] In Puerto Rico, Madame pines for past luxuries rather than specifically for Russia, as demonstrated in her conflation of Britain with Russia in the following nostalgic musing as interpreted by Masha: 'I could guess what she was thinking. She missed the Maryinsky and the Neva [Russian theaters], London and her beautiful house at Golders Green' (p. 121).

[17] In one incident, at a reception in San Juan, Dandré commits the faux pas of raising his glass to 'the Russians' rather than to Madame, whom the governor had just universalized by toasting her as 'one of the wonders of the world' (p. 61). The resulting awkwardness reminds him that his future lies in leaving his war-torn country and its politics behind, and in becoming a citizen of a more generic West.

[18] Madame expresses consternation and then rage at the idea of being made a British citizen: ' "That's impossible. How can you become citizens of one country if you live in another?" she asked. "That's exactly what you'll be doing, Madame, in order to survive," Molinari answered with an unctuous smile. Madame stamped her foot in anger, but couldn't deny what Molinari had said. She would soon be a British subject, whether she liked it or not' (p. 54).

acters from the nomadic subjects[19] of other contemporary novels by women. They struggle to maintain their collective national identity, even in the face of Western pressures to the contrary: 'Talking about our beautiful city made us feel better; it helped us overcome the feeling that we were now unmoored and might drift apart' (p. 37). Thus, the troupe at first turns inward, resisting the opportunities that new geographical settings might offer, clinging to outdated notions of community. At the novel's end, Masha ultimately creates a new home, mooring herself to Juan Anduce and her ballet school in San Juan; and Madame, while forever wandering, does so always as the profitable instrument of Dandré. These plot outcomes demonstrate that rootlessness is an intolerable condition for the novel's women.

Puerto Rico – 'it could also weave its spell around you, and then you'll never want to leave'

The young island nation of Puerto Rico is presented in two contradictory frames throughout the novel: as fertile tropical land of possibility, and as colony of the United States – therefore, simultaneously as a site of unrestrained freedom and as a place of confinement and control. In this conflicted identity lies the central theme of the novel, as the characters partake of both place-typings, and attempt to forge their new identities on this unstable ground.

As tropics, Puerto Rico is presented in quite a stereotyped fashion. In commenting critically about Ferré's representation of the island in her other works, Ronald Méndez-Clark observes her 'esfuerzo … para proporcionar en ciertas entregas una introducción breve … a la realidad politico-cultural del Puerto Rico contemporáneo a lectores norteamericanos a quienes subestima, a quienes no quiere antagonizar y a quienes no les quiere complicar demasiado las cosas' (p. 414). While harsh, his observation does point to the feeling that the reader is looking at a postcard image of Puerto Rico throughout this novel. The island's vibrant green is frequently contraposed to the winter white of St Petersburg, and its sun to Russia's cold (pp. 25, 177). Lust is in the air, dark Latin eyes flash, adventure throbs, and both revolution and carnival constantly threaten to rupture the fragile veneer of daily life. This vitality seeps into the stage space, luring the girls – including Madame – towards the thrill of physical and emotional danger.

On the other hand, the Russians, like the North Americans, are depicted as ill suited to this teeming environment. The governor's wife, Mrs Yager, 'lived like a recluse in the upstairs rooms of the governor's mansion and never came downstairs to any of the parties because she had a neurotic fear of the tropics' and its air infested with germs (p. 74), and later in the novel, the male dancer Novikov does indeed contract pneumonia from the humidity (p. 176). The most compel-

---

[19] Braidotti's term (see the Introduction to this study for elaboration).

ling image of the Russian troupe's inadaptability to their Caribbean immersion is found in the novel's epigraph, which offers a passage attributed to the metafictitious *Memoirs of Masha Mastova*: 'The swan was a symbol of the beauty of our times. ... Then we landed on this strife-torn island and the swan melted under the scorching sun' (frontispiece).

Within this anything-goes environment of natural and cultural tropicality, the novel repeatedly confronts the question of the economic and political colonization of Puerto Rico by the United States. The military presence is ubiquitous, as Puerto Rican citizens are mobilized under the American flag for the theaters of war in both Panama and Europe. The governor, Arthur Yager,[20] is a personal friend of President Wilson's and doesn't even understand Spanish (p. 61), and he ensconces his adolescent daughter far from the tropics, in a site which constitutes San Juan's polar opposite, the Lady Lane finishing school in Massachusetts (p. 66). With sarcasm, Ferré allows the sinister character Molinari to point out that Yager's origins in Kentucky make him knowledgeable about the two central issues facing Puerto Rico: poverty and the 'ins and outs of the liquor business' (p. 60). In spite of these links to Appalachia and moonshine, Yager is clearly depicted throughout the novel as an ill fit for Puerto Rico.[21]

The US agenda within this novel clearly smothers the cultural identity of the island. San Juan is remapped in order to impose the North American military agenda, as Masha describes her city tour in the following terms: 'we turned right on General O'Donnell, formerly Calle San José, and then right again on General Allen, formerly Calle Fortaleza. ... We much preferred the Spanish names, which were several centuries old: San Francisco, San Sebastián, and San José, who are also holy in our Orthodox faith' (p. 58). This geographic renaming corresponds to the economic colonization of the island, as globalization destroys the bases of the Puerto Rican economy. The story of Juan Anduce's family is presented as typical: their local tobacco industry is wiped out by 'American Cigar, General Cigar, and Consolidated Cigar' (p. 191). The family's warehouses are burned, and Juan's brothers killed, by arsonists during the price wars (p. 192), and Juan is eventually forced to move to New York to work for a tobacco factory there (p. 193). Local coffee production is similarly wiped out by US economic interests (p. 60).[22]

The strongest condemnation of the relationship between the 'big white brother' and the 'little brown brother' (p. 237) appears during flying hero Danny Dearborn's visit to Puerto Rico. Presented as a conquering Viking god, he embodies the imposed ideals of progress and globalization: 'Danny's visit was proof that the Americans were able to pilot the destinies of the sleepy-eyed, lazy people of

---

[20] Puerto Rico's governor from 1913 to 1921.

[21] See for example Yager's lack of understanding of the role of carnival king, resulting in the embarrassment of hero Danny Dearborn (pp. 244, 248).

[22] See also Masha's linking of economic globalization to US military control in Nicaragua and Honduras, and the implications for Puerto Rico (p. 237).

the tropics' (p. 236). His soaring plane, the 'Silver Hawk,' provides a diametrical contrast to the 'Dying Swan' as his image supplants that of the dancer. He is steel and strength, while she is feathers and vulnerability. While the Swan gracefully slumps to the floor in the space of the enclosed theater, the Silver Hawk roars through the skies, reducing the island to a 'small crumpled lozenge' from the perspective of Dearborn's birds-eye view (p. 239).[23] It should be noted that this is the episode in which Ferré most clearly confronts the racial issues inherent in US-Puerto Rico relations, as she makes frequent reference to Dearborn's blondness, his Nordic heritage, and his strutting lordship over 'el Jíbarito' (p. 237).

Thus, in spite of Ferré's own pro-statehood stance, she here depicts the US cultural, political, military and economic invasion of Puerto Rico in consistently negative terms.[24] The only character who speaks well of the relationship is the unreliable Dandré, who shares the capitalist ethos with the neighbor-to-the-North, and recognizes the link between military occupation and prosperity: '"Under the American flag there's bound to be progress," he said ... "The island was until recently under military rule. There will be order and discipline and we will be paid in dollars," he added, looking satisfied with himself and plucking at his mustache, as he did whenever he didn't want anyone to contradict him' (p. 14). As the agent of international capitalism, he sees any unexplored territory as a site of potential profit, and Puerto Rico thus becomes a scheduled stop on his Latin American tour.

Within these general images of the island nation, the novel offers close-up perspectives of four primary locations, which are presented in a telescoping order as the plot progresses: the large capital, San Juan; the village of Arecibo; the plantation of Dos Ríos, and the tiny rebel hideout in the island's interior, Otoao. Each site provides the topochrone for different dynamics swirling around the artistic and carnal impulses of Madame, and of the characters who dance in her shadow.

San Juan – 'a marvelous spectacle'

In marked contrast with the other sites, San Juan – like the San Francisco of Allende's *Retrato en sepia* – is presented as a heterotopia, where cultures converge and sometimes clash. As vignettes symbolic of this chaotic space, the

---

[23] Note also the proliferation and popularity of cheap Danny-Dearborn souvenirs, marking the linkage between cultural and capitalist control (p. 238).

[24] It should be noted, however, that the United States produces two of the most positive female figures in the novel, fictional character Ronda Batistini (tomboy daughter of a local aristocrat) and the dancer Isadora Duncan (the American dancer presented as a contrast to Pavlova); both will be discussed later in this chapter. Both figures should be read as positive products of a freer environment for women, available only in the United States. In the novel's final pages, Ferré does present a more positive picture of the US relationship with Puerto Rico during the decades subsequent to the novel's action: 'years later, thanks to President Roosevelt, the Puerto Rican Recovery Act was passed in Washington, and economic aid finally began to flow to the island' (p. 257).

novel draws two related geographic sites: the Casa de las Medias y los Botones, and the locations of the Juan Ponce de León Carnival. Both places offer the opportunity for inversion, for the poor to don the accoutrements of the rich, and for the appropriation of the exotic. It is clear that, for the narrator, the protagonist, and the author, these sites exert a strong attraction as sites for the fluid formation of identity, sites of possibility. Bricolage is the order of the day in the Casa de las Medias y los Botones:

> The display windows looked like something out of *A Thousand and One Nights*: buttons made of ivory, of fake mother-of-pearl, of glass that shone like diamonds, fake gold, silver, all displayed on wooden drawers that rose all the way up to the ceiling. They also sold silk ribbons by the spool and all sorts of feathers: ostrich, marabou, pheasant. The rolls of lace, silk damask, brocades, wools, and linens recently arrived from Europe stood spilled over the mahogany counters like newly discovered treasures. The store was swarming with customers, all of them asking to be helped. Madame and I stood there and stared at what was going on. 'People in San Juan must love to dress up,' Madame said. 'We must come back here soon, to have new costumes made.'   (p. 55)

As Madame notes, the Casa de las Medias y los Botones gives the impression that the whole world is a stage. The site is particularly popular at carnival time, when costume blends with reality (pp. 229–30). Carnival, extending the microcosm of the Casa de las Medias y los Botones, creates a similar space for the discarding of rules and social orders, and – at least temporarily – for the celebration of the disorderly.[25] The carnival takes place throughout the city, turning the official and the controlled over to the spontaneous will of the people, turning San Juan into 'a magical coral reef, spilling fireworks from every rooftop and church belfry … a marvelous spectacle' (p. 244). Most significantly for our study, the carnival overtakes the place of the Teatro Tapia, the site which had hosted the ordered, disciplined presentation of the ballet *The Dying Swan*. Now, Madame plans to dance the exuberant *Bacchanale* there, dressed in provocative red. But even this ballet is far too tame for carnival standards, and Madame abandons the stage, surrendering herself to the lure of the transgressive:

> Madame and I watched from the sidelines when one of the *jíbaros* approached the orchestra and ordered it to stop playing. The brawniest of the group … walked up to the dais, picked up one of the drums, straddled it, and began to play. Suddenly, as if energized by the beat, Madame walked determinedly toward the center of the dance floor, and the girls followed her. I looked on in bewilderment – this definitely wasn't on the program. The drumbeats – hand to hand and skin to skin – penetrated to the bone, and we swayed to the rhythm as if in a trance. The women lifted their skirts and petticoats to the waist, fanning

---

[25] See Bakhtin's in-depth analysis of the carnival trope, in *Rabelais and his World* (1968).

themselves with them, as if directing the fumes of their genitals toward the crowd. Madame, in her red chiffon skirt and golden bra, stepped into the middle of the dance floor. She transformed herself into a flame, writhing and burning before us.   (p. 250)

The stage has been erased, or perhaps broadened, to include the entire theater – by extension, the entire city. When the mob invades the Teatro Tapia, it at the same time subsumes the body of the Swan herself. This disruption is temporary, however. Although Diamantino is shot and killed during the mêlée, subsequently order is restored: the rebels are captured or chased away, Madame safely returns to husband and stage, and the threat of destabilization is once again contained. Ferré's presentation of carnival contains as much threat as it does celebration, and in the end carnival is read primarily not as the expression of desire but as the locus of danger. In the end, the characters are better off on their stages, above the grasping hands of the masses and dancing to orchestras rather than to drums. Madame returns to the discipline of her white costumes and to her *Dying Swan*.

Madame retreats, but San Juan survives as a site of resistance to US occupation. As Juan Anduce tells it, the island's geography itself knows how to fight for its own independence. He describes to Masha the six-hour bombardment of the city by Admiral William T. Sampson in 1898 – in his view, Sampson was just another of the many pirates who had attempted to conquer the defiant island. As the American fleet attempted to overwhelm by firepower, the city's layout nullified the impact of their bombardment. The city lies between the sea and a bay, and the buildings were built low, 'so that cannonballs would sail over the houses when fired by ships out at sea' and fall harmlessly into the bay that lay behind them (p. 190). Although the city did fall to the Americans, Juan prefers to relate the event in a way that presents San Juan as a small but elusive counter-site, whose geography defended it:

> Admiral Sampson's bombardment lasted six hours, but the city, bobbing up and down in the distance, kept friskily cleaving the waves as in a game of tagalong. Sampson strode up and down the deck of the USS *Mississippi*, ordering more and more cannon fire, but no evidence of impact was perceived. ... Sampson was baffled. He didn't believe in magic and he couldn't figure out what was wrong. ... he didn't know there was a bay behind the city and that its waters were swallowing up all his fire and brimstone without a belch.   (p. 190)

Thus Juan Anduce represents the resistance that continues to mock, beneath the surface of the US occupation. The city does surrender to the US Navy, but the population does not, as events such as carnival continue to create spaces for the game of cat-and-mouse against the northern giant.

Arecibo – 'which Diamantino absurdly called a "city" '

In contrast to the bustling San Juan, Arecibo is presented as backward, sleepy, resistant to modernization. Carriages replace cars, and the streets are muddy, with 'no pavement anywhere' (p. 115). As in San Juan, the architecture reflects the character of the residents: here, instead of defying the seafaring enemy, the town huddles together with its back to the water, 'as if the islanders were afraid of the wide open space through which foreigners always reached them – first the Spaniards, then the British, the Dutch, and finally the Americans' (p. 12).[26] The hotel in which the troupe is lodged is depicted as primitive and bug-infested (p. 147), and even the local sugar baron disdains his provincial little capital: '"Why did you come to our little town, Madame? ... I can see why you traveled to San Juan, which is a rich city. But Arecibo! There's absolutely nothing here, except a few families who own run-down sugar mills like our own, and a lot of hungry peasants"' (pp. 128–9). The troupe in general can't wait to leave this provincial town of some fifty thousand inhabitants, and their stay only lasts because Madame escapes its inconveniences – she is ensconced with Diamantino in the more comfortable world of don Pedro, at his sugar plantation Dos Ríos, leaving her dancers behind to cope with the messiness of the tropical town.

There is one oddly cosmopolitan feature to Arecibo, though: the coexistence of many immigrant populations. Its distance from, and difference from, the capital's power center appears to have rendered it somewhat immune to the successive takeovers and impositions of hegemonic cultural identities:[27]

> While in the narrow cobblestone streets of San Juan you heard only the Castilian Spanish of the king's ministers, in the dusty alleys of Arecibo you often heard french, Dutch, German, Italian, and Portuguese. In San Juan, people looked to Spain, *la madre patria*, for their material well-being and spiritual sustenance. But in Arecibo the whole world was *la madre patria*, and immigrants from all over Europe settled in its environs. (pp. 119–20)

In this sense, distance from the capital implies a certain kind of cultural autonomy. Each immigrant group has been allowed to preserve its language, and by implication its identity, because of Arecibo's lesser visibility and lesser strategic significance. Additionally, this feature correlates modernity with homogenization; the streets may be paved with mud, but the people have been left alone. When modernization does come – heralded already by the Pierce-Arrow of don Pedro the sugar baron – it will inevitably scatter the people like geese (p. 125) and

---

[26] See also the subsequent description of Arecibo's layout, a few pages later: 'Arecibeños did everything differently: it was as if every house in Arecibo were trying to sail inland, toward the mountains, instead of away from them' (p. 119).

[27] The exception here is that the town seems overrun with US-flavored military parades, as the troops mobilize for Panama and take pride in their invitation to participate in the European conflict: 'We're a part of the modern world now' (p. 129).

require the paving of the roads; but until then, identity is allowed more heterogeneity than in the capital.

Dos Ríos – *'you and your ballerinas don't belong here'*
The novel does not offer any sustained portrait of the sugar plantation, but the discrete anecdotes are filled with walks on the beach, talks on shaded verandas, interludes in hammocks and a general air of luxury. Juan and Masha establish relationships with the silent and invisible servants – 'pale, thin zombies dressed in rags' (p. 139) – but the plantation also provides a safe place for the development of the illicit relationship between Madame and Diamantino, as well as for the furthering of Diamantino's revolutionary agenda with his childhood *compañero* and don Pedro's godson, Bienvenido Pérez.

For the author, Dos Ríos allows space not only for the advancement of these plot lines but for a representation of Puerto Rican aristocracy. Throughout the novel Masha has observed that the rich are the same everywhere – in Russia as in Puerto Rico – and this pastoral interlude allows her to bear witness to this classism. Race also becomes a factor, as we learn for the first time that Juan Anduce is black; doña Basilisa immediately assigns him servant status and sends him off to the kitchen (p. 138).

For Madame, Dos Ríos is the place of seclusion for her own personal bacchanale, but for less empowered characters it is the site of secrets. Here Masha is raped by the sinister (and never-explained) character Molinari (p. 145). Here also, years before, don Pedro had raped many women, including the mother of his 'godson' Bienvenido, who (predictably) turns out to be his own son. Notably, rape in Dos Ríos does not carry adverse consequences. Masha opts to remain silent about Molinari's abuse of her, again (and absurdly) putting Madame first.[28] And in the episode relating to Bienvenido's conception, a story which is only revealed piecemeal, we learn that don Pedro had greatly admired his foreman Arnaldo Pérez, but this respect had not prevented him from raping Arnaldo's wife Aralia. It appears not only that this action had no consequences for don Pedro – Arnaldo remained his loyal servant – but also that Aralia herself took pride in the encounter, for she names the red-haired offspring Bienvenido ('welcome') (p. 160). These episodes of sexual violence work alongside the ubiquitous side-arms of the men (p. 136) in establishing the parameters of a territory beyond the safety of hegemonic stability. The law of this land is every man for himself, and every woman at their mercy.

The female character who cannot be made to fit into this landscape is don Pedro's daughter Ronda. She has been sent off to Massachusetts, to the Lady Lane Finishing School, in order to return vested as a lady aristocrat. Instead, she

---

[28] In this startlingly unconvincing episode, Masha narrates: 'I should have been thinking of myself, of the terrible thing that had happened to me that day, but I could only think of her. I wanted to bring her out of her depression and didn't know how' (p. 147).

brings back a contrary set of US values, those of the liberated woman. Intentionally she sets about to shatter the concept of a woman's place:

> When she came to Arecibo for vacation in the summer she scandalized everyone with her American tomboy independence. She wore bell-bottomed khaki slacks in public, smoked unfiltered Chesterfields, and took her pets riding with her in her father's Pierce-Arrow. She went to the beach alone at night with her boyfriends to roast marshmallows on an open fire, and never went to Mass on Sundays. Tongues wagged, but she was headstrong and went on doing what she pleased.   (p. 151)

Furthermore, she fraternizes with the peasants (p. 150) and demands her own career, planning a career as a veterinarian.[29] She also insists on buying the kind of horse reserved for men – a spirited, dangerous paso fino (p. 151). On the other hand, Ronda is perceived by Masha to be 'conceited and spoiled' (p. 153), and she proves vulnerable to don Pedro's capitalist bribery when she agrees to renounce her tomboy values and dress as carnival queen in exchange for receiving the coveted horse (p. 225).[30] Ultimately, though, this at least partially transgressive model is not allowed to survive in the novel. In the mêlée following the carnival, she loses control of the fiery horse she had demanded, and both girl and horse are pitched down a cliff to their deaths (p. 257). This plot development contributes to the return to order that governs the novel's ending, as the woman who refused her place is conveniently erased from the landscape. Once again, a potential swan's wings are clipped.

Otaoa – 'one felt safe, with many places to hide'

Otoao – 'one felt safe, with many places to hide'
The hideout of Los Tiznados, the rebel gang, is mapped as a locus of magical power, where there still lurk the indigenous spirits routed by the island's succession of invaders. The site, whose name means 'rock among the clouds,' consists only of shacks and open areas for plotting the next raid; both access and escape are impossible, for the uninitiated, because of the treacherous mountains which have shielded it for centuries. The landscape is ominous: 'Huge boulders with strange inscriptions on them stood everywhere, so that the place had a mysterious look about it. They protruded from the ground like dolmens, with animal shapes and human faces carved on them that looked strangely alive as they stared out of the wet mist' (p. 205). Otoao had been the location of a *taíno* ball court, and the site of the last stand of this indigenous culture against the Spaniards (p. 211); and now, as the refuge of their apparent heirs Los Tiznados, both the land

---

[29] Don Pedro adamantly enforces gender norms, refusing to allow Ronda to attend veterinary school: 'There were no women veterinarians on the island – it was a career for men' (p. 151).

[30] Ronda succumbs to the pressure to dress as the Statue of Liberty and reign as carnival queen, but she does refuse to share the spotlight with a carnival king, insisting that she reign alone, thus defending her turf of independence to some degree (p. 227).

itself and the general atmosphere continue to seep with violence, as Juan Anduce narrates:

> The mist traveled through the area in huge shreds of gauze, as if the mountains had wounds in them that needed to be bandaged. In Otoao the earth was a deep red, and when it rained it seemed to bleed from every jagged hillock and abrupt crag. … Those bleeding mountains around camp made me fear our island would always remain cursed, that it would never heal.   (p. 211)

In terms of literary craft, the symbolism of this place is somewhat forced. Nonetheless, it does have its usefulness in terms of plot development, as it allows for the most stark contrast between Madame's icy formality and the dangers of the island's interior.

For the marginal Juan Anduce, the place feels like home: he notes that 'the terrain was reassuringly familiar' and that 'one felt safe, with many places to hide' (p. 211). He paints an image of a welcoming natural landscape, and a complicitous *campesino* population who 'always gave us shelter or told us where to hide' (p. 211). On the other hand, here Madame is very much an outsider. She soon contracts dysentery, and in the face of this new reality she continues to seek 'a theater or a movie house in which to dance *The Dying Swan*' (p. 212). Los Tiznados, on the other hand, tolerate her as a valuable hostage and a potential source of income (much as Dandré had done earlier). Initially, the novel seems to imply that Diamantino and Madame had fled to Otoao; but the plot reverses course as they are eventually revealed to be prisoners of the gang. Most significantly, Los Tiznados are the only figures in the novel who are immune to Madame's mystique – not only immune, but demythifying: 'they ridiculed her, and whenever they saw her dance *The Dying Swan*, they would guffaw and slap their thighs in merriment, making obscene sounds or gobbling like turkeys' (p. 218). This affront, combined with their propensity to kill innocent travelers during robberies, finally causes Madame to seek escape from Otoao, the indigenous paradise that becomes her hell.[31]

Otoao is mysterious, hidden, protected – except from the relentless eye of the Silver Hawk. Danny Dearborn, the Nordic hero who brings modern surveillance to Puerto Rico, exposes the hideout in less than twenty minutes of searching. Mapping the territory from the air, he can then turn it over to Governor Yager's army, which promptly levels it (pp. 239–40). Ferré displaces the rebellion, mentioning briefly that both Bienvenido and Diamantino narrowly escape the raid, and reconvene in 'a cafetín near Arecibo' (p. 240), but as a source of power

---

31 Juan describes the journeys in and out of Otoao as a kind of *via purgatoria* for the ballet star: 'The trips seemed to be a kind of pilgrimage for Madame, a way to pay for her sins, for having enjoyed a privileged life' (p. 211). On the other hand, and in a most unconvincing reference, he mentions the benefits of her ballet skills in traversing the difficult terrain (p. 212); this improbable line sounds a dissonant note in the overall portrayal of Madame as a fish out of water, in the mountains of Puerto Rico's interior.

and protection, the mountaintop refuge is easily neutralized by the conquering hero from the United States.

The dancing body

The site of the body contains the novel's central paradox. Madame, the bird-like figure dancing on the points of her toes, is pulled in two different directions. On the one hand, her art calls for her to discipline her body, and this discipline involves complete sacrifice and asceticism.[32] On the other hand, this tropical place invites her to shed her tulle and surrender herself to the idea of the body as a locus of pleasure.

The transcendence sought by Madame is that which is achieved by separating the soul from the flesh, if only temporarily: 'classical ballet made the liberation of the spirit possible precisely by disciplining the body' (p. 154) through rigorous training, hunger, and celibacy. The perfect body is both born and made. Madame mercilessly enforces a dietary code among her girls in order to sculpt their bodies in her image, that of the ideal ballet body, and in this sense the Caribbean context is seen as offering a corrupting temptation: 'if someone gained a pound or two – something easy to do in these islands, where the best food is fried by the road-side in smoking black cauldrons by turbaned black women – she [Madame] would immediately call out to us: *"Vaches! How can you pretend to be dancers when you look like chateaubriands!"* ' (p. 16).[33] On the other hand, once freed from Madame's surveillance, Masha indulges her body, not only through sex but by eating freely. While expressing some relief at her liberation ('Now I'm fat and have stopped worrying about my weight' [p. 156]), the narrator still exhibits anxiety about her appearance, confessing at the novel's outset that she is 'fat and sluggish ... wearing muumuus all the time to conceal my size' (p. 6). On the other hand, according to the dictates of this novel the perfect body cannot always be acquired. Masha depicts herself as the ugly duckling to Madame's swan, because she is by nature large and awkward in comparison with her mistress's delicate body type (pp. 28, 199). Madame both signifies and establishes the feminine corporeal ideal, as her mother describes the young prodigy's natural proclivity for ballet: 'Niura was petite and finely boned. Her legs were long and her feet

[32] This image may be traced entirely to Pavlova's self-presentation quoted within Olivéroff's biography: 'There are people who think that the life of a dancer cannot but be frivolous in every respect. In reality, the dancer's profession and a life of frivolity are incompatible. If a dancer lets herself go – if she does not exercise upon herself an iron-like control – she simply cannot go on dancing. She must sacrifice herself to her art' (p. 59). And later: 'People ask me why I do not marry. The answer is very simple. I believe that a true artist must sacrifice herself to her art – absolutely. It is forbidden her to live a life such as most women enjoy' (p. 61).

[33] Masha also narrates the tragedy of fellow dancer María Volkonsky, who commits suicide in despair after gaining ten pounds and facing the wrath of Madame (p. 19).

were beautifully arched. She had a great affinity with birds, quick, darting movements and a light step. The rich black silk of her sleeves made the long, tapered
fingers of her hands look even more delicate' (pp. 38–9). Other female body
types, by comparison, are seen throughout the novel as either weak or clumsy.
Identity is imposed entirely by the physical container. In this sense, Madame
strives to surround herself with a flock of young swans who look like her, who
will dance in her footsteps. She is as much a perpetuating agent of hegemony as
the capitalist enterprise, and the girls chafe under her control, even as they strive
to conform physically to her image.

Celibacy is another ruthlessly enforced rule of the dancer's community.
Dancers – male or female – are warned not to 'let your heart get under your
feet' (p. 50), as the body is turned away from pleasure and towards sacrifice.
Ironically, Madame as a young dancer used her body as a mechanism for gaining
financial security, when she engaged in a daring ménage-à-trois with Dandré and
his friend, the handsome Prince Kotschubei. Referring to this as the time that 'the
Eleusinian spirit took hold of us,' Madame describes this to Masha nostalgically
as a different kind of transcendence: 'I felt wonderfully loose and relaxed as I
floated above both my lovers, light as a dragonfly' (p. 106). Nonetheless, the days
of sleeping her way to the top are now behind her, and she and Dandré maintain a
filial relationship which allows her to dedicate herself entirely to the sublimation
of the dance.[34] By the time of the troupe's arrival in Puerto Rico, the girls have
learned to view her as 'pure as snow, unsullied by the mud of sex and betrayal'
(p. 23) – in other words, her body is imaged to match the artificiality of her frilly
white costumes.[35]

Homoeroticism, on the other hand, offers an intriguing and safe outlet for the
expression of desire. Around her, Madame creates an environment of adoration
that blends admiration with physical attraction. As Masha narrates: 'The girls
and I were constantly pampering her. We would brush her hair, rub Pond's cold
cream on her face, massage her feet. Once a woman has experienced the soft-
ness of another woman's caresses, the delicate fingertips like silk buds on her
skin – even if it's an *amitié en rose* – how can she ever go back to loving a man?'
(p. 23). While most of the expressions of homoerotic desire are directed towards
rather than emanating from Madame, Masha narrates at length one scene where
Madame seems also drawn to the temptation of lesbian desire:

> She bourréed next to me during Chopin's lyric arpeggios, and suddenly she
> leaned forward during an arabesque and her hand brushed my breast. It could

[34] Madame confides to Masha that even when she and Dandré had had a sexual relationship she was unable to 'experience any womanly pleasure,' because of the size of his masculine
body relative to her little-bird figure; nonetheless, their relationship continued to function as a
source of security, both financial and emotional (p. 107).

[35] The dancer's body must also be womb-less. Madame once became pregnant but under-
went an abortion that made her sterile (p. 106), and Masha's maternal drive awakens only after
she has left the troupe.

have been unwittingly, but I felt a shudder of delight rush through me. Madame always made it a point not to touch any of us or let us touch her. ... Her inaccessibility was part of her mystique, and we accepted the taboo without questioning it. For some reason, on the day of our rehearsal she broke her own rule.

The caress surprised me. Maybe I was wrong all along and Madame could love me! (pp. 19–20)

Homosexual desire is more openly embraced by the male dancers in the novel. The fictional Novikov picks up an 'ephebe' at the Governor's reception (pp. 62–3), and at the end of the novel pairs off with a trapeze artist (p. 223); and Madame's mother narrates in graphic detail her version of the real-life Vaslav Nijinsky's love affair with director Serge Diaghilev (pp. 49–50). Female eroticism, on the other hand, is primarily confined to caresses, and desire conflated with the more general adoration that Madame inspired in and required of her girls.

The ardent defense of their homosocial territory lies at the root of the girls' jealousy of Diamantino. Drawn to the irresistible passion of both his politics and his smoldering Latin charm, Madame abandons her own ethos of bodily domination in order to surrender herself to hetero-erotic desire. Physically, Diamantino is the symbolic incarnation of Puerto Rico itself, as fascinating as 'everything else in his baroque, tropical paradise' (p. 81) – he is, in essence, tropicality masculinized, and Madame succumbs at first contact. As Masha observes, 'I could tell she felt powerfully attracted to him because of the dark circles under his eyes and the shadow of a beard on his cheeks' (p. 69). When Masha later spies on their lovemaking, she is consumed with jealousy – but whether this jealousy is based on her own attraction to Diamantino or her desire for Madame is left ambiguous. Significantly, however, her description of the scene focalizes only Madame's nakedness ('a deliberate address to the eyes, a command to envelop and bring close in a consuming embrace' [p. 134]), implying that homoerotic desire lies at the heart of Masha's (and the other girls') resentment of Diamantino's intrusion.

Masha too has an offstage body, as she discovers in the novel. She gives the impression that she only knew her body as a dancing tool, until her encounter with Juan Anduce in Puerto Rico. Once there, Juan decides that he will 'take the Russian fortress by storm' (p. 204), and eventually she does yield physically to his advances. Nonetheless, it is clear that the attraction to Madame would have been stronger than her desire for Juan, had Madame herself not ordered Masha to transfer her loyalty to him.[36] And in the novel's final scene, the pregnant Masha and the aging Madame sit on a bench in Central Park, and Masha admits that the homosocial bond was in fact stronger than her marriage: 'I was going to tell her ... that now I understood perfectly why she'd been willing to go with Diamantino to the ends of the earth, because I, too, had fallen in love, with Juan. But I would

---

[36] In explaining her decision to stay behind when the troupe left Puerto Rico, Masha admits that 'I stayed because Madame ordered me to. I was obeying her for the last time' (p. 254).

have been lying. I had never loved anyone as Madame had loved Diamantino. Except her; I had loved *her* much more' (p. 262).[37]

This confession may be read as the triumph of the artistic connection over the traditional women's role of marriage and family. But more convincingly, given the context of the novel, it may be seen as an admission of the stronger appeal of the gynocentric society created on the stage. Throughout the story, Madame remains the beloved who lies just beyond her lovers' grasp, and the girls all suffer the torments of unrequited passion.[38] Given the primacy of this bond, Madame's yielding to carnal passion betrays the girls as much as it betrays her artistic vows, and Masha's decision to marry and remain in Puerto Rico must also be read as failure, as the renouncing of her life's passion in accordance with the wishes of her beloved.

The dancing body, then, is primarily homosocial, homoerotic, and divorced from issues of fertility. It is a vehicle which must be honed in order for the soul to leave it temporarily and achieve the transcendence of artistic superiority. Its calls for pleasure – either gustatory or carnal – lead only away from the stage.

On the other hand, the novel does present a tantalizing counter-site to the dancing body, in the guise of references to Isadora Duncan, Madame's real-life American contemporary who is today recognized as the founder of modern dance. Duncan presents an alternative embodiment of art, distinct from the disciplined and artificial formality of classical ballet. The novel contains several references to Duncan's rising fame, and Madame's scorn of this upstart brand of bodily expression; her role in the novel should be interpreted as one of tantalizing possibility, a potential vision of the body's freedom to express its desire.

The first reference to Pavlova's American counterpart appears early in the novel, when Masha echoes Madame's disdain of her rival's corporeal freedom:

> Madame was much stricter than the American dancer Isadora Duncan, who at that time was prancing around the world's stages clad in a semi-transparent tunic. It was very difficult to accuse Madame of being a 'loose woman,' as the press often did with the American. ... Isadora Duncan's art ... was the result of improvisation; her dancing was far from the grueling discipline of the Imperial Ballet, and Madame always saw her as an amateur.   (p. 31)

Later in the novel, the rebellious Ronda confronts Madame more directly with the contrast between the two dance styles, evincing her obvious admiration for

---

[37] Notable also is the reference to Sappho, the Greek poet often cited for her descriptions of homosocial or homoerotic desire; according to Masha she describes desire as both contagious and crippling. Masha adds, referring to her own adoration of her mistress, 'Pity the blow, which I had received from Madame but could never return in kind, so that I was condemned to see her harnessed to Diamantino Márquez like a swan to a ballroom tiger' (p. 184).

[38] See Masha's observation early in the novel about the girls' adoration of Madame; her exclamation recalls the expressions of the courtly love tradition throughout Western history: 'Like the rest of the girls in our company, I could have kissed the ground my mistress walked on, dragged myself over a bed of hot coals or needles of ice just to be near her' (p. 5).

the dance that seemed to liberate rather than confine the female form: ' "Why don't you dance barefoot, Madame, instead of with your feet bound like Chinese women? It would make you much closer to nature." And when Madame laughed and insisted she was wrong, that classical ballet made the liberation of the spirit possible precisely by disciplining the body, the girl answered: "Isadora's art is far more advanced than yours" ' (p. 154).

A look at the life and art of Isadora Duncan reveals that she indeed created new inroads for women in both arenas. Rather than following Madame's path of handing her career over to masculine direction, Duncan apparently managed her own tours, thus creating her own geographic and expressive path. She openly had several lovers, and overcame the womb-lessness of Madame's stage world, by bearing two illegitimate children. For a clearer picture of her cultural signifi-cance as public female body, we turn to the illuminating cultural study by Ann Daly, *Done into Dance: Isadora Duncan in America*. In her book, Daly attempts to situate Duncan along similar parameters to those we have used in assessing Madame's role within *Death of a Swan*, as a woman negotiating her identity in particular contexts. 'One of the original "liberated" women' (Daly, p. ix), Duncan created an intentionally provocative style of movement that was intended to free the female body from corsets and toe shoes, and to connect with rather than transcend embodied experience. According to Ann Daly's cultural analysis of Duncan's impact, the famous dancer's body may be read as a cultural map of her time: 'with Duncan, the dancing body became a conspicuous participant in America's social, cultural, and political life. It became a place where contested ground – nation, Woman, culture, self, race, art – was negotiated quite explicitly' (p. 5). In contrast to the learned and repeated routines of Madame's *Dying Swan*, Duncan offered, in Daly's words, 'the illusion of spontaneous freedom' (p. 19).[39] Duncan intentionally furthered this impression, stating in her biography that she strove to reject the constraints of traditional ballet: 'This stiff and commonplace gymnastics which [the ballet teacher] called dancing only disturbed my dream. I dreamed of a different dance' (pp. 21–2).

Ronda's assertion that Duncan's dance style was 'more advanced' than Madame's undermines the novel's surface reading. Ferré, through Masha, appears to admire Madame's sacrifices in pursuit of the perfecting of bodily expression; but the dancing background figure of Duncan implies that there were other paths, to which Madame remained obstinately blind.

---

[39] According to Daly, 'It was important that audiences imagine Duncan to be free from technical training, even from choreographic preparation, for she embodied a vision of sponta-neity and complete freedom, born of 'Nature.' That was a large part of her appeal for a genera-tion of Americans whose ambivalence toward modernism left them longing for things simpler, purer, more seemingly "authentic" ' (p. 75). Daly also talks about the constant comparisons that critics drew between Pavlova and Duncan, when the two diametrically different performers simultaneously toured the United States in 1910. She cites an interview with Pavlova, where the Russian dancer averred, 'I think that my work is harder than that of Isadora Duncan. You see, she never has to get up and dance on her toes, and I do' (quoted in Daly, p. 75).

In one key episode, however, Madame does free her dancing body from its practiced constraints. In a village near Otoao, far from any theater or stage, she observes 'a group of people dancing an atonal, rhythmic dance of African origin,' and she allows her body to respond to the drumbeats in its own fashion. In the words of Juan Anduce:

> For years Madame had danced in pink tights and frothy tutus in deference to the formal etiquette of the czar's court, but now she burst out from all that as from a silk cocoon. She took off her toe shoes and concentrated on the rhythm of the drums. She danced wildly, whips of hair flailing around her. It was as if she were possessed by the spirits summoned by the drums. She choreographed a new ballet to them, which she said she would dance in the next town.
>
> (pp. 216–17)

This daring display of bodily freedom approximates the novel's descriptions of Duncan's style, barefoot and spontaneous.[40] Indeed, this is perhaps the protagonist's most attractive moment, as she demonstrates openness to transculturation and to a broader conceptualization of Art. The moment repeats itself at the height of the carnival celebration, as discussed earlier. However, upon her return to San Juan, Madame immediately dons her toe shoes and takes up her Imperial Ballet School choreography, as she returns to her silk cocoon. Ferré's own stance towards the female staged body thus remains ambiguous.

Conclusion

The frame of *Flight of the Swan* offered promise for the original exploration of female autonomy. The gynocentric space of the stage created an alternative social structure, a kind of laboratory where society could be restructured according to a new set of rules. The spotlight on the female body allowed for an examination of issues of spectacle and performance. Additionally, the concept of Russians on tour in the Caribbean opens up possibilities for situations of encounter and negotiation. Nonetheless, the author opts not to allow the characters to confront these questions. Madame remains locked in a loveless embrace with the corrupt and controlling Dandré, turning her back on Diamantino even before his murder. Instead of the transcendence she sought to embody in her trademark dance, she remains firmly anchored, for she and Dandré have become 'two trees whose trunks had grown into each other' (p. 233). Masha's founding of San Juan's own Imperial Ballet School seems equally backward-looking, a refusal to relinquish the ties that bound her to Madame's servitude. Puerto Rican culture is barred

---

40 It should be noted that Isadora Duncan herself rejected jazz and ragtime as 'this deplorable modern dancing, which has its roots in the ceremonies of African primitives' (quoted in Daly, p. 114); thus Madame's symbolic incursion into the African heritage of Puerto Rico should not be interpreted as imitative of Duncan's specific style or cultural ideals.

from the new Academy. The school may be located in 'an old house, with several wrought-iron balconies that opened onto the shady Plaza de Armas' (p. 4), but the culture constructed and communicated within those walls is unchanged from the one learned years earlier at the disciplining hands of Madame. At the close of the novel's penultimate chapter, Masha eulogizes Madame as the architect of spaces for women's actualization: 'Today, Madame's memory is revered on the island. With her money, several gymnasiums were built for schoolchildren, as well as ballet academies; our Russian Dance Academy is one of them. Most important, she gave many young women the opportunity to become professionals, so they could fly on their own' (p. 259).[41] However, the girls are still encased in 'yards and yards of white tulle ... and two dozen diamanté wings delicately wired' (p. 260), and they still bind their feet in toe shoes. The question of whether the swans can fly, and to where, remains unanswered, as both Madame and Masha ultimately opt for rootedness.

[41] Masha also states at the novel's opening that her dance academy gives young men and women 'self-respect and a sense of who they are' (p. 4); this assertion remains unsubstantiated, however, since through such training Masha, and Madame herself, continue to rely on others for a sense of who they are.

5

In the Garden: Sefchovich's *Demasiado amor*

Introduction

Already well known for her sociological essays on Mexican history and feminism as well as literary studies, Sara Sefchovich gained the immediate attention of the literary community when her first novel, *Demasiado amor* (1990), was awarded the Premio Agustín Yáñez. The novel topped bestseller lists, going through several reprintings during the years immediately following its publication, was reissued by Alfaguara in 2001, and renewed its popularity when its cinematic adaptation was released in 2002 (directed by Ernesto Rimoch). Sefchovich's subsequent novels, *La señora de los sueños* (1993) and *Vivir la vida* (2000), have fared less well in the popular arena but have nonetheless furthered critical interest in her treatment of the confining spaces traditionally constructed for women, and these characters' creative responses to the restriction of their movements. *Demasiado amor* interweaves the two discourses of a single narrator, as a woman both keeps a personal erotic journal and sends letters to her sister. In alternating segments within each chapter, the two narratives begin asynchronously but then overtake each other, intertwining in order to offer mutually illuminating first-person insights into Beatriz's professional and personal explorations.[1]

The geographic scope of the two narrations sets up an immediate dialectic. The first part of each chapter, the personal memoir addressed to the unnamed male lover, creates verbal maps of an impossibly extensive geographical area, as the two travel through dozens of Mexican cities and towns, experiencing the food, customs, politics, and people of the country's present as well as its history. All of these forays into the national territory, chronicling an orgy of sensorial perceptions commingled with the discovery of sexual pleasure, take place during the weekends, and as we shall see, are written largely in the second person. In contrast, the more prosaic letters to her sister – forming the second part of each chapter – chronicle the narrator's weekday life, an office secretary by day and, gradually, a sex worker by night. In these letters, the narrator operates within restricted spatial limits, as she wears a routine path from her apartment to her two workplaces: her office, and the Vips café where she picks up her 'clients.' The artistry of this novel lies in the way the style of the two narratives mirrors and reinforces their spatial mapping. In the sections dedicated to the lover, Sefchovich

---

[1]   Alicia del Campo offers an interesting geographic metaphor for the act of reading the parallel narrations; she concludes that the reader becomes a 'lector "fronterizo" que debe transitar la ambigua línea que separa ambos textos para vislumbrar un sentido total' (p. 65).

creates a poetic litany of phrases through lyrical imagery, anaphora, conjoined clauses, and chaotic enumerations to convey a vertiginous onslaught of sensorial impressions. On the other hand, the letters to the protagonist's sister take on a chatty and commonplace tone, asking the usual mundane questions-without-response that punctuate everyday epistolary discourse. One narrative addresses the intricate cultural identity of Mexico and the joy of erotic extravagance, while the other worries about money, boyfriends, weight and appearance, and the future. One discourse celebrates an apparent freedom of movement, while the other strains against its moorings. This dual narration functions to question, from the outset, the possibilities of female nomadism as a solution for women's spatial and sexual restriction.

Sefchovich's popular novel has been discussed by various critics, particularly in terms of its portrayal of, and confrontation of, Mexican history through the narrator's chronicle of her travels; studies by Alicia del Campo, Javier Durán, and Norma Vega, for example, explore this aspect of the novel.[2] Other critics have focused on various aspects of gender and ethnicity, such as Sandra Messinger Cypess's analysis of issues of Jewish identity in this novel.[3] In relation to our current discussion, the most interesting study to date is the doctoral dissertation of Felicia Fahey, entitled 'Remaking Place: National Space in Late Twentieth-Century Latin American Fiction' (2001).[4] This thesis, which considers works by Luis Rafael Sánchez, Alina Diaconú, and Mario Vargas Llosa as well as Sefchovich, analyzes the search for the creation of new spaces within the trope of the traveling writer. Her study in many ways can serve as a foundation for the present discussion, in its reading of the protagonist's lack of spatial autonomy as the key to the failure of her nomadism: as in Ferré's *Flight of the Swan*, while the female protagonist appears to embrace a celebratory and free-ranging movement across a boundless geographical territory, in fact her sexual and territorial journeys are mapped entirely by a controlling male figure, thus allowing her movement only within areas that are defined and interpreted for her.

However, Fahey's analysis and mine lead us to different interpretations of the novel's ambiguous ending. At the end of the novel, the protagonist simultaneously becomes disenchanted with her erotic and cultural explorations, and invites her lover to break off the relationship; at the same time, she quits her office job and restructures her prostitution enterprise, re-creating within her own

    2   Alicia del Campo, 'Reterritorializando lo mexicano desde lo femenino en el contexto neoliberal: *Demasiado amor* de Sara Sefchovich' (1995); Javier Durán, 'Narrar la nación: (Des)Construyendo el imaginario nacional en *Demasiado amor* de Sara Sefchovich' (1997); Norma Vega, 'Re-Inscribing the Nation under the Global: Mexican Narrative Perspectives after 1968' (1998).
    3   Sandra Messinger Cypess, 'Love Preserves: Ethnicity and Desire in the Narratives of Sara Sefchovich' (2004).
    4   Fahey's chapter on Sara Sefchovich was also published in article form, entitled '(Un)Romancing Mexico: New Sexual Landscapes in Sara Sefchovich's *Demasiado amor*' (2001).

apartment a pre-verbal *chora* environment, reminiscent of a Boschian 'Garden of Earthly Delights'[5] with carnal pleasure as its only object – the sex without the work. Fahey reads this as a victorious ending, in that the character has defined her own realm, populated with both men and women of her own choosing, as well as natural elements and other sensory extravagances. According to Fahey, the narrator's creation of an alternative spatial practice constitutes a victory, as she opts to elide herself into the insterstitial spaces of the city (p. 169). The character does, indeed, create a space of her own, sheltered from the power structures that made other places in Mexico ultimately uninhabitable. However, Fahey reads Lefebvre into this novel in a different way than I do. From the perspective of freedom of movement, the narrator of *Demasiado amor* in fact opts to delimit her own territory. She withdraws inward, creating a kind of infinite space – it seems very large, and the removal of the glass from the windowpane contributes to this sense of an existence without horizons – but in fact she gradually stops moving. The steady deterioration of her mobility is a voluntary one, but in terms of her power to navigate, it has decidedly pessimistic overtones. In fact, the novel's end may be read as entropic, in its portrayal of an inexorable ebbing of energy. In the final chapters, Beatriz bids farewell to both her lover and her sister, and lays down her pen. Her self-silencing reads like a suicide note, as she bequeaths her writings to her sister's daughter. Cynthia Duncan, in her study 'Mad Love: The Problematization of Gendered Identity and Desire in Recent Mexican Women's Novels' (2000), interprets the final chapters as a descent into madness – which is not an uncommon interpretation of a woman's retreat to the *chora* space. But from a spatial perspective, we can read instead that the protagonist has consciously accepted the futility of movement. In contrast to Aurora's accessing of a *chora* in Allende's *Retrato en sepia*, as a source of strength with which she can return empowered to the continued negotiation of a place of her own, Beatriz here locks herself into the *chora*. In the end, the geoplot grinds to a full stop.

All readings of the novel concur that the problem with the narrator's exploration of Mexico – her at first delighted inventories of its color, sound, and taste – originates in the fact that the country is experienced primarily in the second person. The narrator does not explore, but rather accompanies and serves as accessory to a male traveler. From the novel's outset, verbs in the 'tú' form punctuate the narrative; the phrase 'me llevaste' appears four times in the first paragraph, alongside other second-person verbs of physical coercion (p. 11), and this critical sequence is reiterated at several other moments in the novel, with particular repetition of the phrase of incessant motion, 'me llevaste y me trajiste, me subiste y me bajaste' (pp. 11, 32, 42). These verbs (including also 'me hiciste,' 'me enseñaste,' and most notably 'me arrastraste') not only imply a fatigue in response to endless movement, but they also reflect the narrator's

---

5   This and future references are to the painting 'Garden of Earthly Delights,' by Dutch artist Hieronymus Bosch (c. 1504); I postulate a link between the images depicted in that painting and the environment painted verbally by Sefchovich in the novel's final chapters.

passivity. She is quite distinct from the nomadic female character that has offered a positive archetype in other novels by women; on the contrary, she eventually admits the disillusionment of 'sólo seguir y seguir' (p. 213). The quest itself is represented in the second person, 'como si tuvieras una deuda pendiente con el país que fue éste hace cincuenta, hace cuarenta años' (p. 12). And finally, the erotic exploration too is represented largely as a second-person endeavor – 'me tuviste desnuda' (p. 17), 'me enseñaste' (p. 18), 'me acariciaste, me abrazaste y me hiciste el amor' (p. 51). Like Mexico, the narrator's own body – her 'geography closest in' (Rich, p. 212) – is thoroughly mapped by her lover.[6]

The memoir is not written as a diary, reflecting the narrator's progressive realizations, but rather as an extended *post facto* reflection, presumably written around the time of the final letters written to her sister, near the novel's end. This temporal positioning means that the narrator is writing from the point of awareness, when her fantasies of happiness through exploration have already disintegrated. From this vantage point, in the novel's opening sentence the narrator lays blame squarely upon her lover: 'Por tu culpa empecé a querer a este país. Por tu culpa, por tu culpa, por tu grandísima culpa. Porque tú me llevaste y me trajiste, me subiste y me bajaste' (p. 11).[7] By the memoir's end, the accusatory tone has not abated, as the narrator writes – but still does not dare to say aloud – that 'tú no te diste cuenta, tú nunca supiste nada de mí' (p. 207). However, our discussion in terms of autonomy – where is she, who put her there and with what authority? – must recognize that, from the outset, the narrator has opted for her position of follower. The novel's second and third chapters detail the initiation of their romance: he sits alone in the Vips café, and she moves to sit with him. He ignores her, but she unquestioningly follows him out of the restaurant, into his car, and to his hotel. Even so, she blames him for her paralysis of will: 'No sé qué imán tenías que me quedé petrificada' (p. 16). Within this chapter, the narrator repeatedly reiterates her positionality, using the phrase 'detrás de ti' twice, 'conmigo detrás' twice, and 'atrás de ti' once (p. 17). She claims a loss of autonomy as she is subjected to forces beyond her own will: 'Y todo el mundo me empezó a dar vueltas a mí' (p. 17). Desire now chains her to this anonymous lover, but always in the position of accessory, as object rather than subject: 'Sentí miedo porque en esas horas contigo se había tejido dentro de mí la cadena que me ataría a ti por siempre, una que subía por el pecho y bajaba por el vientre para salir entre mis piernas. Me había convertido en una condenada que se dejaba arrastrar y que sentía placer porque el metal le rozaba todas sus partes' (p. 19). Throughout the novel, the narrator prefers to use impersonal verbs or second-person verbs to explain her subordinate position, and even by the novel's end she has not been able to alter her passivity: 'te odié porque por tu culpa olvidé mis sueños, por

---

[6]   This representation of female eroticism stands in marked contrast to those of Allende, Restrepo, and Mastretta, examined elsewhere in this study.

[7]   Several subsequent passages also reiterate the words 'Porque' and 'Por,' harking back to this issue of blame assigned on the novel's first page.

tu culpa me olvidé yo de mí' (p. 210). Since this narrative is written after their breakup, we are meant to understand that she never does acknowledge her own complicity in her 'arrastramiento'; and even when she opts to end the relationship, she does so by bringing the lover to her apartment, her place of sex work, knowing that this will induce him to leave her rather than her having to leave him. Who put her there? She put herself in his restaurant booth, in his room, and in his bed; along with this erotic bonding, she put herself into his car, with his maps and his quests. These issues of autonomy complicate the surface reading of the text as one of Mexican male dominance, and bring to the surface the issues of the complicitous victim who, having other options, nonetheless chooses to become 'encadenada' and 'arrastrada.'

In fact, passivity is the fundamental characteristic that connects the two facets of the narrator – the decadent weekend reveler and the plain office worker/sex worker. In the novel's first letter, the narrator has just said goodbye to her sister, who leaves with their life savings to lay the groundwork for their grand plan: to buy a guest house in Italy, there to live adventurous and happy lives by the sea. Material limitations force their separation: one sister will strike off to set up the new venture, while the other will stay behind to raise money both to send to Italy and, eventually, to purchase her own airfare. Yet the narrator's passivity is immediately apparent; after seeing her sister off, she does not even leave the airport for two hours, and then she takes up the position that she as narrator will occupy throughout the story – she sits by the window, in her apartment, imagining the life of her sister. From the outset, the narrator's stasis is contraposed to her sister's movement: 'Mientras escribo esta carta, tú vas por las nubes. Vas cruzando el mar y quién sabe en qué estás pensando' (p. 15). As she allows her sex work increasingly to replace her office work, she adopts the same kind of secretarial or service role in the bedroom that she played in the office; thus whether in the bed of her lover or her clients, the narrator does not assume agency. Both facets of this narrator opt consistently for the paths of least resistance, of least risk, and of safety in the shadow of another's plan.

At the novel's conclusion, the narrator becomes disenchanted with Mexico, with the sexual adventures, and with the character of her lover. Her chaotic catalogues of Mexico's handicrafts and festivals become instead postmodern accumulations, simulacra of actual history and experience. In a similar vein, the narrator's vicarious travels are exposed as the simulacrum of agency. The novel's most intriguing ambiguity then lies in its ending: as she lays down her pen and redesigns her apartment into a fantastic Garden of Earthly Delights, is she for the first time assuming agency, or for the last time resigning it?

Mexico in the second person – 'imaginando que la felicidad era eso, que la felicidad estaba en los caminos'; 'en todos los lugares hicimos el amor'; 'así es, dijiste, este país'

Several critical studies of this work have focused on the breadth of the national exploration that the first half of each chapter weaves for the reader. In a creative and expressive syntax, Sefchovich constructs verbal postcards of the Mexican geographic and cultural landscape, through the montage of images recorded in the narrator's personal memoir. Hundreds of place names and topographies form the skeleton of this national portrayal, an attempt to capture 'el espíritu del país' (p. 80), and this central armature is fleshed out with images of the people, their food, their celebrations, and the agricultural and artistic products of different regions. Throughout these dizzying catalogues, Sefchovich privileges all five senses of experience: the narrator notices the changes in natural lighting at different times of day (p. 46), celebrates the rich musical heritage of Mexico (pp. 115–16), enjoys a variety of regional foods (pp. 48–9, 99), and notices the smell of candles pervading different towns (p. 39); but primarily the tactile experience is privileged, most notably through the recurrent imagery of water. The following passage serves as one of the best-wrought examples of the vivid sensory imagery that occurs throughout the first forty-two of the novel's fifty chapters; it also serves as a notable representation of the author's technique of encapsulating the entire country through corporeal sensation, represented with a circular syntax that emphasizes repetition and rhythm:[8]

> Me acuerdo cuando te dio por nadar y nos metimos desnudos en cuanto lugar de agua se cruzó por los caminos. Así fue en Montebello, escondiéndonos si alguien pasaba por allí, así fue en Zempoala envolviéndonos después en una sola toalla, así entramos en el mar gris del Golfo, en el mar bravo de Baja California, en el mar azul de Cozumel y en el mar inmenso del Pacífico. Así nos detuvimos en mil aguas por los caminos: ríos y estanques, apantles y albercas, gélidos o hirvientes, sucios o transparentes en Tepoztlán, en Matehuala, en Comanjilla, en Chiapas y en Mazatlán. Me acuerdo de las aguas en la cascada de San Antón y en las cascadas de San Miguel. Un día me enseñaste una cascada artificial que un cacique de Juriquilla mandaba prender cuando quería escenario, otros días me llevaste a los lagos del Valle de Bravo, Pátzcuaro y Zirahuén. Fuimos al ojo de agua de Nu Tun Tun y al de Misol-Ha, a un cenote adentro de una cueva en Valladolid, a los ríos enormes que corren por Tabasco,

---

8   For Fahey, this emphasis on multi-sensorial perception unwrites the traditional romance in which 'the travelling protagonist makes himself master-of-the-land. ... Instead Beatriz ... anchors the couple's experience of place in the body, thus indulging the senses' ('Remaking Place,' p. 156). However, I would argue that since the narrator blends 'tú' and 'este país' so inseparably, neither her sexual experiences nor her geographic encounters allow her to experience any of the places with authenticity. She remains in the passenger seat, enjoying the trip but not discovering anything essential about her own geography-closest-in, about Mexico, or about her lover himself. The novel's final chapters reveal that she was seeing and experiencing through a romantic haze that was self-generated and distorting.

a los riachuelos sin nombre que corren por Morelos y también a los canales
de Xochimilco cubiertos de lirio. Me acuerdo de un camino de agua detrás
de las ruinas de Palenque y de un cenote en Chichén-Itzá. Me acuerdo de un
arroyo bordeado de árboles en San Miguel y de una fuente llena de monedas
en Guanajuato. Me acuerdo de las aguas heladas de la alberca de Santa María,
de las gardenias en la alberca de Fortín, del vapor de la alberca en Comanjilla,
del agua tibia de Tasquillo, del agua sulfurosa de Cuautla, del chorrito que salía
de la regadera en Nautla, de la tina enorme que daba masaje en Cuernavaca.
    ¿Te acuerdas de la lluvia que inundó nuestro cuarto durante dos días en
Nautla? ¿Te acuerdas de las aguas que tomamos en vasitos muy pequeños
en Tehuacan? ¿Te acuerdas de las aguas amarillas de San José? ¿Y del agua
que sacamos de un pozo hondísimo para echarle al motor del coche afuera de
Guanajuato? ¿Y de todas las tinas y regaderas en las que nos bañamos y de
todos los excusados por donde corrieron nuestras aguas antes y después de
hacer el amor?   (pp. 42–3)

This passage, and many others, avail themselves of the depiction of opposite
extremes in order to emphasize the variety of this barrage of images and experiences. As Fahey has observed, these sections of the novel recall Western literary
traditions that link the geography of the fatherland to sensorial exploration: 'The
travelogue therefore makes recourse to the most powerful trope in romantic narratives, metaphorical triangulation, or the process by which the amorous identity of
the couple is sedimented in space' ('Remaking Place,' p. 155). And alongside this
geographic 'incorporation' ('Remaking Place,' p. 156) occurs the recollection of
erotic experience, firmly tied to places, in a style that appears to arouse as powerfully in the retelling of it as in its original performance:

Y todos esos días y todas esas noches me llevaste a pasear, me hablaste, me
acariciaste, me abrazaste y me hiciste el amor. El amor una y otra vez y tres
veces más. El amor parados, sentados y de pie. El amor vestidos, desnudos y
dormidos. El amor con los dedos, con la lengua, con todo tu cuerpo. El amor
de día, de noche, en el silencio, en la luz y en la oscuridad. El amor con frío,
con agua, con lluvia, con calor. El amor en el coche, en la tierra, en el piso,
debajo de la mesa y junto al espejo del tocador. El amor así y como sea, el
amor.   (p. 51)

However, as mentioned earlier and as seen in the above passage, most of the active
verbs appear in the second person, attributing the power of movement and action
to the lover, and representing the narrator as receptacle ('dentro de mi cuerpo
habitaste tú' [p. 18]). In addition to the verbs of movement ('me llevaste,' 'me
arrastraste') she reiterates verbs of telling and teaching: 'me dijiste' (p. 97), 'me
diste' (pp. 99–100), 'te detuviste en cada poblado y en cada rincón para expli-
carme, enseñarme, comprarme y regalarme' (p. 132), 'me compraste' (repeated
twelve times, pp. 133–5). One of the few times that she expresses agency is in the
relinquishment of it: 'entre tus manos había perdido toda voluntad' (p. 23). The
narrator is not only a recipient, but a passive and uncomprehending one; six times

in the aforementioned section she repeats 'Y cuando yo te pregunté para qué ...',
but his responses never address that question (pp. 134–8).[9] Unprotestingly she
receives his sexual attention, his onslaught of national images and experiences,
and his endless, even suffocating gifts. This passive role is from the outset an
indicator that this journey of discovery will ultimately prove disillusioning. Like
Madame in Ferré's *Flight of the Swan* but unlike the other female protagonists
discussed in this study, this narrator records a journey that was mapped for her
('por verte extender el mapa y buscar el camino' [p. 54]); she takes pleasure
neither in movement for its own sake, as does the female nomad archetype, nor
in charting her own parallel path, as will the protagonist of Mastretta's *Mal de
amores*. Instead, even at the writing moment, the moment of supposedly enlightened reflection, she continues to assign agency to her lover.

One geographic place merits particular analysis because of its frequent recurrence within the place-name inventories. On at least seven different occasions,
the narrator mentions with reverence the town of Monte Albán, an archeological
site in Oaxaca that has been identified as the ancient capital of the Zapotec civili-
zation. The narrator describes this place as unique, and as a site of origins: 'Pero
ninguna piedra, ninguna ruina, ningún lugar de entre todos los lugares fue como
Monte Albán, el ombligo del mundo, el centro de todos los centros, el lugar más
bello y el más sagrado de la creación' (p. 44; see also pp. 54, 62, 80, 165). In her
analysis of this novel, Alicia del Campo also notes the recurrent references to
this site, and comments on it as a 'centro mítico heterotópico,' comparing it to
'la vagina, como segunda metáfora fronteriza'; together, these two sites create
a ceremonial center for the protagonist (p. 73). Within a different narrative, this
place might be seen potentially as a source of empowerment, a site where the
female narrator might connect with a pre-Hispanic or even an atemporal sacred
space, and thus find refuge from the hegemony that contemporary Mexico exerts
over her. However, even in this place the narrator's view of the horizon is blocked
by 'tú': 'Sentados en un extreme del gran cuadrado mágico, miramos el mundo
desde el lugar donde nació. ... Tú estás en una orilla y yo en otra, pero nunca
hemos estado tan cerca. Bendito sea, Señor, por haberme dado a este hombre y
en este país' (p. 62). At the novel's close, Monte Albán becomes one more source
of blame for the narrator, as she records her resentment that, even there, her lover
was unveiling for her the Monte Albán he had already discovered, rather than

---

[9]   In contrast to the narrator's inability to find purpose in the quest, she writes that her
lover was in fact purposefully seeking his own roots, defining his own identity through particular journeys to sites that encompassed his history. She mentions his 'búsqueda' (p. 12), meetings with his friends (p. 63), his search for his origins ('mil veces me llevaste al Bajío porque
en sus huertas andabas buscando el olor de tu infancia' [p. 129]); and late in the novel she
expresses her resentment at the second-person nature of their search: 'Te detuviste demasiado
tiempo ... buscando a los fantasmas de este país y en mil otros lugares perdidos te detuviste
buscando a tus abuelos, tíos, amigos y conocidos' (p. 181). Yet the ultimate objectives of his
search, if indeed there were any, remain beyond her ken: '¿Qué andabas buscando tú por los
caminos? ¿Qué querías encontrar ...?' (p. 156).

allowing her to discover it for herself (p. 210).[10] Unlike Emilia in Mastretta's later novel, this female protagonist does not find any more space to roam in Mexico's past than in its present; the dominant makers of place have already reached into, and thus robbed her of, every corner of the country.

Mexico in the first person – 'este país de Dios, tan sufrido y abandonado, tan lastimado y lacerado, tan explotado'

Just as the narrator had discovered Mexico through the skin of her lover, so as their affair grows tiresome she re-visions her national territory, unwriting the exuberance of the first thirty-seven chapters and evoking instead what Fahey terms a 'dystopic rediscovery of Mexico' ('Remaking Place,' p. 157). Throughout the following five chapters, she maintains the same spiraling syntax to encompass a broad spectrum of Mexican territory and experience; but the images now appear as the negative or inverse of their initial presentations. The narrator now identifies the poor as miserable and victimized rather than merely as picturesque; she realizes that the artifacts and handicrafts she had admired are in fact postmodern simulacra mass-produced for tourists (like herself):

> descubrimos que la blusa deshilada no era de Aguascalientes sino del mercado de Tepoztlán, que el rebozo de Santa María no cabía por el aro de un anillo porque no era de seda sino de imitación, que el marco no era de plata sino de latón, el sarape no era de lana sino sintético, el mantel no era del mercado sino de una tienda, el pantalón de manta no lo hicieron los indios sino una gringa de San Miguel […]. La mesa de varas la compramos en una esquina, los cojines bordados en una boutique, los platos pintados a mano en una fábrica enorme.   (pp. 190–1)

Homogeneity and reproducibility, the hallmarks of the postmodern construction of space, now unmask the illusion of cultural specificity that the love-struck narrator had thought she was discovering. Instead, what she has seen is the Mexico that offers itself for sale, that markets itself to just the kind of spectator and consumer that she has allowed herself to become. As Lefebvre notes, 'Under neocapitalism or corporate capitalism institutional space answers to the principles of repetition and reproducibility – principles effectively hidden by semblances of creativity' (p. 354). This facsimile of authentic production, 'mimesis' for Lefebvre (p. 376), creates stability through the semblance of desire, when in fact all of the bodily sensations that have accompanied the spatial practices, while they might have been real experiences, were at the same time safe experiences, experiences which, since they were based on consciously constructed artifice, never really

---

[10] Del Campo's analogy between Monte Albán and the narrator's vagina as ceremonial centers continues to serve here, as the protagonist's discovery of erotic pleasure with her lover was apparently not matched by a similar awakening on his part. See del Campo, p. 73.

threaten the status quo. In Lefebvre's words, 'Mimesis … pitches its tent in an artificial world, the world of the visual where what can be seen has absolute priority, and there simulates primary nature, immediacy, and the reality of the body' (p. 376).

As a male-administered experience, the narrator's 'discovery' of Mexico – and, in corollary, of her own body's capacity for pleasure – merely substituted for authentic encounters. Stripped of the artifice of romance, the country is portrayed in the novel's final chapters as corrupt, polluted, emptied of both natural and human resources, plagued by natural cataclysms, human degradation, and brutal climate cycles. Even the narrator's erotic writing is, in retrospect, made trite – just another fabricated souvenir, a concrete sign that desire has been satisfied.

Early in the novel, the narrator writes: 'Y allí iba yo comprando todas las artesanías que veía, no para adornar mi casa como tú creías sino para traerme pedacitos de los lugares en donde tanto te amé' (p. 30). By the story's end, she realizes that she has created a museum of what never was, a romance that is as mass-produced, and as worthless, as the factories that churn out Mexican handicrafts. A particularly telling scene in the later chapters serves to expose the artifice of the couple's past spatial practices:

> Y entonces fue cuando me hiciste ponerme mi falda de enredo, mi blusa bordada y mi faja a la cintura y me cantaste pirecuas que decías que eran canciones de amor de Michoacán. Y me regalaste un huipil de Mecalapa todo bordado y brocado para que pareciera una virgen y un quexquémetl para que pareciera una sacerdotisa y un rebozo de dos colores azules y un collar de pescaditos para que pareciera una novia tarasca.   (p. 138)

As the male narrator dresses her up and plays that she is a virgin, a priestess, a bride, and (later in the passage) a mother, she realizes the emptiness of the roles she has been performing, and the simulacrum of the window dressing. All of this costuming should be read as analogous to the stark vision of Mexico that the novel's closing chapters present, and equally analogous to the romantic and erotic experiences in which the narrator thought she had participated; once both the national territory and she are stripped of their mimetic overlays, both are seen to be barren.

In the novel's final pages, most of the second-person verbs disappear – with the exception of the occasional accusation – as do the verbs of sensation, which are now replaced with the anaphora of the verb of realization, 'vi' (repeated nine times on p. 199, for example); as the narrator now admits, 'Y yo ahora me fijaba en todo eso, en todo. … Y yo antes no me había fijado en nada de esto, en nada' (pp. 190–1).

The dream of Italy – 'ese país desconocido y nuevo al que te has ido'; 'la casa de nuestros sueños'

One of the novel's most controlling sites is the terrain never visited by the narrator. Through the epistolary discourse that comprises the second half of each chapter, the narrator writes letters to her sister, who has left for Italy to realize the first phase of their dream. As mentioned above, they plan to establish a future for themselves by buying a guest house near the ocean in Italy; one sister leaves to begin that work, while the other stays behind to earn more money. The dream is built upon layers of spatial illusions, which have been gained from poring over travel brochures and other commercialized images of Italy. As the narrator writes, 'lo que más añoro son las horas sentadas junto a la ventana, o las horas en la banca del parque, viendo fotos y libros y soñando con islas y pueblos lejanos y con el mar' (p. 26). From the outset, the sister's freedom of movement is contrasted with the narrator's stasis, as she expresses in successive letters her loneliness, frustration, fatigue, envy, and resentment. This space of her dreams exerts as much influence over her as does her workday environment and her weekend panorama, as in her letters she imagines what her sister might be experiencing, and endeavors vicariously to participate in, even to direct, those enterprises. However, both the illusions about Italy and the implementation of 'el plan' are mired within the constraints of production, as the narrator struggles to produce the necessary capital to underwrite the dream.

The narrator's positionality is reiterated several times; her place is at a table by the window, in the place formerly occupied by maps and brochures – simulacra of Italy – and now occupied by the paper of the narrator's letters – another simulacrum of experience. Hearing only one side of the conversation, we read that the sister is making real decisions, such as which property to purchase, and while the narrator attempts to influence those decisions, her sister's physical distance lends her all decision-making power. So, when the narrator warns that buying too large a house 'nos esclavizaría' (p. 28), her sister is free to purchase it anyway, and the narrator must yield to the impotence that her fixed position, by the window, imposes upon her. In order to continue to participate vicariously in the plan, she immediately alters her view to embrace the revision that her sister has made in their mutual dream;[11] but she spends much of the rest of the novel feeding a dream that has a seemingly bottomless appetite for her wages. Her earnings, first as an office worker and then as a sex worker, do not buy her a passage to Italy, but only a role as continued supplier of capital, as she encloses money with each letter she posts.

Through her letters, the reader gains a view of what may be interpreted as successful spatial practice by the sister. With the support she gains from home,

---

[11] The narrator resignedly accepts her sister's purchase of a large house: 'Demasiado grande y demasiado vieja y demasiado derruida, pero está bien si tanto te gustó. ... Ya me estoy emocionando. ... Lo que me preocupa es que ... nos va a costar mucho dinero echarla a andar. ... En fin, decide tú. Haz lo que creas mejor' (p. 34).

she is able to buy and then to refurbish the home, to open it to interesting guests, and to construct a multi-generational family with an adoptive mother-figure, a husband, and children; she even cultivates the garden she has always dreamt of having. In marked contrast to this space of productive agency, the narrator retreads the same paths each weekday, to her twin places of work, waiting for the weekends to lend her temporary, and still delimited, mobility.

Earlier in this study we have discussed the potential of the liminal space, as a between-ness that can offer possibilities for the creation of a new, consciously constructed identity. The epistolary narrator of *Demasiado amor* identifies herself as living in a liminal state: 'No acabo de organizar mi vida sin ti. Es como si todo fuera provisional, uno de esos sábados cuando te ibas a comprar plantas y yo pasaba el día esperándote en el silencio tan sobrecogedor' (p. 25). The writer of the letters leaves her sister's room empty in Mexico, while in turn her sister sets up an empty room for her in Italy; both create spatial arrangements that signify the transitional state of their plan. And indeed, this liminal state does offer the narrator the opportunity to reinvent herself. However, her options remain constrained by the exigencies of their plan, and by the fact that until near the end of the novel's seven-year time span, the narrator cannot alter her Italian horizon. Instead, she opts to remain tied to the table by the window, and to the workplaces of bedroom and office, sending her thoughts as well as her funds across the ocean to her sister. As the novel concludes, the narrator successfully sheds both her boyfriend and her illusions of Italy: 'A veces me pregunto por qué todavía no me voy y no lo sé, hay algo aquí que aún me detiene' (p. 186). But as long as the plan is in force, as long as she defends the territory of the bedroom reserved for her in her sister's house (pp. 77, 109, 112, 140, 178), the potential of the liminal space remains unrealized.[12]

Italy is signified within the apartment by two concrete symbols. In the kitchen is posted a sign, 'No te olvides del sueño' (p. 113), that exerts vigilant control over the narrator's activity: when her boyfriend gives her a new sweater, 'estuve a punto de quedarme con él [el suéter], pero cuando vi el letrero que colgué en la cocina, el de 'No te olvides del sueño', me lo quité y se lo vendí a una compañera de la oficina. Por eso verás que el cheque de este mes es más grande' (p. 113). She thus converts a gift of affection into pure capital. The gaze of the sign – a sign that she herself had posted – enables the Italian plan, in both its real and its imagined dimensions, to contain the narrator in her assigned role and to exert coercion over her own more immediate reality.

A second and equally controlling object within the apartment, mentioned only once in the novel but serving as a spatial link to the Italian counter-space, is the small basket in which the narrator's 'clients' leave their money (p. 68). This repository for her capital functions as a pipeline that connects the narrator to her

---

[12] Gradually the narrator recognizes that she will never occupy that room in the Italian house, and that her sister can – at first temporarily, and then permanently – fill that room with other tenants and other purposes (pp. 182, 207, 209).

dream of her future; in a sense, it symbolizes the room that has been reserved for her in the Italian house. The problem with this pipeline is its relentless exigency. Throughout most of the novel, no matter how much money the narrator feeds into the basket, the sister's responses indicate the need for more. The basket is voracious and insatiable, and like the sign in the kitchen, it exercises, from Italy, coercive power directly over the most personal activities of the narrator. From Monday through Thursday she retreads continually her assigned space of productivity, working to buy a dream that takes concrete form for the sister, but that never comes closer to realization for the narrator.

Vips diner – 'solitario pero con luz, esa luz nocturna, tan exageradamente blanca, que hacía verse más sola a la poca gente que había'; 'allí me siento bien, como si tuviera compañía'

Perhaps there is no site more reproducible in Mexico than the ubiquitous Vips diner. Like many chain stores and restaurants, once one is inside, regional specificity is lost; one can be in any city and find the same dependable menu of generic and universalized foods, the same lighting and décor, the same feeling of the place. For example, within this novel the narrator, so attached to her neighborhood Vips in Mexico City, finds another one in Cuernavaca as she recovers from an abortion, seeking there the sense of familiarity that will salve her loneliness (p. 139).

The Vips café is a central yet complex site for the novel's narrative kinesis, and its function within the novel is clarified when viewed through the lens of Lefebvre's views on capitalism's structuring of space.[13] The artificiality of the Vips environment is based on two suppositions that are central to the capitalist enterprise: that customers tends towards the familiar and the recognizable, and that reproducibility is more economical than uniqueness. The narrator revisits Vips because of its successful marketing of an environment – one where different

---

[13] Viewed through such a lens, the Vips website sounds almost like a parody of itself. The 'Historia' link of www.vips.com.mx boasts about the Mexican-ness of the chain, now a Wal-Mart subsidiary but still closely identified with the nation's modernization, and also its significance as a site of important personal and professional transactions: '1964 marcó para siempre la historia de México. En ese año, una estrella anaranjada y brillante iluminó el cielo del D.F., allá por la zona norte que apenas empezaba a nacer. ... desde entonces su rojizo resplandor ha llenado de colorido y calidez a nuestra ciudad y a toda la República Mexicana. Poco a poco las estrellas se multiplicaron para formar lo que ahora es todo un firmamento: el universo de restaurantes VIPS. Desde entonces, muchas cosas han cambiado pero la calidad y la filosofía de la cadena de restaurantes más importante del país, se conserva intacta. VIPS es toda una tradición para los mexicanos. Todo el mundo ha ido a VIPS, o lo frecuenta regularmente. En sus mesas, frente a un delicioso y clásico café, se han firmado tratados, conquistado corazones, cerrado negocios, creado campañas de publicidad ...' (<www.vips.com.mx/historia. html>). The chain's slogan takes on special significance when read through the context of this novel: 'Dale sabor a tu encuentro.'

people sit comfortably and safely together, consuming inexpensive but satisfyingly familiar fare. As a meeting place, it satisfies several of the narrator's
needs. She begins to go there in order to remember more vividly her boyfriend
Sergio, who like her sister has left her to pursue his own travels. Thus the place
serves as a repository of memories that console her in the present, 'como si
tuviera compañía' (p. 34). However, Vips soon becomes the geographic hub of
her activity. On the one hand, Vips becomes the weekly pick-up spot where she
reunites every Thursday with her mysterious lover. They may travel throughout
Mexico's territory and throughout its past, glimpsing even its future, but all of
their journeys begin at Vips, thus subtly calling into question their authenticity
even from the novel's outset. More importantly, though, the Vips restaurant
becomes the purveyor of clients for the narrator's growing enterprise as a sex
worker.

While some analyses of Sefchovich's novel describe the narrator's second job
as prostitution,[14] Fahey opts in her study to use the term 'sex work,' 'in order to
signal the subversiveness of Sara Sefchovich's intervention' (p. 147). However,
there is an even stronger reason to use this term here: the consistent equation
of the narrator's sexual enterprise with her office job, and the analogous spatial
practices between Vips and her office workplace.

The continuous flow of resources to Italy requires initially that the narrator
allow the drudgery of her office work to invade her apartment, as she brings
additional typing work home in order to earn extra pay (p. 23). This invasion
of production into her space of reproduction dehumanizes her: 'Voy a la oficina
y luego vengo a la casa, como cualquier cosa y me pongo a trabajar pasando a
máquina los papeles tan aburridos que me da el jefe, pero cuando acabo no tengo
a quién contarle nada y eso es muy feo' (p. 23). Seeking some space that offers
a refuge from the relentless work, she goes to Vips. Yet the work of picking up
men and taking them back to her apartment, for pay, acquires the same sense of
drudgery that the office work involved. On several occasions, the narrator reiterates that one of the advantages of her Vips-based business was that it replaced her
former overtime work (pp. 69, 93). But in fact, it has simply replaced one kind of
service with another, and the new work is not so different from the old.

Vips in another context might be seen as a heterotopia, implying a space of
possibility in terms of unexpected encounters. At several moments in the text, the
epistolary narrator displays to her sister a verbal catalogue of the different kinds
of clients she has met, and we see that many barriers of class and background
are erased under the bright lights of the restaurant. Yet within the context of
this novel, the amalgam of customers seems as recycled as do the trite souvenir
stores of the couple's weekend travels. Instead of Vips serving as a crossroads of
society, the world is instead pulled in and reduced to the size and shape of a Vips.
Between paragraphs, in the midst of one of her catalogues of the diverse 'galanes

---

[14] See for example the studies by Elvira Sánchez-Blake (1998), Cynthia Duncan (2000),
and Anne Gebelein (n.d.).

levantados,' the narrator ends a long and tumbling sentence with the following blunt comment: 'creo que ésa es la especie que más abunda en el mundo o por lo menos en el Vips' (p. 81), revealing that Vips is now the horizon of her weekday world; and the heterotopic excitement is reduced to the four-times-reiterated phrase that encompasses her response to this variety, on the following page: 'me da igual' (p. 82).

Early in the novel the narrator complains to her sister about the repetitive path she wears, from home to the office and back again (p. 31). However, she soon creates the same monotony in her increasingly frequent trips from home to Vips and back again. As office typists are paid by the page, so the narrator is paid per customer; she becomes increasingly efficient, remarking to her sister that she can make two trips from her apartment to Vips per night (p. 79), then three or four per night (p. 102), and finally eight or nine per night (p. 177). Sex 'work,' sex 'industry,' sex 'business' is the clear implication, as the narrator chronicles her progress in selecting her clients more astutely and satisfying them more efficiently, and measures her success by how many pesos have accumulated in the basket. While contemporary critics might be tempted to read the narrator's liberated attitudes toward sexuality and her move into public space as positive – because they are in a sense transgressive, and in a sense successful – a close analysis of her spatial practice reveals otherwise.[15] As a subsidiary of the Vips enterprise,[16] she too has sacrificed authenticity for reproducibility and, therefore, increased profits. The novel's ambiguous ending does involve the simultaneous rejection of both her office space and the Vips visits, thus suggesting that she does free herself from the shackles of the wage slave – but 'in exchange for what' is more difficult to assess.

While at the outset the narrator visits Vips in a more passive way – sitting alone, seeking a kind of invisibility in that openness – she does attempt to exert some control over the place, as she grows more secure in her business. She notes that she parades through the area as she arrives, 'para echar un ojillo y para que me vean a mí' (p. 64), and that the clients then come to her, to sit next to her and transact their business deal (p. 69). Eventually, not only does the Vips commerce feed hers, but she also becomes a draw for customers, as they come there to seek out the woman about whom they have heard (p. 151). Thus the tie is cemented between her bedroom and the Vips café, now linked by capital as well as by her countless treks between the two sites.

The final analogy that ties Vips to the controlled spaces of production involves the Vips manager's demand that he receive compensation for the business that the narrator is conducting there. In contrast to the brightly lit and populated area

15 The image of the sex worker in this novel represents a clear contrast to Restrepo's inhabitants of La Catunga, who spoke repeatedly and proudly of their 'vocación' and their celebration of female sexual pleasure (see Chapter 2 of this study).

16 The narrator develops a business relationship with the employees of Vips, such that she brings in clients for them (p. 151) and they refer clients to her as well (p. 82). Her own apartment, her bedroom, thus becomes an unofficial extension of the Vips corporation.

of the restaurant, the manager forces her back into his bathroom, a place where the power relations are stark and unambiguous: 'Total que se la tuve que pagar. La dichosa comisión duró diez minutos y fue en su baño particular que estaba tan chiquito que no cabíamos más que de pie' (p. 79). Immediately following this encounter, to which the narrator passively submits, she returns to her booth, 'y ni quién se hubiera dado cuenta' (p. 79), thus perpetuating the power structure by protecting its secrecy. Instead of resisting this new form of forced labor, she instead works him into her regular work week, just one more part of the drudgery of her job (p. 108). The analogy between the Vips manager in his bathroom and the exploitative practices of her official employer in his office (p. 183) is clear. Even when constructing her own business, in which her body is the primary commodity, the narrator is unable to construct an alternative spatial practice. As long as she originates her business in the heart of the capitalist enterprise (Vips), that enterprise will constrain her movement. By the novel's end, however, she does find this path – the counterpart to her subordinate positioning with her lover – to be intolerable, thus leading to the self-enclosure of the novel's entropic ending.

Working from home – 'Yo aquí sigo'; 'hay algo aquí que aún me detiene'; 'este nuestro departamento de siempre'

As the national landscape provides the backdrop for the traveling narrator's activity, so the apartment represents center stage for the epistolary narrator. The apartment serves as the site for four distinct phases of the narrator's development, as we have seen: first as the birthplace of 'el plan,' when its tables were littered with Italian travel brochures; second as the extension of the office, the place where overtime typing work is brought in for extra pay, 'peso sobre peso' (p. 20); third, as the extension of the Vips marketplace, the site of the sex work that replaces the office work; and finally, as a *chora*-like sanctuary for the self-silencing narrator. The first phase of this activity takes place before the novel begins, and is referred to only in nostalgic letters to the narrator's sister; and the second function of this place is also referred to only in passing. The third phase, on the other hand, is the novel's spatial anchor, as this is the site from which the narrator writes as well as the place within which she works.

By linking the apartment to Vips through her sex work, the narrator in one sense converts her apartment into a similar heterotopic space, a site where people of different social classes and types come into contact. However, the material pressures of the Italian plan, discussed above, keep that heterotopic quality from being a place of creative possibility, an intermediate site where new identities can be tried, discarded, or reinvented. Instead, the narrator's fundamental spatial practice within her apartment is that of passivity. Because the apartment becomes another workplace, capitalism's external power structures are mirrored within it, and the clients – those with the purchasing power – call the shots. Within Vips the narrator does exert some agency, as she first makes a spectacle of herself in order to attract clientele, and then chooses which customer(s) she will invite home. But once they are inside her apartment, these men assume control of the site. In a sense, they take her place.

The narrator's passivity takes the form of dissociation from her body, when she is with her clients. As she admits to her sister, in describing one of her early encounters for pay, 'yo sólo le sirvo de trinchera pero a mí eso me da igual' (p. 57). Thus she appears to leave her own identity at the threshold, renting out the space of her body and her apartment and waiting patiently until what is for her the climax of the act, the financial transaction that follows the sexual activity. Sefchovich's narration of this space must be read through the lens of metafiction, since the epistolary narrator's references to place are overlaid with what she chooses to reveal to her sister about her new enterprise, which occurs on the margins of social acceptability but which, because of its profitability, remains attractive to the distant, judgmental, but needy sister. In her conflicted letter-writing, the narrator alternately defends and bemoans this business venture; while she defends her right to put her private space to profitable use, at the same time she adopts the same complaints of drudgery and exploitation that she used earlier in describing her office work.

Throughout the letters, she draws attention to what have become for her the two dominant architectural features of the apartment. Both features contribute to a sense of claustrophobia. One is the window, the glass barrier through which the narrator projects her dreams about Italy, her sister, and the imagined future that she is trying to buy. The other is the ceiling of her bedroom; the repeated focus on this image conveys graphically the narrator's will to surrender ownership of her body, at least temporarily: 'simplemente era yo un palo con el que no había ningún placer en estar y que se la pasaba mirando el techo para entretenerse mientras los señores se afanaban en lo suyo' (p. 94). The narrator here paints a stark image of submission, of a woman inert under the weight of her 'client,' eyes wide open, the mind closing off bodily sensation, as she waits patiently on a succession of customers who may seem different – occasionally even interesting – on the surface, but who functionally are interchangeable. The narrator mentions the ceiling on three more occasions, but always in the context of relieving the monotony of her encounters, through increasing use of fantasy and imagination. As we shall see below, these learned techniques eventually allow her to defeat the spatial barrier and to transcend both the ceiling of her apartment and the boredom of her nightly work. She notes, regarding her creative game of seeking that the clients please her instead of just satisfying themselves, 'Si consigo eso, mi trabajo va a ser sabroso siempre y hasta me podré olvidar del techo de mi cuarto que de tanto verlo me lo sé de memoria' (p. 147). Later, talking about visualization techniques as escapism, she repeats: 'Descubrí que ése es un buen método y pienso usarlo de hoy en adelante en vez de mirar el techo y pensar en tonterías mientras mis clientes se afanan en lo suyo' (p. 194). And finally, near the close of the novel, she admits that even the fantasies serve only as a dissociative coping mechanism: 'O simplemente no soy nada más que una trinchera y me dedico a pensar en mis cosas o imaginarme que estoy con un hombre que me gusta (porque ya aprendí eso en vez de mirar el techo)' (p. 204). All three of these mentions of the bedroom ceiling serve as foreshadowing of the novel's conclusion, when the narrator will succeed in transforming her apartment from a workplace into a fantastically boundless *chora* space; but until that time, she remains pinned under that ceiling and those customers.

Solitude had not been a fulfilling use of space for the epistolary narrator as, feeling acutely the absence of her sister in the early letters, she opted to flee to the simulacrum of community that Vips so successfully marketed. But once the apartment becomes a site of productivity, the narrator does in fact establish a room of her own within that structure, eventually taking over the room vacated by her sister, and thus separating the work bed from her place of rest ('para apapacharme' [p. 121]). At another moment, she moves the furniture around in an attempt to exercise control over a place (p. 45). But these spatial rearrangements mark empty assertions of ownership. Throughout the majority of the novel, the rules of the workplace circumscribe her behavior even in what otherwise might have been 'personal space.'

Several incidents reflect the fact that the clients, rather than the sex worker, control the place. She tolerates their presence but hopes that they will depart soon, so that she can repeat the productive cycle; but she does not appear able to force them or even ask them to leave, as she reveals while relating to her sister the story of one unpleasant client. She concludes the letter with the passive observation, 'Di gracias al cielo cuando por fin se fue' (p. 79), demonstrating that she has no mechanism for asserting control or erecting protective barriers, either around her body or around her living place. She tries to convince herself that a neighbor, Gerardo, will serve as her bodyguard (p. 72), but when she finds herself in real physical danger she opts not even to call out to him (p. 131). Repeated thefts by her customers reinforce the idea that her space has been invaded completely by this trade, leaving her defenseless (pp. 83, 107). Within the apartment, her lack of autonomy is based largely on her choice to adopt the passive role, in imitation of the profitable spatial practices of capitalist workplaces.[17]

In other words, the narrator internalizes her own choice to commodify herself. Even while she complains about her fatigue, the punishing impact of these clients on her own body, and the pressure of the 'círculo vicioso' (p. 94), she continues to see a return to take-home office work as the only viable alternative – and that option involves even greater tedium, at less profit. As a result, she continues to yield her domestic and personal space to commercial activity. As her apartment becomes a subsidiary of Vips, she too creates a spinoff business, serving as pimp

[17] Capital brings power, however; on one occasion, the narrator actually pays a client to leave her apartment (p. 197). Additionally, it should be noted that, when offered a safe place to live by her client the architect, she opts to remain in the unsafe location because it offers her greater freedom as well as profit (p. 158).

to her onetime client, the gay architect for whom she serves as heterosexual cover. As she explains, she begins by renting him a room for his own encounters, thus further commodifying her domestic space. She then expands her sex work to include serving as his pimp, luring young men ('efebos' [p. 157]) to the apartment and then turning them over to him, thus profiting via the mechanisms of management rather than labor. Most notably, the narrator even mentions to her sister that some of these clients are unwilling to trade places and, in a sense, be prostituted themselves, implying that the narrator is sanctioning sexual coercion for profit: 'le consigo a sus chavos, pero es una ayuda que no es fácil. El me señala cuál le gusta, yo lo trabajo como si fuera para mí y cuando llegamos a casa, se lo dejo y él me lo paga. Lo malo es que los chavos no siempre quieren' (p. 163). The back room of the apartment now is no longer the place reserved for respite, but rather an additional site of exploitation, this time commodifying the clients rather than the narrator.

According to Braidotti, the nostalgia for home and hearth – for 'fixity' – undermines the potential of the nomadic ideal (*Nomadic Subjects*, p. 22).[18] But neither the epistolary nor the traveling narrator can relinquish this dream completely. In one of the rare convergences between the two narrative personae, Beatriz confesses to her pregnant sister that, even in the face of her transgressive weekends and her unconventional second job, she clings to the traditional image of a domesticated future:

> A veces quisiera también tener un hijo. Detenerme y empezar otra cosa. Vivir con el hombre que una quiere y formar un hogar. Yo tengo un hombre al que amo, te diría que con locura, del que tú sabes que nunca hablo. Con él me quisiera casar. Pero creo que eso no sucederá porque ni él dice nada ni yo estoy hecha para esas cosas.   (pp. 188–9)

The narrator's habitual passivity surfaces here, as she in fact appears made precisely for 'esas cosas,' but cannot move in that direction unless her lover takes the lead. As the narrator tours Mexico, the boyfriend inundates her with objects with which to decorate 'mi casa'; yet, interestingly, these objects never seem to appear in the field of vision of the epistolary narrator.[19] The apartment does undergo superficial decorative alteration, albeit with the narrator watching

---

[18] While the narrator's sister does achieve the dream of traveling, once in Italy she reproduces the ideal of fixity, turning her independent boarding-house business instead into a domestic space filled with her husband and a growing number of children that gradually push out the heterotopic tenants. Nonetheless, it should be noted that this domestic ideal is achieved, literally, at the expense of her sister. While it would be misleading to sum up Beatriz as a 'prostitute,' it is much more accurate to observe that her sister does indeed prostitute her, continuing to demand the profits at the same time that she officially disapproves of the industry.

[19] There is one telling reference to a traditional image of home, in the narrator's memoir of her travels with her lover; she mentions that he buys her decorations 'para cuando tuviera mi casa' (p. 138), an imaginary home in the future, in contrast to the commercial space of her

passively, as her client appropriates the place and adapts it to his own tastes (p. 162). Fundamentally, however, this single woman's apartment remains a place to work, and to rest in order to work harder. Her home is not a place which either reflects or allows her to create an identity – until, at the end of the narration, she breaks with her lover and her dreams of the traditional female domestic space, and opts instead for a different future, in a self-designed apartment.

The profitable body – 'la herramiento de trabajo'

This discussion has already clarified the images of the narrator's body as a site of erotic sensation, a canvas on which her lover inscribes all he knows of Mexico. As we have noted, in spite of the fact that she records her pleasurable experiences in a syntax that represents the verbal equivalent of ecstasy, nonetheless her eroti-cized body, like Mexico, exists primarily in the second-person:

> dentro de mi cuerpo habitaste tú y todos los objetos de ese cuarto y de entre mis piernas salieron frutas y panes que tu boca mordió. ... Tus ojos me miraron todo el tiempo mientras tus manos se deslizaban y se detenían por mi cuerpo y mientras tus dedos me tocaban despacio. Fuiste buscando, conociendo, movi-endo, midiendo, pesando y calculando todos mis tamaños, todas mis formas, todas mis temperaturas y mis texturas. ... Y tú te diste cuenta muy pronto de ese poder que tenías sobre mí y me hiciste enloquecer una y otra vez ...
> (pp. 18, 22)

In recalling her erotic education at her lover's hands, the narrator notes that he took possession of her body by naming each of her parts, recalling the masculine paradigm of territorial claiming; she even wonders whether those parts existed before he named them (p. 65). Later in the novel, she correctly refers to herself as 'la poseída' (p. 168), a condition that increasingly problematizes her erotic pleasure.[20] Concurrently – and indeed correspondingly – at home her body becomes a place that can be leased, for profit. In both cases, the narrator cedes control of her most personal territory, and her body is then inscribed both figura-tively and literally with the vestiges of these functions.[21]

Throughout the majority of the narrative, erotic pleasure is contraposed to the sensations of sex for pay. While the traveling narrator creates her hymns to

apartment. However, as she later clarifies, even though the implications of marriage excite her (p. 141), neither her lover nor she ever discusses that prospect explicitly (p. 189).

[20] The narrator also notes that the travels across Mexico have now inscribed themselves upon her body, in what Fahey refers to as her 'incorporation' of Mexico (Sefchovich, p. 159; Fahey, p. 157).

[21] See for example the references to the scars left by both an abusive client and a careless doctor (pp. 132, 205); her references to an abortion ('no existe nada más espantoso en la vida' [p. 139]), and her repeated comments on the uncomfortable physical after-effects of her job as a sex worker (e.g. pp. 107, 108, 193, 197).

the joys of the flesh, the epistolary narrator on the other hand describes in blunt and graphic detail the distasteful side of the sex trade, her aversion to the bodily odors and secretions of her many clients, and the traces these possessors leave on her body (pp. 93–4). However, both narrative voices increasingly interrogate the question of corporeal agency, reducing the weekend lover to the same exploitative level as the paying customers, and ultimately leading the narrator to reject both of them in order to assert control of her own body.

The concept of sex work as drudgery dominates most of the narrator's letters to her sister; however, coincident with her disillusionment with her weekend lover there occurs an increased pleasure in the performative possibilities of sex work. From the outset, the narrator has taken shelter in the idea of corporeal dissociation, as noted above, concentrating on the ceiling tiles or, in the case of the Vips manager, the smell of the man's cologne (p. 79), in order to block out the ceding of her body to this temporary user. However, as she observes, bodily dissociation can also set the mind free, and once she closes her eyes to the ceiling tiles, she finds enjoyment in fantasizing, imposing alternate identities or characteristics onto her clients; from that point on, 'la cosa es cada vez más fácil' (p. 68). Finally, as her success continues, and as the energy formerly directed at her lover continues to redirect itself towards her own body, she finds her own sexual desire to be insatiable: 'Quisiera tener a todos los hombres del mundo. ... Quisiera probarlos a todos y no me alcanza el tiempo, la noche se pasa rápido' (p. 200). Thus, as economic security and professional expertise enable the narrator to become the buyer rather than the seller, she does take the 'work' out of sex work.

The question of corporeal agency is not limited to the erotic arena. Both narrations record other social dictates that constrained the narrator's bodily self-expression: the weekend lover told her how to dress and how to wear her makeup (p. 55), and her sister directed how she should cut her hair (p. 73). The epistolary narrator's comments about her own weight as well as her gossip about mutual friends indicates that a larger societal gaze also judged individuals by their bodies. As we shall see, in the novel's apparently triumphant ending, all dictates regarding weight and clothing are set aside, along with the constraints of comportment. The narrator opts to withdraw completely from the surveillance of outsiders, and to defy cultural ideals by displaying and celebrating her body as it is: naked or wrapped only in a caftan (p. 222), with 'mi cuello corto, mi cintura ancha, mis pechos caídos, mi piel café, mi vientre y mis nalgas tan grandes' (p. 218).[22]

---

[22] The narrator's expression of renewed confidence in her body is reinforced by the calendar of nude photos of her, published by one of her clients, in direct confrontation to the 'muchachitas flaquitas y etéreas' that typify the genre (p. 212).

The Garden of Earthly Delights – 'aquí estoy yo, dispuesta siempre'

The novel's sudden shift towards what Fahey terms 'surreal' (p. 162) and Duncan interprets as 'eccentric' begins when the traveling narrator opens her eyes to the realities of Mexico and her lover and, at the same time, the epistolary narrator closes her eyes to the ceiling of her apartment, instead exploring the possibilities of fantasy as an escape from geographic and corporeal reality.

Even though the narrator's Mexican travels might be construed as somewhat fantastic in scope, the majority of the novel is nonetheless narrated with veri-similitude. But chapter 47 marks a shift toward the improbable, and the final three chapters narrate a spatial restructuring of radical proportions. Somehow, by purchasing the neighboring apartment, tearing down partitions, and removing the glass from the window, the narrator creates an infinite space within the walls of her building. Ceasing to go out at all, she instead invites countless seekers into her space, which is now filled with exotic fish, butterflies, fountains, and lovemaking of all varieties. Significantly, the narrator in these chapters sheds the capitalist drive that has governed her epistolary messages. Instead, the final images are clearly meant to imply that, at last, and after seven years of operating in the space of others, the narrator has finally made a place for herself.[23]

There is no doubt that the ending of the novel is intended to be open, ambig-uous, subject to multiple potential readings. Both Fahey and Gebelein interpret this ending as positive, as establishing a creative and successful model of female agency for the Mexican woman, within the hidden interstitial spaces of the city. The narrator appears free from constraints, physically satisfied, and finally treading a path of her own choosing. Her active role as architect of this site, in erasing all of the relics of her past life, and successfully blocking out society's judgmental surveillance, might support such a conclusion. Like Rosario Ferré in *Flight of the Swan*, Sara Sefchovich has posited that the female character who chooses her own space might indeed construct a 'happy ending.'

However, as with *Flight of the Swan*, if we return to the paradigm of socio-spatial construction, we must arrive at a more critical interpretation. In order to help decipher the symbols of the novel's closing scene, two concepts prove useful: the model of Hieronymus Bosch's painting 'The Garden of Earthly Delights' (c. 1504), and the platonic concept of *chora* as reinterpreted by Kristeva and subsequent feminist theorists.

Bosch's work has become a favorite of the postmodern culture. Generally interpreted as ahead of its time, it depicts a visual panoply of carnal pleasure, some 100 naked human figures in various erotic interactions with each other, with animals, or with natural symbols. As the central panel of a biblically-inspired triptych, it represents the epoch of existence that lay between the Garden of Eden and the deformations of eternal Hell; it is therefore meant to represent earthly

---

[23] See Fahey, pp. 162–6, for a full discussion of the apartment and one interpretation of its symbolic significance as a space of celebratory female agency.

existence, and humanity's enjoyment of a world that, within Judeo-Christian symbolism, could only be interpreted as sinful.[24] From a contemporary perspective, however, the representation can be submitted to more positive readings, as humanity's fullest celebration of 'earthly delights.' The resonances between this painting and Sefchovich's final image of her narrator's apartment are very strong. The narrator describes the open and outdoor feeling of the place, naked bodies so numerous that they crowd the apartment, an immense variety of erotic experiences occurring within a kind of timelessness, and even the fish, water images, and butterflies that pervade Bosch's painting: 'Sólo se escucha el aleteo de las mariposas que se posan en una oreja, en el pelo. Sólo se ve la neblina del incienso densa y perfumada. Sólo se huelen nuestros cuerpos, nuestros líquidos, nuestros deseos. Lo que se ve, se huele y se oye son nuestros placeres' (pp. 223–4).[25]

Bosch's work has been described in the same terms as Sefchovich's – as surreal, as a representation of desire freed from the restraints of the conscious. Most famously, Carl Jung described Bosch as 'the discoverer of the unconscious' and 'the master of the monstrous.' Some interpretations of the painter's work consider the possible influence of psychotropic drugs, to explain the clarity of his visions of the human psyche and its drives. Significantly, the influence of drugs as a mechanism for warding off the normative power of the panoptical gaze is also considered by Sefchovich. Early in the novel, the epistolary narrator mentions in passing, one of her favorite clients who, after bathing her tenderly, set up a kind of hookah and shared the experience of smoking an unspecified drug with her: '¡Ay, hermanita, no sabes lo que es eso! Un humito que me llevó al paraíso. Veía yo lucecitas de colores, sentía todo muy grande y muy despacio y no podía ni moverme. Fue increíble' (p. 73).[26] Near the end of the novel she mentions the return of this friend, as she plans to make his experience of escapism, and of heightened sensory pleasure, a regular part of her future life. She dreams of having 'un cuartito para fumar los humitos que me enseñó hace tiempo un cliente árabe que hace poco regresó a buscarme y que cada vez me gustan más' (p. 174). As she at the same time narrates her progressive cessation of movement ('Ya casi no salgo de la casa' [p. 214]), her increasing focus on pleasure, and the shedding of concern for the outside world ('Nunca voy a la oficina, ni llamé siquiera para avisar' [p. 214]), it is clear that she is slipping into a kind of 'high.'

Both the Boschian influence and the references to psychotropic drugs lead us

24 It is also notable that the opening panel in Bosch's triptych references the Judeo-Christian fall from grace, traditionally attributed to Woman. The central panel, the 'Garden of Earthly Desires,' may therefore be read as the result of unrestrained female desire.

25 It should be noted that the sites painted by Bosch and (verbally) by Sefchovich are not identical. For example, Sefchovich's narrator mentions a bed, a window, and a carpet that gets wet when it rains (pp. 223–4); she also describes herself as adorned with either a caftan or a necklace of shells (p. 222). None of these particular images appear in Bosch's painting; however, the ambience she evokes is identical to that of the Dutch painter's work.

26 The narrator wistfully recalls this hallucinatory experience at another point in the novel (p. 153), reminding the reader of its allure.

to a consideration of the *chora* space as a framework for interpreting Sefchovich's closing scene.[27] The *chora*, the pre-verbal space often equated with the subconscious, has been defined by Kristeva as 'an essentially mobile and extremely provisional articulation constituted by movements and their ephemeral stases' (*Revolution*, p. 25) – in other words, a state in which impulse and immediacy take priority over reason. As Dina Felluga interprets it, Kristeva's *chora* represents the stage of development during which 'you spent your time taking into yourself everything that you experienced as pleasurable without any acknowledgment of boundaries … when you were closest to the pure materiality of existence. … At this stage you were, according to Kristeva, purely dominated by your drives.'[28] Clearly, this is the imagery that Sefchovich evokes in her structuring of the novel's ending; as the narrator writes:

> Hay veces que me quedo todo el tiempo acostada, entre las sábanas blancas y ellos vienen a mí. En otras ocasiones camino por la casa y los voy atendiendo donde estén. … Ellos esperan, pacientes, tranquilos. Saben que así es y desde que llegan a la puerta del edificio y conforme suben los seis pisos hasta mi casa, se van despojando de la calle, de la rutina, de la prisa, la culpa y el hastío y entran en la paz, en la calma, en la serenidad, listos para el placer.
>
> Y aquí estoy yo, dispuesta siempre. Con algunos es el cuerpo lo que doy, con otros el oído. Algunos quieren caricias mías, a otros los dejo hacer. … Todos pueden entrar y salir a voluntad de la casa, de la habitación, de la cama, de mi persona. …
>
> Sólo se escucha el aleteo de las mariposas que se posan en una oreja, en el pelo. Sólo se ve la neblina del incienso densa y perfumada. Sólo se huelen nuestros cuerpos, nuestros líquidos, nuestros deseos. Lo que se ve, se huele y se oye son nuestros placeres.   (pp. 222–4)

Thus Sefchovich has appropriated the environment of Bosch's painting and merged it with twentieth-century conceptualizations of feminine space, the semiotic space where societal structures yield to the primacy of the corporeal drives. In a final assertion of the joyful potential of such a solution, the narrator in the novel's final sentence reveals her name – Beatriz – recalling Dante's guide to Paradise.[29] But the question remains: in spite of the narrator's declaration of satisfaction, does this novel create a space of creative possibility for women within Mexican society, or a final surrender?

As mentioned earlier, the silencing of the narrative voice simultaneous with the physical enclosure of the protagonist imply that Beatriz has realized the futility of her dreams, but has not been able to create any new strategies for nego-

---

[27] See Chapter 1 of this study, as well as the chapter on Allende's *Retrato en sepia*, for further discussion of the *chora* as conceived by Plato, Kristeva, and contemporary spatial theorists.

[28] Felluga, 'Introductory Guide to Critical Theory.' <http://www.cla.purdue.edu/academic/engl/theory/psychoanalysis/definitions/chora.html>

[29] For a further discussion of this intertextual reference, see the study by Antonio Arreguín Bermúdez (2002).

tiating within the existing hegemonies of capitalism and gender. Like Restrepo's Sayonara, she opts to disappear. However, unlike Sayonara, she does not continue the search, but withdraws to a place of stasis. She finds satisfaction in meeting her clients' needs – physical and psychological – as well as in the pleasure of accepting and experiencing her own body; but she will not effect change from there, nor will she attempt to do so, as she is resigned to the failure of such attempts: 'En adelante voy a desaparecer, a perderme en las sombras, a dejarme llevar por los amores fáciles, gozosos, que son los únicos que no hacen daño, que no lastiman' (p. 226).

The character's final act of agency is to write the story of her illusory romance and send it to her infant niece in Italy, as 'both an invitation to dream and a warning' (Fahey, 'Remaking Place,' p. 166). But the decision to silence and to immobilize herself demonstrates a subtle but deeply critical message from Sefchovich. *Chora* without *choros* might be read as schismatic, renunciatory, even fetal. As we have seen, her final writings carry the tone of self-erasure: 'Hoy ha terminado mi historia de amor y con ella todo el sentido de mi vida. ... Estoy tranquila como hace mucho no lo estaba. La calma perfecta y el silencio absoluto, con el espíritu alejado de todo, sumida en una serenidad indecible' (p. 226). Beatriz's withdrawal is the entropic result of the fact that she, if real experience cannot live up to the rosy glow of her illusions, the only option is to renounce all movement:

> Ya no quería ver rostros ni rezos, plazas ni iglesias, niños ni magueyes, chozas ni parajes agrestes. Ya no quería ruinas ni montañas ni primaveras ni inviernos, ya no quería ni siquiera el mar. Porque ya no podía ver sólo lo bello, sólo lo verde, lo luminoso, lo asoleado, lo erguido, lo transparente, lo artesanal de este país.   (p. 221).

As the dizzying momentum of the novel's opening slows to this final stop, the perceptive reader must question the possibility of resistance, of contesting existing spatial practices. While many female protagonists do chart new paths and challenge the hegemonies that attempt to control their autonomy, Beatriz finds Paradise in withdrawal.

Conclusion

In 1989, Lois Parkinson Zamora's study *Writing the Apocalypse: Historical Vision in Contemporary US and Latin American Fiction* posited that American fiction tended to address society's potential annihilation, privileging the apocalyptic rather than the entropic. As Zamora insightfully observes, apocalypse, with its dramatic finality, can sometimes signal not just erasure, but energy, as well as the consoling implication that this erasure might form some incomprehensible part of a larger plan for the universe. No such consolation exists in entropic endings, where energy decays inexorably until the protagonists simply give up.[30] Entropy measures loss, randomness, and 'inevitable or steady deterioration.'[31] Sefchovich's Beatriz confronts many of the issues that threaten to constrain her, as she breaks taboos by imagining a gynocentric future with her sister, and then by finding pleasure in her sex work, and finally by exploring female erotic pleasure with her weekend lover. However, Sefchovich leaves ambiguous the question of whether such quests can triumph in Mexico. While many readers seek to impose positive female role modeling onto the protagonists of novels written by women, some in fact ultimately do not offer images of energetic hope, of the possibility that hegemonic space can be rebuilt in a way that offers women a place of their own. In *Demasiado amor*, Sefchovich posits that excess leads ultimately to disillusion, and further contestation is futile, as she leaves her protagonist floating silently in a permanent liminal space.

[30] Zamora cites as an example of entropy the fiction of Thomas Pynchon (Chapter 3). Her discussion articulates the 'extreme ... hostility toward human value and potential' in the entropic vision (p. 55). Sefchovich's view is not quite so nihilistic; the narrator does not suffer the 'heat death' to which Zamora refers (p. 54) but, instead, simply opts to drift through the rest of her days, allowing the world to pass on outside her pane-less window.

[31] *American Heritage Dictionary*, 4th edn.

6

Revolutionary Paths: Mastretta's *Mal de amores*

Introduction

The archetypal novel of the Mexican Revolution, *Los de abajo* (Mariano Azuela, 1915), represents the fighters and their womenfolk as storm-tossed leaves, victims of the national winds of chaos and change. In what has become one of the most classic scenes in Latin American literature, protagonist Demetrio Macías faces his wife's question, '¿Por qué pelean ya, Demetrio?' (p. 207).[1] In lieu of an explanation, the inarticulate revolutionary tosses a small stone down the walls of a canyon, and observes, 'Mira esa piedra cómo ya no se para ...' (p. 207). The characters do not make choices as to where they will go or stay; instead, they are swept along by the random and relentless forces of the Revolution.

In *Mal de amores* (1996), Angeles Mastretta offers a very different mapping for the individual players in this national drama. Mastretta views the Revolution not as an entropic slide toward the national chaos of a 'raza irredenta' (Azuela, p. 135) but as a moment of immense creative possibility. As she asserts in a 1997 interview with Barbara Mujica, 'Yo creo que la Revolución mexicana es una época que funda cosas, funda actitudes. ... Yo te puedo decir que las mujeres mexicanas de los años cuarenta y cincuenta no tuvieron de ninguna manera la libertad que tuvieron las mujeres de los [años] veinte' (p. 37); she later adds that, in her view, this cataclysm gave Mexican citizens the 'habilidad de soñar un país diferente' (p. 39). While in Azuela's novel the Revolution descended on a couple who seemed unaware of its imminence or its potential, *Mal de amores* traces the gradual apprehension, and cautious optimism, of a middle-class family in Puebla, as the *porfiriato* draws to a close. Throughout the buildup of opposition and of increasing political awareness, both male and female characters participate in discussions and debates, stay closely tuned to newspapers and rumors, and make the choices that situate them once the Revolution does occur. The primary locational questions of this novel are not 'Where is she?' or 'Where is she from?' but rather 'Where does she go?' The paths of her movement reflect the increased possibilities for female autonomy, both geographic and social, in post-Revolutionary Mexico.

Mal de amores is second only to *Arráncame la vida* (1985) as Mastretta's most widely read and widely studied novel; while the earlier work continues to mark Mastretta's place in popular readership, the more recent novel demon-

[1]   This and subsequent references are to Mariano Azuela, *Los de abajo*, ed. Marta Portal (Madrid: Cátedra, 1984).

strates a sophistication of character and style that make it far richer for analysis. In terms of existing critical dialogue, several studies that include consideration of *Mal de amores* focus on the appropriation of the Mexican Revolution as a *topos* for current women's narrative in Mexico (see, for example, articles by Carmen Rivera Villegas and Carlos Coria-Sánchez);[2] others explore the question of women's education, most notably addressed in Judy Maloof's 1999 study '*Mal de amores*: Un bildungsroman femenino.'[3] Mastretta's own comments on the possibilities offered by the disintegration of hegemony during the Revolution reinforce both of these foci, but also invite analysis through a geographic lens, as the characters watch places disintegrate, and help to build new structures to take their place.

Indeed, Mastretta's characters demonstrate that traditional pressures of career and family responsibility are set aside when revolution erupts. As one of the male protagonists, Daniel Cuenca, joins up with the revolutionaries, he does so from the (ad)vantage of education and volition, following the different factions both as work and as adventure, since he is serving as a correspondent to both Mexican and US newspapers. Periodically, donning women's garb, he is able to sneak back to Puebla in order to visit his family and his girl. In other words, he is the architect of his own revolutionary path, stepping beneath the radar whenever his needs dictate or when the situation grows too dangerous. The female protagonist, Emilia Sauri, is depicted as equally able to chart her own course through the storm. Rather than remaining as the passive lady-in-waiting, she sometimes opts to travel alongside her peripatetic lover not merely as company for him, but carving out a role and, correspondingly, a place for herself in each of the sites they visit. Eventually, she opts to travel without him, as she pursues her own course of studies in the United States and he returns to the disorder of the Revolution. And finally, she freely chooses to re-root herself in Puebla, welcoming Daniel when he returns but purposefully not constructing her own lifecourse around those visits.

Emilia, unlike Daniel or her counterparts in earlier novels of the Revolution, grows in knowledge and maturity as she travels. The knowledge gleaned in each site – rural towns, the heterotopia of Mexico City, the protected laboratories of the United States – equips her for survival in her next destination. Thus, while Daniel might in some ways follow the course of the archetypal Demetrio Macías, Mastretta carefully plots Emilia's journey as a series of encounters which are self-directed, and ultimately productive both for herself and for the sites through which she travels.

---

[2]   The focus on the Revolution in this novel draws increased attention as it recalls the setting of the other blockbuster Mexican novel by a woman author, Laura Esquivel's *Como agua para chocolate* (1989), as well as other works by Elena Garro, Elena Poniatowska, Sabina Berman, and Brianda Domecq (see Maloof, p. 36).

[3]   See also Virginia Hernández Enríquez, 'Educación femenina y transgresión en *Mal de amores*' (1999), and Eva Núñez-Méndez, 'Mastretta y sus protagonistas, ejemplos de emancipación femenina' (2002).

Mal de amores offers a different spatial paradigm than do the other novels here examined. In the novels by Restrepo, Allende, and Ferré, female autonomy was linked to the nomadic model. In order to free themselves from the located-ness of traditional femininity – the roles of good girl, wife and mother – the protagonists had to 'walk away' from notions of assigned space, and create a new site in which they could, in a sense, write their own tickets. Restrepo's Sayo-nara becomes a prostitute and then disappears over the horizon; Allende's Aurora leaves her husband and takes an apartment for herself and her lover; and Ferré's Madame stays perpetually on tour (albeit under the capitalist and male-domi-nated restrictions discussed earlier). In Mastretta's novel, the nomadic model is attempted but ultimately rejected, and a more original, more accommodating solution is offered.

Emilia does follow the nomadic course in the United States, traveling alone to pursue the study of medicine, and defying both family pulls and gender norms in order to satisfy her own passion for learning. But unlike the paradigmatic female nomad, she maintains her longing for home and hearth – specifically, for a home like the one her mother had created. In the face of opportunities for adventure and achievement, she continues to yearn for stability and security. In the end, she opts to go home again, 'urgida de abrazarse una hilera de días al regazo inaplazable del mundo que la creció' (p. 342). If the novel ended here, it would have to be read spatially as a path of failure and renunciation. However, as the novel frequently indicates, the world of Emilia's parents is the world of the nineteenth century; and in this new century and after this Revolution, returns are not possible. Instead, at the novel's end Emilia has reconfigured the architecture of her domestic space. She creates three nests for her homing impulse, and each of the three places satisfies a distinct but equally relentless passion: she creates a home with husband, children, and grandchildren along traditional female lines; she operates a hospital in which she serves as a primary physician and constructs a curative heterotopia of alternative treatments; and she maintains a private dwelling where she can continue her trysts with the adventurous and sensual Daniel. Thus, she exercises the nomad's defiance and creativity, the autonomy of creating one's own place according to her own rules, but in contrast with previously examined female nomads, she does not have to make the sacrifices that accompany physical itinerancy in order to do so. In the novel's penultimate chapter, Daniel – the only character unsatisfied with Emilia's creation of this all-inclusive social order – asks her aunt, '¿Qué es lo que quiere esta mujer?' (p. 370), expressing his frustration at her refusal to assume a single assigned place; but Emilia's complicit aunt Milagros answers simply that what Emilia wants is 'Todo' (p. 371). By assuming control of three loci of action and power, Emilia does attain what she seeks.

Of course, such an option requires some degree of acquiescence on the part of the dominant social structures. Emilia is fortunate to find a husband (Antonio Zavalza) who will tolerate this kind of individualism. Most significantly for our study, the surrounding society also tolerates her geography. In contrast to the other novels, capitalism is not seen as a primary engine of *Mal de amores*. Poverty and social injustice are depicted – and in spatially effective ways, as we shall see – but blame is assigned to the socio-economic structures of the *porfiriato* in particular rather than capitalism in general. Thus, post-Revolution Puebla is seen as a place of free movement during this phase of reconstruction, rather than as an engineered construct of social reproduction.

The aesthetic success of Mastretta's novel lies in her ability to manage both the macro- and the micro-spatial planes of the Mexican Revolution: both the national arena of political and military activity, and the individual drama of a woman negotiating her way through the cataclysm. Allende attempted to accomplish something similar, as the narrative eye followed Severo del Valle through Chile's war with Perú; but Mastretta more effectively brings the Revolution into the living rooms of middle-class families, by repeatedly interweaving personal and national conversations within the households of the Sauri family and the Cuenca family.

The *botica* of Emilia's father Diego and the *salón* of Daniel's father Octavio Cuenca function as counter-sites of resistance, housing activity and conversation that both reflects and brings about the end of the *porfiriato*. Subsequently, the Sauri home functions as the place where letters and newspapers make national events the stuff of dinner conversation and debate. The characters' own travels through Mexico offer further opportunities to blend personal quest with the larger forces of the Revolution.[4] Most effectively, Mastretta in a central episode locates Emilia and Daniel in a train, a hurtling chronotope that offers them a panoramic view of the revolutionary landscape. Within that train, Emilia sets up an ad hoc medical clinic, thus creating an oasis of healing within a landscape of devastation. In this way she takes her father's *botica* on the road, and increases her own medical knowledge at the same time that she offers shelter – albeit temporary – to the wounded wanderers of the Revolution.

A further structuring device that Mastretta uses to merge national and individual landscapes is the representation of the Revolution as Daniel's other lover, a rival to Emilia. Spatially, Daniel is frequently drawn from conversations with Emilia to dialogues with the numerous, nameless characters of the Revolution. The most effective example occurs in a Mexico City café, significantly just after Emilia's and Daniel's improvised wedding ceremony. At this place where he finally seems to have committed himself to one lover, Daniel is irresistibly lured to the other; rather than conversing with his new wife, he instead observes the café filling with the Revolution's typical cast of characters, 'generales con facha de políticos y de políticos con garbo de generales' (p. 315). Mastretta dramati-

---

4 In her article on *Mal de amores*, Rivera Villegas highlights the 'acto de feminizar el espacio histórico nacional ... [privilegiando] la psicología, las experiencias y la conducta del ser femenino para representar literariamente un aspecto histórico cuya representación ha sido reservada, en exclusiva, para la supuesta seriedad y profesionalismo crítico de la cultura masculina' (p. 37).

cally sketches the scene in the café to portray Daniel's torn loyalties: while dining with his new wife, 'Daniel los observaba con la avidez de quien ha sido arrancado de ese cogollo y no tardó ni cinco minutos en descubrir varios amigos con los que había hecho la guerra contra Huerta en el norte' (p. 315). With the permission of his jilted bride, Daniel crosses the café and spends the next hours across the room, with his co-revolutionaries. Ultimately, he returns to her table only to summarize the conversations and dismiss her to her own errands, while he opts to stay on in the café, to continue the discussions. In various locations, this dynamic is repeated throughout the novel, as Daniel oscillates between his desire for Emilia and the allure of the Revolutionary drama. The rivalry is again positioned spatially when Emilia, having left Daniel, characterizes him as 'un traidor que se subía al caballo de la revolución para irse a hacer la patria, como si pudiera haber patria en otro lugar que no fuera su cama en común' (p. 275). In its spatial interweaving of the national and the individual, Mastretta's award-winning novel thus offers a vivid and complex revision of the Mexican Revolution as well as its destabilizing effects on individual spheres of activity.

The plot of the novel is anchored in Puebla, but as the home base of several travelers, the city becomes a site of intersection for various traditions. The novel opens not with the birth of Emilia, but with the childhood of her father Diego Sauri, in Isla de Mujeres. His kidnapping at the age of nineteen and the subsequent travels turn him into a cosmopolitan whose journeys through some ten countries have added European and Eastern science to his knowledge of indigenous pharmaceuticals. His involuntary exile is filled with nostalgia for home, and his honeymoon trip with Josefa Veytia is represented as his last journey. Nonetheless, he remains a kind of virtual nomad, satisfying his 'ambición de viajes' through reading:

> Haber recorrido medio mundo y llevar la mayor parte de su vida en el mismo sitio, atado a los mismos ojos y el mismo delirio por la misma mujer, a veces lo traspasaba de inquietud. Entonces, seguro de que intentar cualquier otra cosa hubiera sido ridículo, Diego Sauri hundía la nariz entre las estampas de sus libros y viajaba tardes enteras por la India y Marruecos, Pakistán y China. Tras varios días perdido en la querella con sus deseos, regresaba completo a la estancia de su casa y al mostrador de su botica, renovado y excéntrico, seguro por todos lados de que no había elegido mal quedándose tras la invisible muralla que cercaba la ciudad de Josefa Veytia. (pp. 225–6)

The young doctor Antonio Zavalza, Diego's eventual son-in-law, possesses a similar spirit; having traveled the world accumulating medical knowledge, he too becomes spatially grounded by his love for Emilia. Thus the two men follow the traditionally female path of surrendering their geographical mobility in order to wait on a woman: 'A uno la madre y al otro la hija los habían vuelto locos por su mundo mentido de sencillez y lleno de recovecos, quieto y alrevesado, temerario y sonriente, trémulo y poderoso' (p. 226).

Thus, while Mastretta's portrayal of her female protagonist is innovative, particularly in the eventual bigamous solution she proposes, her representation of male figures is even more radical. Diego's wife, Josefa Veytia, comes from a long line of anti-nomads,[5] so the voluntary renunciation of his mobility is somewhat explicable. But Zavalza, and another male character (Manuel Rivadeneira, the companion of Josefa's sister Milagros), opt for an even more radical spatial and social positioning. In both cases, their women assert their independence to travel along their self-mapped routes, and the men create a home and hearth to which the women occasionally return. As we shall see, Milagros is a free-spirited woman who 'prefirió negarse al matrimonio antes que abandonar lo que juzgaba el privilegio de vivir como los hombres' (p. 35). In contrast to the archetype of the dominant male Latin figure, the poet Rivadeneira opts to live in patient loyalty to Milagros, and to content himself with her occasional nocturnal visits to his home and his arms. She is the mobile and active figure, running a resistance newspaper, raising support among the poor, and rescuing political prisoners, and he stands as the pole around which she oscillates. She maintains a separate residence in Puebla and another in Mexico City, but his bed is open to her when she wants it. Similarly, Antonio Zavalza waits in the wings while Emilia pursues her passion for Daniel. He builds a home with space for her, and a hospital in which she will eventually house her own medical practice, but he does not constrain her timetable or her movements. Both Zavalza and Rivadeneira present revolutionary models for the male figure, and their assumption of the traditionally female role enables the novel's wandering women to 'have it all.'

Finally, Emilia does return to the place that her second husband, Zavalza, has constructed for her. However, this cessation of movement is seen as triumphant rather than renunciatory, as their hospital becomes a creative and curative heterotopia. In his discussion of this concept, Michel Foucault refers to the hospital as a 'crisis heterotopia' because of the juxtaposition of patients from various milieux and their isolation from society due to disease ('Of Other Spaces,' p. 24). However, in this novel the encounter, the blurring of traditional hierarchical distinctions, occurs among the healers as well as the patients. Emilia's past travels and her questing spirit draw to that spot all of the practitioners of medicine and of paramedicine that she has met in her journeys: Teodora the *curandera*, don Refugio the intuitive listener, Hogan the North American physician, combined with the knowledge of indigenous herbs inherited from her father's own exploratory journeys. In sum, the hospital becomes a site of power and possibility.

---

[5]   The narrator details emphatically the anti-nomadic character of the Veytia family: 'Los Veytia descendían de un señor Veytia que emigró de España para ayudar a la fundación de la ciudad en el año de 1531. Y desde que aquel primer Veytia se había atrevido a cruzar el océano del modo en que se cruzaba por esos años, todos los que heredaron su apellido, con la reciente excepción del tío Miguel, heredaron con él la certeza de que Puebla era el mejor lugar para vivir y morirse que ser humano alguno pudiera escoger. Así que ninguno tuvo jamás entre sus ambiciones la de viajar y nadie, en trescientos cincuenta y dos años, había tenido la ocurrencia de emprender una luna de miel que acarreara el peligro de perder de vista los volcanes' (p. 39).

The novel's geography is centered on Puebla, but is filled in by forays – primarily Emilia's – to rural villages, to Mexico City, and to three cities of the US – San Antonio, Chicago, and New York. Each of these destinations is verbally sketched as a site of encounter between Emilia and an Other culture, thus offering a scenery in which various social classes of Mexico can be examined as well as the feeling of estrangement from Mexico. These locations anchor the novel's geoplot, as Emilia maps her independent lifecourse through and beyond the Revolution.

Original sites: Isla de Mujeres – 'audaz y solitaria'; 'como la gloria misma'

In contrast to the images of exile and homelessness that dominate Allende's and Ferré's novels, Mastretta's novel places great importance on the concept of origins. Diego Sauri does not know from which people he comes (his father speculates that they were pirates [p. 10]), but he does know from which place. Isla de Mujeres, off the Yucatán Peninsula, is depicted as a *locus amoenus* to which Diego's parents, among others, fled to escape the *guerra de castas*[6] on the Peninsula. In *The Anatomy of Criticism*, Northrop Frye describes the Edenic *locus amoenus* as a typical birthplace of the literary hero, and as a 'place of seed' which nourishes the young hero (pp. 200, 205). This trope is taken up by Mastretta as she paints Diego growing up in a sheltered island paradise, which geomorphically turned him into a youth who was 'brillante, pulido, cubierto de sol y heredero de un afán sin explicaciones' (p. 10). Most significantly, the island offers the basis for the syncretism that pervades the novel. In this fertile place, traditional wisdom thrives alongside the plethora of natural herbs, so that Diego evolves into a natural healer with a vast knowledge of nature's curative powers and the value of indigenous culture. Here he learns to place the goddess Ixchel alongside the Catholic pantheon (p. 10), thus creating a female-friendly worldview which will later serve to empower his daughter.[7]

Isla de Mujeres offers Diego the cultural framework into which he will later weave the knowledge gleaned from his globetrotting. In the face of all his later acquired knowledge, and his yen for virtual travel, Diego retains a fundamentally Mexican identity, due to his rootedness in Mayan heritage and in the sands of the Yucatán gulf.

The island is depicted as unpopulated, awaiting cultivation by Diego's parents

---

6 The *guerra de castas* (1847–54) was a rebellion by those who considered themselves indigenous or of Maya descent, in an attempt to recover land taken from them by the 'colonizing' *campesinos*. Many non-indigenous inhabitants of the Yucatán Peninsula fled in the face of this movement, which at one point is said to have gained control of 80% of the Peninsula. For further information, see José Luis Preciado Silva, 'La guerra de castas en Yucatán, 1847–1901'.

7 Diego's first words to his infant daughter are 'Eres más valiente que Ixchel' (p. 22), as he hearkens back to his Mayan cultural – if not racial – roots.

and the other refugees. The novel's opening paragraphs note that the original inhabitants – or the early colonizers – had left the island because of its vulnerability to pirate attacks; thus, when the refugees arrive in 1847, they find an open space in which to carve out their own place, work, and prosper: 'cada quien sería dueño de la tierra que fuese capaz de chapear' (p. 10). Diego thus learns the values of ambition and hard work, in an environment apparently free of social class divisions or the encumbrances of unjust, inherited economic systems. Again, this geosocial environment offers a contrast to the other novels of this study, in which inhabited space is seen as a creation of capitalist hegemony and assigned roles of reproduction, and in which natural space is gradually overtaken by expanding industry. Mastretta opts not to interrogate these issues. The adult Diego, the product of this island utopia, will settle into a comfortable middle-class career as a pharmacist, inheriting a house and continuing to live by the values learned alongside his hardworking and well-rewarded parents in Isla de Mujeres.

Also of note in the portrayal of this *locus amoenus* is the natural beauty, which creates in Diego a lifelong yearning for his place of origin. In a lyrical passage, the narrator establishes an analogy between childhood innocence and the unspoiled landscape: 'El primer color que vieron los ojos de Diego Sauri fue el azul, porque todo alrededor de su casa era azul o transparente como la gloria misma. Diego creció corriendo entre la selva y rodando sobre la invencible arena, acariciado por el agua de unas olas mansas, como un pez entre peces amarillos y violetas' (p. 10).[8] Diego opts not to return to this paradise, instead staying in his wife's place (Puebla); but this decision is repeatedly viewed as a sacrifice made for love. Diego and his wife often debate the virtues of their own native places (pp. 21, 103), and Josefa recognizes that her husband spends many afternoons consumed by longing for his island roots (p. 161). In contrast to the novels by Sefchovich, Restrepo, Allende, and Ferré, here place does not expel its inhabitants, but rather continues to emit the siren-call of nostalgia. Diego's daughter Emilia will follow the same pattern, when she leaves Puebla but is eventually lured back home, neatly completing a geographic circle.

Sites of transition: voyages and Veracruz

In spite of his idyllic surroundings, Diego does long for geographic exploration, for 'un horizonte no cercado por el agua' (p. 10). However, his one-way ticket out is not one of his choosing. Kidnapped by an interloper with a vendetta, Diego is

---

[8] A later reference identifies the state of Quintana Roo (to which Isla de Mujeres belongs) as the place where political prisoners are sent, thus setting up a contrast with the idyllic portrayal of the novel's outset. In the later reference, the tropical sun becomes an instrument of torture rather than light, but Josefa struggles to reconcile this political news with her husband's nostalgic recollections: 'Por más que le daba vueltas, Josefa no podía creer que tal paraíso fuera considerado un lugar de castigo' (p. 161).

forced into the hold of a ship, 'rumbo a quién sabía dónde' (p. 11). The sketchily narrated tale constitutes a turning point in the novel, as the ship is depicted as a kind of womb from which Diego will be reborn: 'Nunca supo cuántos días pasó en aquel encierro. Una oscuridad y otra y otras muchas le cruzaron por encima hasta que perdió el sentido del tiempo' (pp. 11–12). Since 'who you are' is inextricable from 'where you are,' Diego emerges with no identity at all, when he is dumped in an unknown port of northern Europe (p. 12). A *tabula rasa*, Diego now faces limitless horizons and the freedom to create himself, to the extent that once he returns home, 'no se reconoce' (p. 12). He spends several years as an itinerant, gathering information about other medical traditions. His route constitutes a narrative ellipsis, as the narrator opts to summarize his explorations as 'varios años y muchos aprendizajes' (p. 12). However, this journey turns him into 'un cosmopolita y un excéntrico' (p. 12) on whom the world has left an indelible imprint. His later open-mindedness to his daughter's autonomy of travel and custom can be directly attributed to the geographic breadth of this second adolescence. The omission of specifics invites the reader to imagine an endless array of landscapes, such that Diego has in fact traveled the entire world and come home again.

Mastretta again reasserts the pull of nostalgia, as in spite of his travels Diego 'ambicionaba como nadie que su última peripecia lo llevara de la mano a la misma sopa bajo el mismo techo por el tiempo que le restase de vida' (p. 12). Unlike the nomads of earlier novels, Diego seeks to put down roots; and once planted, he indeed never travels again, except through books, maps, and imaginings. Establishing the pattern that his daughter will follow, he remains a nomad in spirit but not in space, thus establishing that freedom of inquiry is not incompatible with traditional notions of home.

Diego finds his anchor in the port city, Veracruz, described in typically heterotopic terms: 'se metió al puerto que hacía un ruido desordenado y caliente. Fue hasta la plaza y entró en un hostal bullicioso' (p. 12). Through a visually effective technique, Mastretta brings a telescoping vision to that colorful scene; within one paragraph the narrative eye focuses on the broad vision of the port, then the hotel, then the people seated at tables, and finally 'los ojos de Josefa Veytia' (p. 12). This aesthetic device gradually screens out the noise and visual interference of the cityscape, reducing the scene ultimately to one pair of eyes seeing another. No further descriptions of Veracruz are offered, since the city has been reduced to the presence of that one individual, and the plot soon turns to its primary site, the Sauri home in Puebla.[9]

---

9 This telescoping method for narrating space occurs again later in the novel. Emilia's musings take her from distant countries ('que Emilia creía sólo vivos en la imaginación de su padre' [p. 75]) to Mexico, then to Puebla itself, then to 'los pasos de su madre' and 'la lengua inclemente de su tía' (p. 75). In both passages, the technique serves to underscore the significance of individual experience within a global context.

Puebla – 'recatada y tediosa como una iglesia'

Cityscapes are far less significant to the novel than are the more intimate domestic landscapes. Nonetheless, with regards to the city of Puebla, two general inferences can be drawn by the nexus between space and power. The first is the structure of a society unjustly controlled by the rich, under the *porfiriato*.[10] In terms of concrete narration of spaces, this image is represented most directly during Rivadeneira's visit to the governor's home, where he pleads for the release of Milagros from prison; the home is described as 'el palacio en que vivía el repartidor de bienes y desgracias en el estado de Puebla,' and is represented as an ostentatious fortress of power (p. 166).[11] This snapshot is one of the few Puebla scenes that ventures outside the domestic space of the novel's central characters. The second concrete image is that of a city anxiously watching the approach of the long-anticipated Revolution. Political unrest drifts in the air for years, in the form of rumors and newspaper editorials, and increasingly in the form of covert conversations in meetings disguised as social gatherings. But in general the city holds the violence at bay for as long as possible. Politics are purely theoretical, until they burst in on the Sauri household in the form of danger to their own family members. Only once the Revolution knocks on their front door do the protagonists realize that 'la paz de su casa podría perturbarse' (p. 104). Yet even as the novel progresses, real violence never does reach the city.[12] In broad strokes, then, the Revolution happens above and around Puebla, and characters exit and enter the city as they alternately participate in and take refuge from the Revolution's violence.

Three primary domestic places encompass most of the action, in the sections of the novel that take place in Puebla: the Casa de la Estrella (home of Diego and Josefa), the home of the doctor Octavio Cuenca, and the home of Josefa's sister Milagros. Alongside and in contrast to these structures, the novel relates occasional forays into more unstable sections of Puebla, most notably the poor *barrio* of Santiago, but also the circus and the prison. Finally, near the novel's conclusion, the hetero-utopic place of the hospital is established. Each of these spatial arenas is a careful verbal construct designed both to explain and to constrain the actions of the characters.

---

[10] Mexican president Porfirio Díaz served as president and *de facto* dictator of Mexico from 1876 until the Revolution broke out in 1911 (with a four-year hiatus, 1880–84); under his rule, land ownership was consolidated among the wealthy, and the poor were granted few opportunities for advancement.

[11] In this scene, Rivadeneira buys Milagros's freedom by signing over his own lands to the governor, thus elucidating the strategies by which the wealthy had consolidated their own power.

[12] A notable exception is the police raid on the home of the Serdán brothers, covert supporters of the Revolution; a siege ends with their violent death (Chapter 15).

La Casa de la Estrella – *'no hay mejor cobijo'; 'regazo inaplazable del mundo que la creció'; 'el lugar más tibio y grato del mundo'*

The Casa de la Estrella contains two nerve-centers of activity: Josefa's workplace of the kitchen-dining room, and Diego's workplace of the pharmacy. The single structure serves as both residence and businessplace, thus allowing for easy commerce between the two. Following tradition, the kitchen is established as the female space and the pharmacy as the male place – the former welcoming the family's intimates and the latter primarily clients[13] – but several characters, and most notably the protagonist Emilia, operate equally in both spheres, thus breaking down the gendered division of space.

All of the notions of hearth, of the home as refuge, are centered around Josefa's homeplaces. As mentioned earlier, the Veytia dynasty for generations has been anchored in Puebla, with no desire to roam (p. 39). The house, inherited from Josefa's uncle, further cements their stability, guarding them against the insecurities of the future: 'No se sabía bien a bien de qué vivirían, pero al menos ya tendrían en dónde vivir' (p. 39). Geomorphically, the structure thus reflects the earth-mother character of Josefa.[14] During her nomadic years, Emilia often draws upon memories of this archetypal hearth as a source of solace and strength (pp. 268, 323, 342).

Nonetheless, the hearth structure does not appear to be reproducible in the modern age; ultimately the novel offers Josefa's homey place as the *last* site of Veytia stability. The walls prove permeable to the new age, as Daniel's irresistible flute music wafts in through the window and lures Emilia from her engagement dinner with the safe and stable Antonio Zavalza. The two lovers flee from the Casa de la Estrella, and take refuge in a domestic counter-site of resistance, the 'casa de soltera' of Josefa's sister Milagros. The move from Josefa's space to Milagros's marks the disintegration of the past domestic architecture, and the beginning of open confrontation with a new social, and geographical, reality, as from that point forward, the novel never portrays Emilia as sitting still anywhere.[15]

The *botica* on the house's lower levels is a particularly fortuitous literary device, as it creates a counter-site in several different spheres of activity.[16] As a laboratory (pp. 40–1), it becomes an intellectual heterotopia, harboring both

---

[13] Activities within the home also follow traditional gender lines; Josefa reads novels while Diego reads the newspaper (p. 27), or Josefa embroiders while Diego – still – reads the newspapers (p. 64).

[14] Josefa guards the family against instability, 'como si de ella dependieran la paz y la condición eternal de la vida humana' (p. 261).

[15] Additionally, the growing tensions of political change alter the domestic peace of the Casa de la Estrella: '[A Diego] No le gustaba su casa convertida en campo de batalla verbal, temía más que la guerra, que la contingencia lastimara el refugio sedentario y paradisiaco de su armoniosa vida conyugal' (p. 110).

[16] Mujica's study discusses the author's observation that Diego Sauri was based on Mastretta's own father, who worked actively to develop his daughter's independence of thought (p. 41).

books and medications that address an array of Other cultures and approaches. As mentioned above, it is established as a male zone of activity, but Emilia is as much at home in the pharmacy as she is in the kitchen. She takes a co-constructive role in the design of this space, as she alphabetizes and orders the bricolage of resources – in a reversal of gender archetypes, she imposes order on Diego's intuitive arrangements (p. 121).[17]

As a place of knowledge as well as of healing, the *botica* reflects and extends the syncretism in which Diego's youth was steeped. Within this space Diego furthers his vocation as an intellectual nomad, continually seeking new remedies, and expressing his own view of science as perpetual quest: 'Hacen más por la medicina quienes buscan que quienes concluyen' (p. 58). Isolated from the Catholic space of Josefa, Diego teaches the same kind of nomadism to his daughter:

> Enseñaban catecismo en su colegio, pero los Sauri contrarrestaban esa información diciéndole a Emilia que era una teoría como cualquier otra, tan importante aunque tal vez menos certera que la teoría sobre los dioses múltiples que predicaba la cabeza de Milagros. Por eso Emilia creció escuchando que la madre de Jesús era una virgen que se multiplicaba en muchas vírgenes con muchos nombres, y que Eva fue la primera mujer, salida del costado de un hombre, culpable de cuantos males aquejan a la humanidad, al mismo tiempo en que sabía de la paciente diosa Ixchel, la feroz Coatlicue, la hermosa Venus, la bravía Diana y Lilith, la otra primera mujer, rebelde y sin castigos. (p. 59)

Josefa resists this postmodern indoctrination, fearing that Diego will raise Emilia as 'una insatisfecha permanente' (p. 60); and in fact this is the desired, and ultimately achieved, result. In her own hospital, the adult Emilia re-creates the open and liberal environment of her father's *botica*, establishing a gathering place for practitioners of paramedicine as well as the latest scientific advances.[18]

The pharmacy also functions as a political counter-site, a place where the controversies which upset Josefa can be openly debated:

---

[17] Defending herself against Diego's complaints that she has interfered with his ordering system in the *botica*, Emilia responds: 'Me he pasado la vida viendo cómo revoloteas para encontrar algo. Yo me tardaría años en entender lo que tú manejas con intuiciones y recuerdos' (p. 121).

[18] Diego clearly equates the questing spirit with the modern age. When Josefa points out that she has been satisfied with what life offers, Diego concludes that this is because she was born in the light of a full moon, while in contrast Emilia was born 'con luz eléctrica. ... Quién sabe cuántas cosas vas a querer de la vida' (p. 64). Later, when Emilia announces her intention to follow in her father's professional footsteps ('Yo voy a trabajar en la botica'), Diego reinforces that decision by announcing that 'Ella vivirá en otro siglo' (p. 71).

Hacía más de tres años que en la botica habían empezado a reunirse todos aquellos que por motivos justificados, viejos anhelos democráticos o pura vocación conspirativa, tenían algo en contra del gobierno. Primero los acercó el azar, luego el acuerdo, después la necesidad. Y para ese momento, un día sí y otro también, había en la botica algún parroquiano dispuesto a insultar al gobernador delante de cuanto cliente la pisaba.   (p. 27)

Emilia's at-homeness in the pharmacy offers her access to these increasingly dangerous and covert discussions, and ultimately equips her to ignore the traditional gender barriers of political conversation. In this way the place of business functions as an important counterpart to Emilia's official schooling. Raised in this volatile environment, she can capably assume an intellectual footing equal to Daniel's in their debates about the Revolution.[19]

The Cuenca home – 'todo el que llamaba tenía derecho a entrar y buscarse un sitio'
The home of the widowed Octavio Cuenca and his sons offers many parallels to Diego's *botica* site. Two paragraphs near the novel's opening are dedicated to a description of the house's layout and environment; while the front door remains physically closed, as with most houses in Puebla, it is in fact a place of free access (p. 32). This is the only place in the novel where the existence of a *chora* space is implied, as Octavio Cuenca frequently evokes the presence of his dead wife 'a rozarle la frente con sus pestañas y a escuchar su silencio diciendo todo lo que le pesaba' (p. 30).

This environment of openness revolves around two primary sites: the salon, where artistic *tertulias* slowly give way to political discussions, and the patio, the site of encounter for Daniel and Emilia.

As the political danger grows, the covert meetings are moved from the pharmacy to Cuenca's salon (p. 27). Because the doors are open to all, the meetings blend revolutionary dissidents with federal spies, and the salon as a place of 'theater' takes on a double meaning. While children or adults present their musical or dramatic offerings, another kind of acting is occurring behind the scenes, since the primary vocation of its attendees becomes 'el disimulo': 'No

---

[19] An important spatial contrast is drawn between the environment of Emilia's childhood and that of Daniel Cuenca. After his mother's death, he spent the first three years of his childhood in the care of Milagros, who might have raised him in the same dual environment of stability (kitchen) and volatility (pharmacy) that Emilia experienced. However, his father sends him away 'para enseñarlo a ser hombre' (p. 33), and with the absence of a 'home' he develops a nomadism opposite to that of Emilia: physical restlessness without the intellectual questing spirit. He spends years traveling with the forces of the Revolution, but never takes sides and never evolves in his political views. Instead, he develops an 'incapacidad para detenerse demasiado en el mundo privado' (p. 321) that costs him Emilia, a family, and an 'asidero' (p. 93). At the novel's end, he is the one who has lost most. As the wise doña Baui observes about his frenetic but pointless movement, 'aunque corras, te vas a morir a la misma hora' (p. 344).

se hablaba con frecuencia de los problemas sociales ni se hacían críticas al gobierno, todo parecía cosa de canción y poemas, pero todos los que debían saber
algo lo sabían y cuanto secreto creció en ese mundo de conspiradores se guardó
entre ellos como se guardan los tesoros' (p. 79). The Sunday salon becomes the
center of a covert network: 'Entre semana, los tambores escondidos el domingo
llamaban a guerra de boca en boca y de carta en carta' (p. 79). The fact that this
revolutionary space exists in the home of an upper-class citizen of Puebla makes
it a particularly effective counter-site of resistance.

This is a heavily gendered space, into which Josefa does not dare enter (p.
34). In contrast, her sister Milagros does cross the gender boundary, by adopting
masculine styles of engaging in discussion:

> Todo en esa sala olía al mundo de los hombres. Las pocas mujeres que discur-
> rían entre ellos, era porque se habían hecho al ánimo de parecérseles en el
> modo de razonar y equivocarse. No porque ése les resultara el mejor de los
> modos, sino porque tenían claro que el mundo de los hombres sólo se puede
> penetrar portándose como ellos. Lo demás genera desconfianza.   (p. 34)

This division is associated with Puebla's upper class, under the *porfiriato*. Such
coded notions of space do not affect the middle-class Casa de la Estrella, much
less the poorer towns and *barrios* encountered in Emilia's later travels. But in
1907, the doctor's salon is still exclusively a sphere of male, or masculinized,
activity.

The patio, on the other hand, offers a kind of natural refuge from the rigidity
of social mores. Frequently mentioned are the gardens, the trees, and the pool
beside which all of Emilia's significant conversations with the young Daniel
take place (p. 90). As a young girl, Emilia climbs a tree there, stripping off her
frilly party dress to do so (p. 50); such scenes characterize the patio as a place
of innocence and, later, of sensual attraction. The combination of patio and
salon makes the Cuenca home the site of Emilia's simultaneous intellectual
and emotional maturation, as she grows aware of the possibilities offered by
Daniel's world.

*The 'casa de soltera' – 'Todo lo demás tenía también una razón de ser y un
destino en aquel lugar. Todo estaba regido por una silenciosa pero deliberada
armonía'; 'vivir como los hombres'*
The narrative eye only examines the structure of Milagros's house once, when
Josefa visits in order to ensure that Milagros is safe after her subversive activities
of the night before (pp. 119–20). On this occasion, we see that the style of the
home once again reflects the character of its inhabitant – orderly, harmonious,
without feminine frills. However, the existence of the site itself is of significant structural importance to the novel. Milagros maintains her own residence
because she has opted not to marry, preferring to exercise 'el privilegio de vivir
como los hombres' (p. 35). While for most of the novel she moves only within

Puebla,[20] in fact the entire city is a space accessible to her. She defiantly negotiates not only the masculinized salon of Octavio Cuenca, but also the governor's
home (p. 164), the city's poor *barrios* (p. 129), and the city streets at night (p.
120), always in constant, fervent revolutionary activity. The true female nomad
of the novel, Milagros issues her statement of identity in terms of freedom of
movement, in what she calls her 'edicto implacable': 'Para que tú me veas quieta,
tendrán que enterrarme' (p. 164).[21]

The novel's spatial constructs underscore the relationship between Milagros
and her patient suitor Manuel Rivadeneira. On the occasional nights when she
desires his company, she visits his bed, 'la cama que compartían cuando las
noches eran avaras con el resto de su destino' (p. 76); there is no mention of his
visiting her territory.[22] Eventually they do decide to live together, in his house,
'la gran casa de la avenida Reforma que olía a papeles guardados y a hombre
solo' (p. 198), but while she does accede to live in the masculine space, she never
renounces ownership of her house, the concrete sign of her independence.

Milagros owns another 'casa de soltera' in Mexico City, and both places, as
love nests for Emilia and Daniel, function as social counter-sites of resistance.
Spatially, Milagros has marked off territories where the restrictive rules of society
do not apply, where the young couple can construct their own relationship apart
from the normalizing eyes of 'proper' society. The door key to her Puebla house
becomes Daniel's talisman, his link to the only place that he can call 'home,'
which in his mind he transforms into the traditional hearth site of the mobile man
and the stationary woman:

> Daniel tenía consigo la llave y no la soltó ni en los momentos de guerra en que
> se pierde todo con tal de salvar la vida. La llevaba colgada del cuello y era su
> certidumbre de que tenía un hogar, de que alguien lo esperaba siempre, de que
> por más líos y muerte que tragara, tenía la vida a la vuelta de la esquina y no
> necesitaba sino correr a buscarla. Emilia estaba guardada para él. (p. 239)

His sense of security is illusory, of course, since Emilia does not remain in the
'casa de soltera.' As a respected wife to Zavalza, a mother, doctor, and eventually grandmother, she does not confine herself to a place where she waits for her
lover. Nonetheless, she and Daniel continue their trysts in Milagros's house for
the rest of their lives.[23] Milagros, by occupying and then retaining the 'casa de

[20] Milagros does travel once to Mexico City, with Emilia, and at the end of the novel to
New York, with Rivadeneira.
[21] Milagros intentionally passes on to Emilia her nomadic vocation. After delivering to
her infant niece the traditional women's blessing (wishing her patience, generosity, and 'la paz
de los que no esperan nada'), she delivers her own blessing, in her own image: 'yo te deseo la
locura, el valor, los anhelos, la impaciencia' (p. 25).
[22] Similarly, when Milagros and Rivadeneira travel through the city in his car, she is at
the wheel (p. 146), a reflection that she directs their relationship as well as their revolutionary
activities.
[23] Ironically, at the novel's end Daniel assumes the role of the 'soltera,' envying Zavalza

soltera,' thus serves as the architect of an alternative domestic order, creating a place where the woman can make her own rules and live 'como los hombres' (p. 35).

Santiago – 'aquel paisaje empolvado y chaparro'; 'el otro lado del mundo suave y aromático'
The section of the novel that focuses on the poor neighborhood of Santiago, on the outskirts of Puebla, offers the most direct vision of urban space as a construct of social reproduction, at the service of the hegemonic forces of economic power. Santiago is explicitly characterized as Other, in contrast to the 'centro luminoso de la ciudad' (p. 130) where the primary action of the novel takes place.

As we observed in the Introduction to this study, novels are often plotted on the basis of encounters, as a protagonist crosses liminal areas and confronts an Other. In this critical scene of the novel, Emilia, with Daniel and Milagros, loses the naïveté of her youth as she sees, apparently for the first time, the space of poverty. The *barrio* of Santiago is described as 'un lugar que acunaba las viviendas de adobe y tierra, la desesperanza y el lodo de familias muy pobres' (p. 129). Most notable in the landscape she describes is the homogeneity of the streets and dwellings, causing for her a disorientation akin to being lost in a labyrinth (p. 131). The narrator also highlights the profusion of sounds and smells, which assault the senses of this resident of middle-class Puebla (p. 130). Emilia realizes that she is now seeing the other face of 'her' city, and in a reversal of the roles that she has learned, she is now the outsider: 'por primera vez al verlos en su refugio, sin los edificios y las calles en los que se les trataba como intrusos, Emilia sintió vergüenza y culpa' (p. 130). The inclusion of this alternative urban construction offers one of the few direct examinations of the *porfiriato*'s economic effects.

A similar urban landscape is presented in a later episode, when Emilia attempts to save the life of a young woman who is in some senses presented as her inverse twin, only two years older than she is but trapped in 'el otro lado del mundo suave y aromático en el cual habían crecido las pasiones y certezas que a Emilia le parecían primordiales (p. 221). In a rambling, chaotic sentence reflecting an accumulation of shocking images, the narrator describes a dantesque world across the river from the Casa de la Estrella:

> Cruzaron frente a un grupo de niños que jugaban sobre un cerro de basura, frente a una mujer que volvía de ir en busca de agua caminando con la espalda doblada, frente a una cantina que olía a vómito y un borracho que dormía sus pesares acostado sobre un pedazo ennegrecido de crinolinas viejas, frente a dos hombres que echaban a otro de una tienda y lo alcanzaban para patearlo hasta hacerlo llorar y pedorrearse pidiendo clemencia.   (p. 221)

his wife and grandchildren; finally surrendering his mobility, he ends up cornered in the 'casa de soltera,' waiting for Emilia instead of expecting her to wait for him (p. 375).

These two landscapes of poverty serve to create a kind of Bildungsroman within the larger story of the Mexican Revolution, for in confronting this other world the adolescent Emilia realizes the limitations of acquiring knowledge only through text. Her theoretical knowledge of medicine is useless when she confronts these conditions of poverty. The images of urban squalor give Emilia, for the first time, critical distance from the Casa de la Estrella, and play a role in pushing her beyond Puebla in a search for both medical and political solutions to the sickness of the society that lie just beyond her own threshold. These two spaces function ultimately to embolden Emilia's nomadic spirit, so that when she next reunites with Daniel, she insists on accompanying him into the Revolution rather than resuming her static role of lady in waiting.

Urban heterotopias: the circus and the prison – 'el mejor sitio para estar y no estar'
Between the episodes of Santiago and the *barrio* across the river, and juxtaposed within a single chapter, the narrator presents two heterotopic spaces, the circus (a political fundraiser for the redemption of political prisoners) and the prison (where Daniel is briefly held). The parallels between the two sites, and the intricacy of their connections, create one of the most deftly constructed episodes in the novel.

Swallowed up in the 'bullicio de la carpa,' Emilia and Milagros interweave their tensions about the trapeze artists' act with commentary on the dangers of the political situation (p. 137). Their dialogue figuratively brings the prison into the circus tent, as they discuss the tenuousness of the prisoners' potential freedom between gasps of thrilled fear at the acrobats. Finally, in this carefully constructed atmosphere of tension, Milagros reveals to Emilia that the theoretical has become very personal, since Daniel is the prisoner whose release they will buy that night. Still under the circus tent, Emilia practices the art of dissimulation, 'con los dientes apretados y una sonrisa de mentiras … como si también ella anduviera brincando de un caballo a otro' (p. 138). Their visit to the prison becomes a continuation of the circus routine, as Daniel plays the role of a gringo tourist mistakenly arrested, and Emilia, 'vestida como una muñeca' (p. 141), flirts her way through the guards in order to effect his release. The episode in the prison becomes a trapeze act of skill, daring, and feigned confidence, theater mixed with danger, thus blending the prison into the preceding circus scene.

Both sites are represented as heterotopias. Emilia observes that the hubbub of the circus makes it 'el mejor sitio para estar y no estar que pudiera encontrarse,' as the bright colors of both spectators and spectacle blend into a 'puño de confeti contra la cara' (p. 137). This carnival atmosphere finds its opposite dimension in the prison, the place where individuals are and are not, until they are erased entirely. The narrator thus describes the holding cell of the jail:

Aún no habían encontrado tiempo ni de tomarles los nombres. Los habían echado ahí a esperar la mañana siguiente. O la semana siguiente. Muchos pasaban meses dentro, antes de que su nombre se apuntara en la lista de llegada. Desaparecían y ya. De nada servían sus mujeres todos los días preguntándole por ellos al guardia del portón. Aún no estaban registrados. Tal vez no los registrarían nunca.   (p. 141)

This place of disappearing acts again makes tangible those theories debated in the Casa de la Estrella. Milagros, the bridge figure, regularly crosses between one territory and the other, between political discourse and the realities of the Revolution; but like the episodes of Santiago and the *barrio* across the river, this circus act within the prison functions as part of Emilia's initiation into the real arena of revolutionary activity.

A healing place: Zavalza's hospital – 'un sitio en el que todo era posible'; 'un circo de tres pistas'
As mentioned earlier, the hospital established by Antonio Zavalza becomes not a segregated heterotopia of disease, but rather a culturally diverse place of healing. It is significant that the hospital is built within an old *finca* abandoned by its owners during the Revolution; thus a construct of the *porfiriato* is redesigned into a gathering place of knowledge.

This place 'en el que todo era posible' (p. 358) is intended as a triumphant counter-site to Emilia's impotence in the face of the poverty of Santiago and the *barrio* across the river. She, with Zavalza, has created a locus of empowerment: 'No sabía darse por vencida, no usaba nunca la palabra incurable. … Diagnosticaba los males de la gente con sólo verle el color de la piel o la luz en los ojos, con sólo detenerse en el tono de la voz o el modo de mover los pies. Zavalza la consideraba tan eficaz como un laboratorio ambulante' (p. 357). The hospital is also an extended version of Sauri's *botica*, but instead of bookshelves lined with texts, the place contains streams of visiting healers and scientists, in constant movement and conversation, 'enriqueciéndose con el intercambio indiscriminado de sus conocimientos' (p. 358). The hospital provides her with a workplace to complement the home she establishes with Zavalza, and in this way offers an alternative to the restricted hearth-world of Josefa.

As a female-ordered space, the hospital operates on the basis of dis-order. Emilia's intuitive approach to healing, her openness to a variety of ideas, and her emotional responses to success or failure create a different sense of space from that of a traditional hospital. The narrator notes that the hospital was 'parecido a un circo de tres pistas' (p. 358) and 'parecía más un consejo de locos que un centro científico' (p. 357). In this sense the hospital, although constructed by Zavalza, becomes a female place, of open exchange rather than authority, and ordered around principles traditionally (albeit stereotypically) associated with women.

The structure continues to nourish Emilia's nomadic spirit, for while she does not continue to roam aimlessly, she samples the great variety of approaches that the world offers for healing, in a satisfying substitute for physical travel:

'recorrió el lugar con más entusiasmo del que hubiera puesto en todos los días de sorprenderse con las maravillas de Europa' (p. 254). Mastretta thus offers an alternative to the nomadic option of flight from a restrictively built society; in the space of possibility opened up by the Revolution, her female protagonist can construct a place of her own empowerment and, at least figuratively, a place without boundaries.

In contrast to the other novels we have examined, the hand of capitalism is not apparent in this spatial construction. The *finca* was inherited from the *porfiriato*, the operating room was set up with help from the smiling North American consul in Puebla (pp. 254–5), and continued funding is obtained through Emilia's colleague Arnold Hogan in Chicago (p. 358). In this sense, the idyllic site side-steps many of the real issues surrounding the construction of space as an instrument of control by larger forces of production, an idea that was apparent in her pre-Revolutionary visions of places like the *barrios* of Puebla, but that Mastretta implies was – at least in some areas – erased by the Revolution.

The towns of the Revolution – 'no son para mujeres'

The novel offers two snapshots of towns beyond Puebla in which the poverty of the *porfiriato* and the violence of the Revolution are starkly portrayed. As a kind of 'honeymoon' after their unofficial marriage, Emilia accompanies Daniel to the town of Izúcar, in an attempt to wage the Revolution alongside her lover; and later, when a rumor reaches her in Texas about Daniel's death, she wanders through ravaged northern Mexico until she locates him in a small unnamed town, the home of doña Baui. These two towns are similarly portrayed in the novel, as dusty and unstable sites ruled by desperation and the struggle for daily survival. But in both sites, Emilia overcomes initial immobilization in order to construct gynocentric loci of power.[24]

Emilia's first experience in Izúcar is one of spatial segregation, as she is barred from entering a cantina, because 'las cantinas no son para mujeres' (p. 243). Taking the exclusion as a challenge, Emilia enters the dank space, only to be attacked by a drunk patron; emerging into the sunlight, she petulantly blames Daniel for standing by. This portrayal underscores that Emilia is out of place here, and reinforces stereotypes of space and power. However, shortly thereafter Emilia finds a place within the women's world, befriending Carmela Milpa and Dolores Cienfuegos (p. 246). The three women play the role of caretakers of the place, while their three menfolk go off to war for days at a time. The town's description recalls the images immortalized in so many visual representations of rural Mexico in the early twentieth century: 'Eran calles con casas chaparras

---

[24] In his discussion of Mastretta's connections to the feminist movement in Mexico, Carlos Coria-Sánchez emphasizes Mastretta's preoccupation with the socio-economic conditions in which rural women still seem entrapped.

por las que andaban hombres vestidos de calzón blanco y sombrero de petate, mujeres descalzas y palúdicas, con los hijos colgando como frutas en sus brazos (p. 241). The role of the women hearkens back to the earth-mother stereotype, as Carmela and Dolores raise their grimy but playful children in the skeletal town, and teach Emilia the art of tending the home fires (pp. 246, 248). But after three sentences beginning with 'Aprendió …,' the narrator inserts the verb 'Enseñó …,' as Emilia begins to alter the space around her (p. 246). Most notably, she converts the male space of the cantina into a female space of healing: 'Todas las mañanas instalaba un consultorio improvisado junto a la puerta de la cantina y revisaba cuanto enfermo quería ponérsele enfrente, cuanto niño con tos o diarrea le llevaban su [sic] madres, cuanta llaga, herida, vientre abultado, dolor en la espalda, infección o moribundo quisieron acercarle' (p. 247). Thus she not only inserts herself into the gynocentric society left by war, but she begins to exercise the power to alter that space.

A similar phenomenon occurs in the town where Emilia finds Daniel hiding, after three more years of the Revolution's devastation. The countryside has become a hostile environment, 'esa extensión negra y seca que recorrió durante días sin encontrar nada' (p. 280). This time Emilia is not a young bride but an experienced nomad, having traveled through the United States pursuing her medical studies; and when faced with the dark door of a cantina, she negotiates the space differently than she had in Izúcar: 'El lugar estaba lleno de hombres bebiendo, pero ella no se intimidó con eso que le parecía un paisaje poco inquietante' (p. 283). Once she has located Daniel, she establishes a friendship with the proprietor doña Baui, and again establishes a medical clinic, this time to receive the war wounded (p. 291).

Emilia also carves a hearth-place out of this ruined town; again along stereotypically female lines, she hangs a few cloths and arranges a few plants to create 'un hueco festivo en cuyo ambiente se olvidaba la vida tosca y triste del pueblo todo' (p. 291). By establishing her clinic and her home, Emilia takes a directive role in the Revolution, asserting both her stability and her ability to improve the space directly around her. Significantly, Daniel here becomes her assistant – for the first time in the novel, he stands in the wings waiting on her. By coming to this place, Emilia dis-places the Revolution in favor of her own, more constructive agenda: 'Viéndola transitar entre los enfermos, Daniel supo que Emilia era más fuerte que él, más audaz que él, menos ostentosa que él, más necesaria en el mundo que él con todas sus teorías y todas sus batallas' (p. 288). In Izúcar, Daniel had pushed Emilia to the borders of the Revolution: 'Esta guerra no es tuya' (p. 249), but here she takes over, and fills up the space left by the war's devastation. In response, in the apartment that she has created for the two of them, he paces restlessly back and forth and kicks the walls (p. 295), in fruitless movement, in contrast to her directed travels through the town. For the male half of the couple, the spatial reassignment is not tolerable.

The United States – 'la paz y los pasteles gringos'; 'un futuro que no pensara en la guerra'; 'huir de su destino'; 'buscando, buscando'

Among the novels of this study, *Mal de amores* offers by far the most favorable portrayal of the United States. With no criticism of capitalist hegemony or globalization and threatened cultural lifestyles such as was seen in the novels by Restrepo, Allende, and Ferré, the novel instead presents the United States as a refuge of safety in time of war (the first World War, contemporaneous with the Mexican Revolution, is not referred to), and as a place where learning can be freely pursued, by women as well as men. In this safety Emilia 'perdió el miedo de perderse' (p. 263), and instead finds her own footing. In contrast to the intricate landscapes of Mexico that the novel offers, the representation of its northern neighbor is quite one-dimensional. The United States plays a purely functional role in the development of the plot; it may be read as the liminal space where Emilia is allowed to develop independently of the confining options of the Casa de la Estrella or her two suitors.[25] Thus, as represented geography, the United States is of less interest. Nonetheless, three cities – San Antonio, Chicago, and New York – offer different kinds of space in which Emilia learns to navigate her own course.

San Antonio houses Emilia's last attempt to re-create her mother's domestic architecture. Reunited with Daniel (now working as a correspondent for US newspapers), Emilia re-creates the Casa de la Estrella for herself and Daniel, leading him to observe that the change of site has not altered her: 'traes a cuestas tu mundo' (p. 263). The failure of this transplantation of her mother's world marks a critical point in Emilia's evolution, as the new culture makes her comfortable for the first time to free herself from loyalties both to Daniel and to Zavalza. In a scene that involves both verbal and physical struggle with Daniel, she announces the initiation of her true autonomy: 'Estoy cansada de ir y venir según el vaivén de tus antojos y los de la república' (p. 265). The safety that is depicted in this San Antonio, in contrast to the Mexican sites, plays a crucial role here, as Emilia discovers that the protective male presence is unnecessary to her future pursuits.[26]

The representation of Chicago continues the development of Emilia in the 'neutral zone' of the United States. Once again, the landscape is marked by its contrast to Mexico – most notably in the hostile environment of winter (p. 268),

---

[25] Van Gennep's key study of liminal spaces postulates geographic 'neutral zones' that mark the transition from adolescent dependence into adulthood (p. 18; see also the Introduction to this study for further discussion of the 'limen' concept); in this novel, the United States plays a similar role in Emilia's maturation. However, she does not remain trapped in the liminoid region of transition, but rather opts to return to resume 'su destino' in Mexico (p. 267).

[26] Stepping off the train in San Antonio, Emilia observes that the overriding odors of Mexico were either of gunpowder or of death, in stark contrast to San Antonio's atmosphere of 'galletas con mantequilla' (p. 262).

but also in the characterization of Northwestern University as an innovative and
welcoming environment for learning; here, under the tutelage of Arnold Hogan,
Emilia refines her abilities to treat illness, both physical and psychological,
through careful listening (p. 270). The University becomes a site of interchange
of knowledge rather than just of Emilia's tutelage, as Hogan learns both from
her intuitive way with patients and from her knowledge of indigenous cures
(pp. 269–70). Chicago is also depicted as culturally open, since Emilia's cultural
influence converts Hogan's solitary home into a salon like that of the Cuenca
home, of Emilia's childhood – a gathering place for poetry, music, and political
discussion (p. 271). Thus, instead of the image we have seen in prior novels, of
US cultural hegemony threatening local tradition, this novel offers the US as a
place of mutual cultural interaction and reinforcement.

Finally, New York City functions as a carnivalesque zone where Emilia can
free herself from responsibilities. Emilia visits the city on two occasions: first to
attend a party with a friend from Chicago (p. 276), and the second time ostensibly
to attend a medical conference but, in effect, to celebrate a passionate reunion
with Daniel.

The first visit involves a masterfully narrated scene similar to the conflation
of circus and prison discussed earlier. Emilia attends a dance, but carries in her
purse an unopened telegram from Mexico, and dreads the knowledge that its
news will draw her ineluctably back home, marking the end of her profitable
time in the neutral zone. The space of the dance contrasts dramatically with the
psychological weight of the sealed envelope:

> Esa noche, mientras Helen bailaba foxtrot, Emilia se empeñó en no cerrar
> los ojos, en mirarla reír o en tararear el ritmo juguetón que seguían sus
> pasos sin dejarse siquiera parpadear, porque temía hundirse en el recuerdo
> de las batallas, persecuciones, horrores y perseverancias que llenaban
> los escritos de Daniel. Pero mientras la música la hacía sentir mansa-
> mente cobijada, le tomaron el cuerpo las palabras de Daniel en su envío
> una semana antes: 'Como están las cosas, aquí ya no importa qué bando es
> más valiente, ni quién tiene la razón. Hace tiempo que todos la perdimos
> y que sólo son cobardes quienes huyeron con su causa a otra parte.'
>   Una mano frente a sus ojos interrumpió el pesar de sus pensamientos y sigu-
> iéndola se levantó a bailar foxtrot como quien hace la guerra, divertida con sus
> pies y su brío, con el abrazo que la llevaba de un lado a otro, con la mezcla de
> castellano y escocés en que su pareja le preguntaba por su vida, con la sonrisa
> que iba acompañándola a oírse hablar de sí misma como de otra mujer.
>
>   (p. 277)

This scene calls upon carnivalesque tradition, with Emilia donning a forced
mask of gaity to combat the sense of tragedy that has tracked her all the way to
New York. She is represented as an outsider at the place of celebration, and she
unwillingly bears out Daniel's earlier observation, 'traes a cuestas tu mundo'
(p. 263). The neutral space disintegrates in the face of the missive from Mexico,

and she returns to search for Daniel – but not without the strengths gained from her time in the US.

The second visit to New York carries even more of a carnival flavor, when Emilia and Daniel reunite after several years of her presumably fulfilled life as Zavalza's wife and a Puebla doctor. They find in New York the anonymity and celebratory atmosphere that make their hiatus from real life possible, the 'mundo desordenado y hospitalario de esa ciudad siempre dispuesta a ofrecer refugio a las pasiones irremisibles' (p. 368), as they spend the first days locked in their hotel room, and then roam the streets enjoying their freedom:

> Las semanas siguientes recorrieron la ciudad como una feria, como si fuera un tiovivo el rodar de tantos coches motorizados y una rueda de fortuna subir la cuesta de sus edificios. Entraban a los teatros como a cajas de sorpresa, miraban como una oferta las embarcaciones que llegaban de otros mundos, comían extravagancias hasta que les salía por las orejas el olor a mares remotos.
>
> (p. 366)

Notably, for the first time in all of her travels, Emilia does not try to construct a hearth-place here. Equipped now with the knowledge that she will not stay with Daniel, that she has a home elsewhere and that Daniel is her present but not her future (p. 366), she celebrates in a space where she assumes no responsibility and takes no control: 'Daniel ... vivía en un departamento pequeño, cuyo desorden Emilia no intentó trastocar. Ahí se instalaron a dormir y besarse mientras el mundo trabajaba' (p. 368). This spatial reference has significance only in the context of the other domestic spaces of the novel, where Emilia had repeatedly set down roots; this escapist New York serves merely as a holiday. This spirit of place will be preserved in Milagros' 'casa de soltera', where the couple will continue to celebrate occasional passionate encounters outside the bounds of productive and responsible social structures, thus enabling Emilia to 'have it all.'

Mexico City – 'la ciudad sitiada, peligrosa y fandanguera en que se había convertido la capital'

Mexico City appears at two distinct moments in the novel, reflecting two phases of the Revolution as well as of Emilia's personal development. The first visit to Mexico City, by Emilia and her aunt Milagros, marks the occasion of Madero's triumphant welcome following the departure of Porfirio Díaz. On this occasion Mexico City resembles the New York described above: a city on holiday. Again the upside-down environment of the carnival prevails: 'todo era un bullicio sin orden y sin tregua' (p. 210). During this brief episode, Emilia spots Daniel in the parade, and the two of them embrace, thus forming part of the spectacle themselves (p. 211). However, the brevity of their reunion reflects also the brevity of the nation's celebration; Daniel disappears, and shortly thereafter Madero is assassinated.

Mexico City is perhaps only narrated in the above episode in order to provide a contrast with its depiction several years later, when it has been battered by the shifting power struggles of the Revolution. In its second appearance in the novel, it is described as 'sitiada, peligrosa y fandanguera' (p. 306), a place of chaos and danger: 'Todos los días aparecían cadáveres regados, sin más dueño que el aire, muertos en mitad de la noche por quítame de allá estas pajas. Al anochecer no les recomendaba que salieran, porque según [el cochero] a esas horas los revolucionarios andaban aún más sueltos que en el día y más borrachos que en la mañana' (p. 307). The apartment owned by Milagros provides the couple with an oasis of safety and cleanliness,[27] but every time they step out, they are within the Revolution itself, in an even more vivid way than they were in the town of doña Baui.

Again the circus imagery is invoked to characterize the perilous nature of this war-enveloped city, 'como si la faramalla del circo fuera la perfecta gemela del desvarío en que vivían. ... la ciudad toda parecía suspendida entre un columpio y otro' (p. 332). The theater is also identified as a site of escapism, with its offerings of light musical *zarzuelas* with their consistent happy endings (p. 331). But outside these controlled arenas of spectacle, the city is represented as a 'vorágine' in which 'cada día era el último' (pp. 332–3).

Within this heterotopia of crisis, Emilia – building on the lessons of Izúcar, the United States, and the town of doña Baui – does construct a navigable world in which to function on both a personal and professional level. Domestically, she constructs a 'casa de naipes' (p. 335) within which she can pretend that she and Daniel are a happily married and stable couple, along the lines of the models from the Casa de la Estrella. She also establishes friendships with two fellow wanderers, don Refugio and Ignacio Cardenal, who fill the personal void left by Daniel's frequent absences. More significantly, she creates a workday routine for herself as a doctor in the Red Cross hospital, fighting against the destruction of the Revolution (pp. 322–3).

Her medical vocation provides the basis for one of the most effective narrations of space in the novel. Emilia leaves her conjugal bed in order to work at the hospital; Daniel, consumed with jealousy, delivers a diatribe against her 'profesión de mierda, profesión que todo lo abandonaba para no abandonar a un enfermo,' and departs to his own pursuits, leaving only a note; fifteen minutes later, Emilia rushes back to their apartment, hoping to tell him about her experiences in order to draw him into that aspect of her life, but finds only the note. The scene is easily visualized in dramatic terms; the narrative eye remains only on the apartment, with each partner rushing around to find the other but equally drawn

---

[27] Notably symbolic is the scene in which Daniel and Emilia bathe away the horrors of the Revolution, 'su mugre de casi un mes' (p. 310); this space of purification within the place that Milagros had prepared fortifies them for their continued revolutionary work in the capital city.

to adventures and responsibilities that lie offstage. This scene marks a shift in Daniel's and Emilia's relationship. For the first time, both he and she admit that 'ella también tenía quehaceres y destino,' and she recognizes that she does not have a real place in the capital city, as her nostalgia for Puebla begins to call her home (pp. 322–3).

This episode in the capital city brings to the fore again Mastretta's talent for blending the landscape of the Mexican Revolution with the personal lifecourse of her protagonist. The images of the couple huddled in a café, taking refuge in a theater or a circus, or blocking out the city by making love in their apartment, are juxtaposed to the brutal and violent exterior of the Palacio Nacional, the streets, and the hospitals. Within this theater of operations, as in the town of doña Baui, Daniel's movement to and fro loses significance, as Emilia struggles to find her vocation and put it to use in the rebuilding of the nation.

The space of the Mexican Revolution – 'un bullicio de odio desatado'; 'un país en destrucción

The larger theater of the Mexican Revolution is effectively constructed by the snapshots of small towns or of Mexico City; but it is spatially configured in other ways as well. One literary mechanism for the penetration of the Revolution into domestic or personal space is the use of letters or, later, newspaper articles, as a way for the bystanders to map Daniel's itinerant experience. The letters make the Revolution optional; Emilia can refuse to open them – as she does with the telegram in New York – or she can contain them – as when she locks a letter from Daniel in a cedar cigar box: 'Una vez encerrada entre aquellas paredes aromadas, el mensaje de Daniel dejó de entrometerse con su futuro' (p. 235). The voluntary nature of this textual participation is emphasized by Daniel's written question to her, '¿quieres oír?' (p. 233), before listing the horrors he has witnessed in person. These missives, and the newspaper articles that replace them once he ceases to write to her, bring the scenes of the Revolution rhetorically into the space of the Casa de la Estrella (for example, pp. 231–3).

Certainly the most effective discursive strategy for portraying the visual spectacle of the Revolution is the chronotope of the train, as Daniel and Emilia travel from doña Baui's town to Mexico City. This chapter perhaps best exemplifies the artistry that won for *Mal de amores* the Premio Rómulo Gallegos, as it adopts cinematic techniques to capture the feeling of mobs of desperate citizens fleeing into or away from the horrors of the revolutionary landscape.[28] Scenes of despair assault Emilia both within and outside the train. Outside, the train hurtles past

---

[28] The scene of the Revolution's train should be contrasted with a pre-Revolutionary train trip, a lyrically described excursion to Veracruz by the still-innocent Daniel and Emilia; the passage describes an idyllic landscape and the young people's enjoyment of the journey (p. 62). Against this dreamy portrayal, the later train ride is seen as a nightmare.

one tragedy after another, kilometer after kilometer, from a row of hanged men to massacres to burned-out villages (p. 298). Emilia is condemned to, and frustrated by, her forced role as passive onlooker on these scenes (p. 299), yet she cannot look away: 'Se abrazaban incapaces de cerrar los ojos, con el asombro de la primera visión negándoles el derecho a perderse las siguientes' (p. 298). From a narrative perspective, the moving train is a brilliant mechanism for communicating the scope of the Revolution's destruction and the conversion of the countryside into an infernal spectacle.

The interior of the train offers another space of horror, as in a continual transfer the healthy men jump off to join the Revolution and are replaced with the bodies of the wounded and the dying. The train is thus a fluid space, an encapsulated version of the Revolution itself. Emilia attempts to adopt her navigational strategy of setting up a healing space, but in this case the need overwhelms her, and she finds herself without any resources with which to respond (pp. 299–300). Trapped on the train and confronted with her own impotence, Emilia becomes simply another victim of the onrushing Revolution.[29]

Within this space, the only ray of hope comes from the *curandera* Teodora, who can heal through touch or mysterious chants, thus offering some relief to the suffering passengers without the aid of herbs or medical resources. This figure offers Emilia the chance to employ the navigational mechanisms that have functioned in the past, to create a space where she can, to some degree, resist the situation that threatens to engulf her. Exchanging medical information, she and Teodora create a 'curso de medicina itinerante' that functions as a mechanism of survival, until she can leave behind the hellish landscape within and outside the train (p. 303).

The wounded body and the eroticized body

The body as a site of encounter forms a leitmotif that connects the two main focuses of the novel: Emilia's vocation for healing and her desire for two very different men. In terms of the medical vocation, it should be noted that the bodies represented are not just diseased, but wounded, either from war or from the effects of poverty. The damage is generally physical, but can also be psychological. In either case, the protagonist views the human body as a decipherable entity, if only the physician can learn to see and hear closely: 'no hay casos perdidos, sino médicos que no encuentran' (p. 270). She views the body as a complex

---

[29] Within the inescapable atmosphere of the train, the people descend to the level of their survival instincts: 'Al principio, Emilia se había empeñado en mantener en alto las dotes civilizatorias que con tanto cuidado habían puesto en ella sus padres, pero con el tiempo aprendió a guiarse como los otros pasajeros, según sus necesidades se lo pedían. Incluso se hizo al ánimo de esperar a la oscuridad de la media noche para levantar su falda y cobijar a Daniel bajo ella, en un juego que sobre la certeza de la muerte, revaluaba la vida en la trabazón de sus cuerpos' (p. 299).

machine, and 'sabía dónde quedaba cada tornillo' (p. 192). Her confidence in the comprehensibility of the human body provides the basis for her confident and consistent movement in the direction of the study and practice of medicine. At the same time, in her approach to healing, Emilia adopts the traditionally feminine attributes of empathy and intuition, often letting instinct rather than science direct her diagnostic process.[30] The innate affinity that Mastretta paints, between the body of the healer and the wounded or sick body, reinforces traditional gender stereotypes that, by associating women with instinct, by implication grant the field of reason to men. Mastretta attempts to combat that limitation by having her character move in masculine professional circles, traveling to deliver medical talks and to attend conferences, but the legacy of the nature/reason binarism still problematizes the representation of the woman as healer.

The eroticized body and female desire also play a dominant role in directing the protagonist's lifecourse. By associating her female character with two men, Mastretta is able to portray two different types of desire: one purely carnal and physical (as Emilia has been physically drawn to Daniel since childhood) and the other stemming from platonic affection (Emilia works alongside Zavalza for several years before entering his bed). While at the novel's end Emilia announces 'Soy bígama' (p. 348), in fact she does not officially marry either man. She side-steps the traditional matrimonial vows, which would renounce one man for the other and one kind of bodily satisfaction for the other, instead accepting – and forcing the men to accept – that her needs exceed the territory that Western matrimony would grant her.

The sweeping forces of passion are, of course, essential elements of the melo-dramatic genre, and Mastretta exploits that magnetism to the fullest, as Emilia is led into nomadism by Daniel's incessant movement, and then twice forces herself to abandon him because he is unable to satisfy her needs. Nonetheless, her final solution, the occupying of two marital beds, dissatisfies only Daniel. While in some senses he – the only character fully engaged in the war – represents the cutting edge of the Revolution, he alone demands that she occupy the space of the traditional woman, either standing by his side or waiting alone for him. For this backward-looking view of female autonomy, he is thus the character that is left behind in the new Mexico since, as Emilia repeats, 'No entiendes nada' (pp. 368, 375).

Mastretta thus constructs an original domestic design for the satisfaction of female desire. Her protagonist Emilia does not silence the demands of her body, nor is she willing to sacrifice the advantages of her mother's hearth-based system

---

[30] It is interesting that, while her 'talking cures' embody many characteristics tradition-ally associated with women, she learns her techniques at the side of three men: the doctor Octavio Cuenca, the North American doctor Arnold Hogan, and the slightly dotty don Refugio in Mexico City. Only one of her medical mentors – the *curandera* Teodora – is female. None-theless, the novel repeatedly asserts that Emilia surpasses her teachers in her intuitive grasp of both psychological and physical maladies, thus reinforcing the stereotypical associations of women with intuition and men with reason.

in order to follow the dictates of passion.[31] Instead, on the empty canvas of post-Revolutionary Mexico, she stakes out the triple territory of the hospital, the homeplace, and the 'casa de soltera,' in order to make her own body whole.

Conclusion

By constructing three centers of activity, Emilia destabilizes the notion of female locatedness. In many ways, this protagonist does not have to struggle against the limitations of Restrepo's, Allende's, Sefchovich's, and Ferré's protagonists. She does not face a society hostile to her nomadic experimentation, and within the chaos of the Revolution, as well as the neutral space of the United States, she actually finds it easier to establish her own footing. All of the male characters of the novel (with the exception of Daniel) are willing to play a complicit role in her search, and she has physically before her the trailblazing model of her aunt Milagros, who faced similar challenges in a much more restrictive social environment. The censure of Church and tradition seems absent, although in one passing reference the narrator notes that she did not have 'tiempo ni ganas de preguntarse por la opinión ajena' (p. 355). Thus Emilia works within a pliable social structure, against the backdrop of national reconstruction and social justice.

In order to accommodate the destabilizing movement of Milagros and Emilia, Rivadeneira and Zavalza must adopt the stationary position formerly allotted to women; they 'keep house.' Rivadeneira acknowledges this reversal of space, in a typically female utterance of frustration against his partner's frequent and perilous absences: 'Estoy harto de condescender, harto de que me trate como si no existiera, de que me tome y me deje como si yo fuera la esposa de un general en campaña' (p. 165). In this sense, the novel offers spatial reversal rather than a complete dismantling of assigned social spaces. Emilia occupies the traditionally male arenas of the workplace, the home, and the bed of her occasional lover. Yet in this imaginative reconstruction of Mexican society at a time of maximum possibility, at the close of the Revolution, the men are ultimately content with these women who do not belong to them, but who, finally, consent to share their space.

---

[31] Perhaps over-emphasizing the function of maternity as an ideal, Martha González discusses the lure of the 'hogar' in her study '*Mal de amores*: la génesis de un espacio materno' (1998–9).

Conclusion

Novels may be spatial practices, but narrated spaces are, in the end, verbal constructs. The study of space and place in literature must include not only what spaces are presented and how space functions upon and from the actions of the characters, but also the aesthetic structuring of space. Contemporary novels do not generally contain long, digressive passages detailing a landscape or a layout. A few words and sentences serve to convey the image of places, the tension involved in struggles for control of those places, and the change in those places over time. This study has attempted to identify not only the spaces constructed in these novels by women, but the discursive strategies used to evoke those spaces. In setting the stage for the novels' actions, the authors triangulate the story, adding the third dimension to the sequence of events.

Popular fiction is a literature of broad consumption. The best-sellers included in this study not only reflect the locatedness of their authors, but also potentially influence the way their readers perceive space. By reading with an eye on space, we follow the novelists in questioning the social construction that built those places, thus reading the text as an exploration of mechanisms of power. The novelists discussed here share a strong sense of their national context. Four of the five novelists choose to set their stories in the early twentieth century, a time when rapid industrialization seemed either to threaten or to renovate existing notions of locatedness. For Restrepo and Ferré, this modernization is seen as negative, in its inevitable erasure of what it builds upon. For Allende, Sefchovich, and Mastretta, the rapid changes bring excitement and the possibility of renovation, although Sefchovich's protagonist can only partially realize this transformation. The early twentieth century was also the period in which the United States made its presence more directly felt in the construction of Latin American societies, and this positioning, and its effect on local and national issues of identity, is also apparent in the ways societies are built within the novels.

In all five novels, traditional domestic architecture collapses, as female protagonists confront the options of increased mobility that accompany modernity. Across all of these novels, one observation is clear: marriage no longer works as a framework for the life of the questing woman. Even exclusive heterosexuality is rare, as these protagonists reject images of fixity. Instead, unsatisfied desire, and attempts to address the demands of the female body, are a constant in all of the novels. Similarly, in all five works the woman protagonist seeks not just to work but to fulfill a vocation. The brothel, the photography lab, the remodeled apartment, the stage and the hospital become places where the woman becomes agent, where she puts herself rather than being located by the expectations of ordered production.

The spatial practice common to all five works is restlessness. Like trying on new suits, the female protagonists try out different places, and experiment with the restrictions of each of those places. Ultimately, no place—not even home—is 'home.' Restrepo and Allende leave their protagonists on the brink of an exciting and unknown future, filled with continued movement. Sefchovich's narrator withdraws inward, in what might be read as satisfaction but is more convincingly read as self-erasure. Ferré and Mastretta, more optimistically, close with epilogues that portray their characters as old women, who look back without regret on a lifetime of incessant movement.

When we read the spaces in these novels, we arrive not only at a more intricate understanding of the structuring of a work of art, but also at a more precise interpretation of the characters' fictional actions. Feminist criticism has often challenged women writers to present positive role models, female protagonists who dare to construct new solutions to shared dilemmas of autonomy and identity. However, writers cannot write to the agendas of critics, but instead craft images that express their own views about the obstacles that women face and the possibilities of surmounting them. A spatial analysis allows for a critical and acute reading of these—and other—novels, in order to see beyond the superficial balm of a 'happy ending.' As we have seen, while the characters may feel satisfied at the end of their stories, and while therefore a casual reading might imply triumph on the part of the protagonist, an analysis of autonomy in the face of hegemony, viewed from the perspective of spatial practices, sometimes implies a bleaker response. In the cases of those characters who do negotiate more successfully, a spatially based discussion exposes the tools and strategies that led to their ability to fashion a tolerable place for themselves. In answer to the spatial question 'Who put her there?' all five characters would respond that they took charge of their own paths, and demystified the idea of separate public and private or separate male and female space. By resisting attempts at control, by building new homes, schools, or hospitals, or through continued traveling, they construct and then defend their own places.

Henri Lefebvre noted that 'new social relationships call for a new space, and vice versa' (p. 59). As these women writers invent the characters that will serve as counter-figures to earlier ways of negotiating gender and class, they will also redesign the sites of those negotiations. A critical reading through this three-dimensional lens allows for a greater appreciation of the layers of architecture that undergird their artistic visions.

WORKS CITED

Allende, Isabel, *Retrato en sepia* (Barcelona: Plaza & Janés, 2000)

American Heritage Dictionary of the English Language, 4th edn (New York: Houghton Mifflin, 2000)

André, María Claudia, 'Breaking through the Maze: Feminist Configurations of the Heroic Quest in Isabel Allende's *Daughter of Fortune* and *Portrait in Sepia*', in *Isabel Allende Today*, ed. Rosemary G. Feal and Yvette E. Miller (Pittsburgh: Latin American Literary Review Press, 2002), pp. 74–90

Arboleda, Carlos Arturo, 'Lenguaje e identidad en *La novia oscura*, de Laura Restrepo', *Cuadernos de ALDEEU*, 17, 1 (2001), 193–200

Ardener, Shirley (ed.), *Women and Space: Ground Rules and Social Maps* (New York: St. Martin's Press, 1981)

Arreguín Bermúdez, Antonio, 'La intertextualidad en la novelística de Sara Sefchovich y Luis Spota: Los escritores crean a su precursor, Dante', Diss. University of Arizona, 2002

Azuela, Mariano, *Los de abajo*, ed. Marta Portal (Madrid: Cátedra, 1984)

Bachelard, Gaston, *The Poetics of Space*, trans. Maria Jolas (Boston: Beacon, 1994 [1st edn 1958])

Bakhtin, M. M, *The Dialogic Imagination*, ed. Michael Holquist, trans. Caryl Emerson and Michael Holquist (Austin: University of Texas Press, 1981)

——, *Rabelais and His World*, trans. Helene Iswolsky (Cambridge: MIT Press, 1968)

Barnes, Trevor J. and James S. Duncan (ed.), *Writing Worlds: Discourse, Text, and Metaphor in the Representation of Landscape* (London: Routledge, 1992)

Bhabha, Homi, *The Location of Culture* (London: Routledge, 1994)

Blunt, Alison, and Gillian Rose (eds), *Writing Women and Space: Colonial and Post-colonial Geographies* (New York: Guilford, 1994)

Bondi, Liz, 'Locating Identity Politics,' in *Place and the Politics of Identity*, ed. Michael Keith and Steve Pile (London: Routledge, 1993), pp. 84–101

Bordo, Susan, *Unbearable Weight: Feminism, Western Culture, and the Body* (Berkeley: University of California Press, 1993)

Braidotti, Rosi, 'Embodiment, Sexual Difference, and the Nomadic Subject', *Hypatia*, 8, 1 (1993), 1–13

——, *Nomadic Subjects: Embodiment and Sexual Difference in Contemporary Feminist Theory* (New York: Columbia University Press, 1994)

Brooker-Gross, Susan R., 'Teaching about Race, Gender, Class and Geography through Fiction', *Journal of Geography in Higher Education*, 15, 1 (1991), 35–47

Brueggemann, Walter, *The Land: Place as Gift, Promise, and Challenge in Biblical Faith* (Minneapolis: Augsburg Fortress, 2002) [1st ed. 1977]

Butler, Judith, *Gender Trouble: Feminism and the Subversion of Identity* (New York: Routledge, 1999 [1st pub. 1990])

Casey, Edward S., 'Body, Self, and Landscape: A Geophilosophical Inquiry into the Place-World', in *Textures of Place: Exploring Humanist Geographies*, ed. Paul C. Adams, Steven Hoelscher and Karen E. Till (Minneapolis: University of Minnesota Press, 2001), pp. 403–25

Caviedes, César, 'The Latin American Boom-Town in the Literary View of José María Arguedas', in *Geography and Literature: A Meeting of the Disciplines*, ed. William E. Mallory and Paul Simpson-Housley (Syracuse: Syracuse University Press, 1987), pp. 57–77

Coria-Sánchez, Carlos, 'El discurso feminista de Angeles Mastretta en *Mal de amores*', *South Carolina Modern Language Review*, 3, 1 (2004) (n.p.)

Cosgrove, Denis and Mona Domosh, 'Author and Authority: Writing the New Cultural Geography', in *Place/Culture/Representation*, ed. James Duncan and David Ley (London: Routledge, 1993), pp. 25–38

Cypess, Sandra Messinger, 'Love Preserves: Ethnicity and Desire in the Narratives of Sara Sefchovich', *Modern Jewish Studies*, 14, 1 (2004), 26–49

Daly, Ann, *Done into Dance: Isadora Duncan in America* (Middletown, CT: Wesleyan University Press, 1985)

Daniels, Stephen and Simon Rycroft, 'Mapping the Modern City: Alan Sillitoe's Nottingham Novels', *Transactions of the Institute of British Geographers*, 18, 4 (1993), 460–80

de Certeau, Michel, *The Practice of Everyday Life*, trans. Steven Rendall (Berkeley: University of California Press, 1984)

del Campo, Alicia, 'Reterritorializando lo mexicano desde lo femenino en el contexto neoliberal: *Demasiado amor* de Sara Sefchovich', *New Novel Review / Nueva Novela/Nouveau Roman*, 2, 2 (1995), 60–75

Derrida, Jacques, 'Khōra,' in *On the Name*, ed. Thomas Dutoit, trans. Ian McLeod (Stanford: Stanford University Press, 1995 [1st pub. 1993]), pp. 89–127

DiBattista, Maria, Review of *Flight of the Swan*, by Rosario Ferré, available from: <www.counciloftheamericas.org/as/literature/br65ferre.html> [Accessed Dec. 2004]

Dickson, Samuel, 'Isadora Duncan (1878–1927)', in 'San Francisco Kaleidoscope' (Stanford University Press, 1949), available from: <http://www.sfmuseum.org/bio/isadora.html> [Accessed Dec. 2004]

Duncan, Cynthia, 'Mad Love: The Problematization of Gendered Identity and Desire in Recent Mexican Women's Novels', *Studies in the Literary Imagination*, 33, 1 (2000), 37–49

Duncan, Isadora, *My Life* (New York: Liveright Publishers, 1955 [1st edn 1927])

Duncan, James and David Ley (eds), *Place/Culture/Representation* (London: Routledge, 1993)

Duncan, Nancy (ed.), *BodySpace: Destabilizing Geographies of Gender and Sexuality* (London: Routledge, 1996)

Durán, Javier, 'Narrar la nación: (Des)Construyendo el imaginario nacional en *Demasiado amor* de Sara Sefchovich', in *La seducción de la escritura: Los discursos de la cultura hoy*, ed. Rosaura Hernández Monroy and Manuel F. Medina (Azcapotzalco, Mexico: Universidad Autónoma Metropolitana, 1997), pp. 355–63

Fahey, Felicia, 'Remaking Place: National Space in Late Twentieth-Century Latin American Fiction', Diss., University of California-Santa Cruz, 2000

——, '(Un)Romancing Mexico: New Sexual Landscapes in Sara Sefchovich's *Demasiado amor*', *Inti: Revista de Literatura Hispánica*, 54 (2001), 99–120

Feal, Rosemary G. and Yvette E. Miller (eds), *Isabel Allende Today* (Pittsburgh: Latin American Literary Review Press, 2002)

Felluga, Dina, 'Introductory Guide to Critical Theory', available from: <http://www.cla.purdue.edu/academic/engl/theory> [Accessed Jan. 2005]

Ferré, Rosario, *Flight of the Swan* (New York: Penguin Putnam, 2002)

——, Rev. of *Flight of the Swan* (Libreros Reunidos, SL), available from: <www.barataria.com/novedades/200210.html> [Accessed Dec. 2004]

Fitter, Chris, *Poetry, Space, Landscape: Toward a New Theory* (Cambridge: Cambridge University Press, 1995)

Foucault, Henri, 'Of Other Spaces', trans. Jay Miskowiec, *Diacritics*, 16 (1986 [1st pub. 1984]), 22–27

——, *Power/Knowledge: Selected Interviews and Other Writings 1972–1977*, ed. and trans. Colin Gordon (New York: Pantheon, 1980)

——, 'Questions of Method', in *The Foucault Effect: Studies in Governmentality*, ed. Graham Burchell, Colin Gordon, and Peter Miller (Chicago: University of Chicago Press, 1991), pp. 73–86

Fowles, John, *Daniel Martin*, 2nd edn (London: Little, Brown, 1978)

Franco, Jean, 'Going Public: Reinhabiting the Private', in *Critical Passions: Situated Essays by Jean Franco*, ed. Mary Louise Pratt and Kathleen Newman (Durham: Duke University Press, 1999 [1st pub. 1992])

Friedman, Susan Stanford, *Mappings: Feminism and the Cultural Geographies of Encounter* (Princeton: Princeton University Press, 1998)

Frye, Northrop, *The Anatomy of Criticism: Four Essays* (Princeton: Princeton University Press, 1957)

Gebelein, Anne C., 'Sara Sefchovich', in *Encyclopedia of Latin American Women Writers*, ed. María Claudia André and Eva Paulino Bueno, available from: <http://www.hope.edu/latinamerican/Sefchovich.html> [Accessed Jan. 2005]

Gershenbaum, Barbara Lipkien, Rev. of *Flight of the Swan*, available from <www.bookreporter.com/reviews/0452283310.asp> [Accessed Dec. 2004]

González, Martha, '*Mal de amores*: La génesis de un espacio materno', *Revista de Literatura Mexicana Contemporánea*, 4, 9 (1998–99), 87–92

Griffin, Susan, *Woman and Nature: the Roaring Inside Her* (New York: Harper Colophon, 1978)

Grosz, Elizabeth, 'Bodies-Cities', in *Sexuality and Space*, ed. Beatriz Colomina (Princeton: Princeton Architectural Press, 1992), 241–53

——, 'Inscriptions and Body Maps: Representations and the Corporeal', in *Space, Gender, Knowledge*, ed. Linda McDowell and Joanne P. Sharp (London: Edward Arnold, 1997), pp. 236–47 [1st pub. 1990]

——, *Volatile Bodies: Toward a Corporeal Feminism* (Bloomington: Indiana University Press, 1994)

——, 'Women, *Chora*, Dwelling', in *Postmodern Cities and Spaces*, ed. Sophie Watson and Katherine Gibson (Oxford: Blackwell, 1995), pp. 47–58

Guerriero, Leila, 'Nómade por naturaleza', *Suplemento Cultural La Nación*, 30 May 2004.

Hansen-Löve, Katharina, *The Evolution of Space in Russian Literature* (Amsterdam: Rodopi, 1994)

Haraway, Donna, 'Situated Knowledges: The Science Question in Feminism and the Privilege of Partial Perspective', *Feminist Studies*, 14 (1988), 575–99

——, *Simians, Cyborgs, and Women: The Reinvention of Nature* (London: Free Association Press, 1991)

Harley, J. B., 'Deconstructing the Map', in *Writing Worlds: Discourse, Text and Metaphor in the Representation of Landscape*, ed. Trevor J. Barnes and James S. Duncan (London: Routledge, 1992), pp. 231–47

Harvey, David, 'Between Space and Time: Reflections on the Geographical Imagination', *Annals of the Association of American Geographers*, 80 (1990), 418–34

——, 'Class Relations, Social Justice and the Politics of Difference', in *Place and the Politics of Identity*, ed. Michael Keith and Steve Pile (London: Routledge, 1993), pp. 41–66

——, *The Condition of Postmodernity* (Oxford: Blackwell, 1990)

——, *Justice, Nature and the Geography of Difference* (Oxford: Blackwell, 1996)

Hayden, Dolores, *The Power of Place: Urban Landscapes as Public History* (Cambridge: MIT Press, 1995)

Hernández Enríquez, Virginia, 'Educación femenina y transgresión en *Mal de amores*', in *Las miradas de la crítica: Los discursos de la cultura hoy*, ed. Rosaura Hernández Monroy, Manuel F. Medina, and Javier Durán (Mexico: Universidad Autónoma Metropolitana, 2001), pp. 275–89

hooks, bell, *Feminist Theory: From Margin to Center* (Boston: South End Press, 1984)

——, *Yearning: Race, Gender, and Cultural Politics* (Boston: South End Press, 1990)

Johnston, R. J. et al. (eds), *The Dictionary of Human Geography*, 2nd edn (Oxford, Blackwell, 1986)

Jones, John Paul, III, 'Segmented Worlds and Selves', in *Textures of Place: Exploring Humanist Geographies*, ed. Paul C. Adams, Steven Hoelscher, and Karen E. Till (Minneapolis: University of Minnesota Press, 2001), pp. 121–8

——, Heidi J. Nast and Susan M. Roberts (eds), *Thresholds in Feminist Geography* (Lanham MD: Rowman & Littlefield, 1997)

Jung, Carl G., *Man and his Symbols* (London: Aldus, 1964)

Keith, Michael and Steve Pile (eds), *Place and the Politics of Identity* (London: Routledge, 1993)

Kristeva, Julia, *Revolution in Poetic Language*, ed. Leon S. Roudiez, trans. Margaret Waller (New York: Columbia University Press, 1984 [1st pub. 1974])

——, 'Women's Time', *Signs*, 7, 1 (1981), 13–35

Lagos, María Inés, 'Female Voices from the Borderlands: Isabel Allende's *Paula* and *Retrato en sepia*', in *Isabel Allende Today*, ed. Rosemary G. Feal and Yvette E. Miller (Pittsburgh: Latin American Literary Review Press, 2002), pp. 112–27

Lawrence, D. H., *Studies in Classic American Literature* (New York: Thomas Seltzer, 1923)

Lechte, John, '(Not) Belonging in Postmodern Space', in *Postmodern Cities and Spaces*, ed. Sophie Watson and Katherine Gibson (Oxford: Blackwell, 1995), pp. 99–111

Lefebvre, Henri, *The Production of Space*, trans. Donald Nicholson-Smith (Oxford: Blackwell, 1991 [1st pub. 1974])

Levine, Linda Gould, *Isabel Allende* (New York: Twayne, 2002)

Levins, Richard and Richard Lewontin, *The Dialectical Biologist* (Cambridge: Harvard University Press, 1985)

Lindsay, Claire, '"Clear and Present Danger": Trauma, Memory and Laura Restrepo's *La novia oscura*', *Hispanic Research Journal*, 4, 1 (2003), 41–58

——, *Locating Latin American Women Writers: Cristina Peri Rossi, Rosario Ferré, Albalucía Angel, and Isabel Allende* (New York: Peter Lang, 2003)

Lutwack, Leonard, *The Role of Place in Literature* (Syracuse: Syracuse University Press, 1984)

Mallory, William E. and Paul Simpson-Housley, ed. and Introduction, *Geography and Literature: A Meeting of the Disciplines* (Syracuse: Syracuse University Press, 1987)

Maloof, Judy, '*Mal de amores*: Un bildungsroman femenino', *Revista de Literatura Mexicana Contemporánea*, 5, 11 (1999), 36–43

Massey, Doreen, 'Politics and Space/Time', in *Place and the Politics of Identity*, ed. Michael Keith and Steve Pile (London: Routledge, 1993), pp. 141–61

——, *Space, Place, and Gender* (Minneapolis: University of Minnesota Press, 1994)

Mastretta, Angeles, *Mal de amores* (New York: Random House, 1996)

McDowell, Linda, *Gender, Identity and Place: Understanding Feminist Geographies* (Minneapolis: University of Minnesota Press, 1999)

——, 'Spatializing Feminism: Geographic Perspectives', in *BodySpace: Destabilizing Geographies of Gender and Sexuality*, ed. Nancy Duncan (London: Routledge, 1996), pp. 28–44

—— and Joanne P. Sharp (ed.), *Space, Gender, Knowledge: Feminist Readings* (London: Edward Arnold, 1997)

Medina-Rivera, Antonio, 'La aniquilación de las bellas artes y de la aristocracia en las obras de Rosario Ferré', in *Selected Proceedings of the Pennsylvania Foreign Language Conference* (Pittsburgh: Duquesne University Press, 2003), pp. 173–84

Méndez-Clark, Ronald, 'Reescritura, traducción, cambio de voz en Rosario Ferré', *Torre: Revista de la Universidad de Puerto Rico*, 5, 17 (2000), 387–417

Mitchell, W. J. T. (ed.), *Landscape and Power*, 2nd edn (Chicago: University of Chicago Press, 2002 [1st ed. 1994])

Mujica, Barbara, 'Angeles Mastretta: Mujeres tenaces en el amor y la guerra', *Américas*, 49, 4 (1997), 36–43

Nash, Catherine, 'Remapping the Body/Land: New Cartographies of Identity, Gender, and Landscape in Ireland', in *Writing Women and Space: Colonial and Postcolonial Geographies*, ed. Alison Blunt and Gillian Rose (New York: Guilford, 1994), pp. 227–50

Navascués, Javier de (ed.), *De Arcadia a Babel: naturaleza y ciudad en la literatura hispanoamericana* (Madrid: Iberoamericana, 2002)

Núñez-Méndez, Eva, 'Mastretta y sus protagonistas, ejemplos de emancipación femenina', *Romance Studies*, 20, 2 (2002), 115–27

Olivéroff, André, *Flight of the Swan: A Memory of Anna Pavlova* (New York: E. P. Dutton, 1932)

Olwig, Kenneth Robert, *Landscape, Nature, and the Body Politic: From Britain's Renaissance to America's New World* (Madison: University of Wisconsin Press, 2002)

Ordóñez, Montserrat, 'Angeles y prostitutas: Dos novelas de Laura Restrepo', in *Celebración de la creación literaria de escritoras hispanas en las Américas*, ed. Lady Rojas-Trempe and Catharina Vallejo (Ottawa: Girol, 2000), pp. 93–101

Pile, Steve, *The Body and the City: Psychoanalysis, Space and Subjectivity* (London: Routledge, 1996)

Pimentel, Luz Aurora, 'The Ideological Value of Description in Latin American Narrative', *Latin America as its Literature: Selected Papers of the XIVth Congress of the International Comparative Literature Association*, ed. María Elena de Valdés, Mario J. Valdés, and Richard A. Young (Whitestone, NY: Council on National Literatures, 1995), pp. 55–67

Postlethwaite, Diana, 'Roadies', *New York Times*, 29 July 2001

Pratt, Annis, *Archetypal Patterns in Women's Fiction*, with Barbara White, Andrea Loewenstein, and Mary Wyer (Bloomington: Indiana University Press, 1981)

Preciado Silva, José Luis, 'La guerra de castas en Yucatán (1847–1901),' *Antropoética* (2001), available from: <http://www.antropoetica.com/rebelion/castas.html> [Accessed Jan. 2005]

Restrepo, Laura, *La novia oscura* (Barcelona: Anagrama, 2000)

Rich, Adrienne, 'Notes toward a Politics of Location', in *Blood, Bread, and Poetry: Selected Prose 1979–1985* (New York: W. W. Norton, 1986), pp. 210–31

Rivera Villegas, Carmen M., 'Las mujeres y la Revolución Mexicana en *Mal de amores* de Angeles Mastretta', *Letras Femeninas*, 24, 1–2 (1998), 37–48

Rivero, Eliana, 'Of Trilogies and Genealogies: *Daughter of Fortune* and *Portrait in Sepia*', in *Isabel Allende Today*, ed. Rosemary G. Feal and Yvette E. Miller (Pittsburgh: Latin American Literary Review Press, 2002), pp. 91–111

Rodríguez, Ileana, *House/Garden/Nation: Space, Gender, and Ethnicity in Postcolonial Latin American Literatures by Women*, trans. Robert Carr and Ileana Rodríguez (Durham: Duke University Press, 1994)

Rose, Gillian, *Feminism and Geography: The Limits of Geographical Knowledge* (Minneapolis: University of Minnesota Press, 1993)

Sack, Robert David, *Homo Geographicus* (Baltimore: Johns Hopkins University Press, 1997)

Said, Edward, 'Invention, Memory, and Place', in *Landscape and Power*, ed. W. J. T. Mitchell, 2nd edn (Chicago: University of Chicago Press, 2002), pp. 241–259

Sánchez-Blake, Elvira, 'Mujer y patria: La inscripción del cuerpo femenino en *Demasiado amor* de Sara Sefchovich', *Confluencia*, 13, 2 (1998), 105–13

Schouten, John W., 'Personal Rites of Passage and the Reconstruction of Self', *Advances in Consumer Research*, 18 (1991), 49–51

Schwartz, Marcy, *Writing Paris: Urban Topographies of Desire in Contemporary Latin American Fiction* (Albany: State University of New York Press, 1999)

Sefchovich, Sara, *Demasiado amor* (Mexico: Alfaguara, 2001) [1st ed. 1990]

Sharpe, Scott, 'Bodily Speaking: Spaces and Experiences of Childbirth', in *Embodied Geographies: Space, Bodies and Rites of Passage*, ed. Elizabeth Kenworthy Teather (London: Routledge, 1999), pp. 91–103

Shaw, Donald L., *The Post-Boom in Spanish American Fiction* (Albany: State University of New York Press, 1998)

Smith, Neil and Cindi Katz, 'Grounding Metaphor: Towards a Spatialized Politics', in *Place and the Politics of Identity*, ed. Michael Keith and Steve Pile (London: Routledge, 1993), pp. 67–83

Soja, Edward, 'The Socio-Spatial Dialectic', *Annals of the Association of American Geographers*, 70, 2 (1980), 207–25

——. *Thirdspace: Journeys to Los Angeles and Other Real-and-Imagined Places* (Oxford: Blackwell, 1996)

Teather, Elizabeth Kenworthy, *Embodied Geographies: Spaces, Bodies and Rites of Passage* (London: Routledge, 1999)

Thrift, Nigel, 'Literature, the Production of Culture and the Politics of Place', *Antipode*, 15 (1983), 12–24

Tindall, Gillian, *Countries of the Mind: The Meaning of Place to Writers* (Boston: Northeastern University Press, 1991)

Todorov, Tzvetan, 'The Journey and its Narratives', trans. Alyson Waters, in *Transports: Travel, Pleasure, and Imaginative Geography, 1600–1830*, ed. Chloe Chard and Helen Langdon (New Haven: Yale University Press, 1996), pp. 287–96

Tuan, Yi-Fu, 'Space and Place: A Humanistic Perspective', *Progress in Geography*, 6 (1974), 211–52

——, *Space and Place: The Perspective of Experience* (Minneapolis: University of Minnesota Press, 1977)

Turner, Victor, 'Liminal to Liminoid in Play, Flow, and Ritual: An Essay in Comparative Symbology', *Rice University Studies*, 60, 3 (1974), 53–92

van Gennep, Arnold, *The Rites of Passage*, trans. Monika B. Vizedom and Gabrielle L. Caffee (Chicago: University of Chicago Press, 1960 [1st pub. 1908])

Vega, Norma, 'Re-Inscribing the Nation under the Global: Mexican Narrative Perspectives after 1968', Diss., University of California-Los Angeles, 1998

Vilches, Patricia, 'La violencia pública/íntima hacia la subjetividad del cuerpo femenino en Julia Alvarez y Rosario Ferré', *Taller de Letras*, 32 (2003), 99–112

Villa, Raúl Homero, *Barrio-Logos: Space and Place in Urban Chicano Literature and Culture* (Austin: University of Texas Press, 2000)

Vips Inc. website, available at: <www.vips.com.mx> [Accessed Jan. 2005]

Webster's 1913 Dictionary, available at: <http://www.hyperdictionary.com> [Accessed Jan. 2005]

White, Hayden, *Tropics of Discourse: Essays in Cultural Criticism* (Baltimore: Johns Hopkins University Press, 1978)

Winchester, Hilary P. M., Pauline M. McGuirk, and Kathryn Everett, 'Schoolies Week as a Rite of Passage: A Study of Celebration and Control', in *Embodied Geographies: Spaces, Bodies and Rites of Passage*, ed. Elizabeth Kenworthy Teather (London: Routledge, 1999), pp. 59–77

Wolch, Jennifer and Michael Dear (ed.), *The Power of Geography: How Territory Shapes Social Life* (Boston: Unwin Hyman, 1989)

Yaeger, Patricia (ed.), *The Geography of Identity* (Ann Arbor: University of Michigan Press, 1996)

Young, Iris Marion, *Justice and the Politics of Difference* (Princeton: Princeton University Press, 1990)

Zamora, Lois Parkinson, *Writing the Apocalypse: Historical Vision in Contemporary US and Latin American Fiction* (Cambridge: Cambridge University Press, 1989)

INDEX